FROM RIVALRY TO PARTNERSHIP?

From Rivalry to Partnership?
New Approaches to the Challenges of Africa

Edited by

TONY CHAFER
University of Portsmouth, UK

and

GORDON CUMMING
Cardiff University, UK

ASHGATE

Published by
Ashgate Publishing Limited
Wey Court East
Union Road
Farnham
Surrey, GU9 7PT
England

Ashgate Publishing Company
Suite 420
101 Cherry Street
Burlington
VT 05401-4405
USA

www.ashgate.com

British Library Cataloguing in Publication Data
From rivalry to partnership? : new approaches to the
  challenges of Africa.
  1. Great Britain--Foreign relations--France--Congresses.
  2. France--Foreign relations--Great Britain--Congresses.
  3. Great Britain--Foreign relations--Africa--Congresses.
  4. Africa--Foreign relations--Great Britain--Congresses.
  5. France--Foreign relations--Africa--Congresses.
  6. Africa--Foreign relations--France--Congresses.
  7. Economic development--Africa--International
  cooperation--Congresses. 8. Great Britain--Military
  policy--Congresses. 9. France--Military policy--
  Congresses. 10. Humanitarian assistance--Africa--
  International cooperation--Congresses.
  I. Chafer, Tony. II. Cumming, Gordon, 1965-
  327.1'7'096-dc22

Library of Congress Cataloging-in-Publication Data
From rivalry to partnership? : new approaches to the challenges of Africa / [edited] by Tony Chafer
and Gordon Cumming.
    p. cm.
  Includes bibliographical references and index.
  ISBN 978-1-4094-0517-7 (hardback) -- ISBN 978-1-4094-0518-4 (ebook)
  1. Europe--Relations--Africa. 2. Africa--Relations--Europe. 3. United States--Relations--Africa.
4. Africa--Relations--United States. I. Chafer, Tony. II. Cumming, Gordon.
  JZ1570.A56F76 2011
  327.604--dc22

                                                                              2011005820

ISBN 9781409405177 (hbk)
ISBN 9781409405184 (ebk)

Printed and bound in Great Britain by the
MPG Books Group, UK.

Contents

Notes on Contributors

Niagalé Bagayoko is a political scientist. She has done extensive field research in several francophone countries in Africa and has studied the impact of Western security policies (France, United States, European Union) on African conflict management mechanisms. She has taught at the Institut d'Etudes Politiques in Paris and been a Research Fellow at the Institute of Development Studies at Sussex University, where she studied security sector reform processes in Francophone Africa.

Daniel Bourmaud is Professor of Political Science and Director of the Centre Montesquieu de Recherches Politiques at the University Montesquieu Bordeaux IV. He specialises in comparative politics, with emphasis on African political regimes, and the analysis of French African policy, a topic on which he has written widely. He is currently preparing a new edition of his book *La politique en Afrique* (Eds Montchrestien).

Theresa Callan is Principal Lecturer in International Politics at the University of Portsmouth. She specialises in IR Theory, Security Studies, and Ethnic Conflict. She has published on security provision within Europe, human rights, and ethnic conflict.

Tony Chafer is Professor of Contemporary French Area Studies at the University of Portsmouth and Director of its Centre for European and International Studies Research. He has published widely on Franco-African relations in the late colonial and post-colonial era. He is the author of *The End of Empire in French West Africa: France's Successful Decolonization?* (Berg, 2002).

Gordon Cumming began his career in the Africa Research Department of the Foreign and Commonwealth Office. He is now Reader in the School of European Studies, Cardiff University. He is a *professeur invité* at the Centre d'Etude d'Afrique Noire, Bordeaux and has published widely on French and British foreign and development policies as well as on civil society capacity-building. He has written monographs entitled *Aid to Africa* (2001) and *French NGOs in the Global Era* (2009).

Marie V. Gibert is a postdoctoral Research Fellow in the department of international relations at the University of the Witwatersrand, Johannesburg, South Africa. She holds a PhD from the School of Oriental and African Studies

(SOAS), University of London. Her research focuses on multilateral cooperation between Europe and West Africa in the security field and has led her to carry out field research in both West Africa and Europe.

Gorm Rye Olsen is Professor of Global Politics and Head of Institute, Institute of Society and Globalisation, Roskilde University. He has published extensively on the EU and Africa, development issues and Danish foreign and development policy.

Ian Taylor is a Professor in International Relations at the University of St. Andrews' School of International Relations and a Joint Professor in the School of International Studies, Renmin University of China and an Honorary Professor in the Institute of African Studies, Zhejiang Normal University, China. He is also Professor Extraordinary in Political Science at the University of Stellenbosch, South Africa.

Alex Vines is Director of Regional and Security Studies and Head of the Africa Programme at Chatham House, London. He is also a part-time Lecturer at the Department of International Studies and Social Science and an Associate of the African Studies Centre, Coventry University.

Paul D. Williams is Associate Professor in the Elliott School of International Affairs at the George Washington University, USA. His research interests lie in contemporary peace operations, Africa's international relations and British foreign policy. His books include, *War and Conflict in Africa* (Polity, forthcoming); *British Foreign Policy under New Labour, 1997–2005* (Palgrave Macmillan, 2005); *Understanding Peacekeeping* (Polity, 2nd edition, 2010); and *The International Politics of Mass Atrocities: The Case of Darfur* (Routledge, 2010).

First Preface:
A UK Perspective.
The December 1998 Saint-Malo Declaration on Africa

Eighteen months in office, Mr Blair had, like his predecessors, started off wanting to place the United Kingdom at the centre of EU policy making. But domestic politics hampered this aspiration. European Security and Defence Policy offered an option which met the objective while providing some low risk benefits. This was particularly true of the Saint-Malo declaration on European Security, which was intended to produce more real defence capability in Europe and to send EU policy in a NATO-friendly direction. New Labour ministers had the confidence to believe that the UK could shape the EU's foreign policy by taking a leading role and drawing on a particular national asset – its diplomacy.

France was the natural partner. The two states had the foremost defence capabilities in the EU. Both were Permanent Members of the UN Security Council and members of the G8. A joint positive initiative within the EU, in an area where they had a particular expertise, would be likely to prevail in Brussels. This was particularly true when member states were disappointed by the lack of progress in implementing the Maastricht Treaty.

However, although the Saint-Malo Franco-British summit is mostly remembered for its declaration on defence cooperation, this was not the only area in which the two countries promised enhanced cooperation. The second part of the declaration promised to put an end to Anglo-French rivalry in Africa. Geographically, Africa was the continent ripest for cooperation between the United Kingdom and France. The two countries had a long history of engagement there, often as competitors. Between them, they had diplomatic missions in most of the African states. Increasingly they shared an appreciation of the challenges facing Africa – conflict prevention, post conflict reconstruction, security, tackling poverty and promoting economic development, governance, to mention some. In the Security Council they were much occupied with African issues, and in the G8, in working out a response to the New Partnership for African Development. The EU was itself prominent in supporting African development through the European Development Fund under the framework of the Lomé (now Cotonou) Agreement.

Moving EU policy forward and fostering real bilateral cooperation was welcome to the foreign ministries in both countries. Policy was anchored on substance, which sat comfortably in a more strategic approach to both the EU and Africa. For their part the French Ministry of Foreign Affairs may also have hoped for a stronger role vis-à-vis the Presidency in French policy towards Africa. The areas chosen for cooperation were also intended to be non-threatening to key partners. Germany welcomed the Declarations and the United States was positive on the African development, if never fully reassured about defence.

The two parts of the Declaration were negotiated between officials, that on defence in a six-hour session in Saint-Malo between the Political Directors. The above factors shaped the agreements but the negotiations were eased by personal relations, especially the rapport which Robin Cook and Hubert Védrine had established. Tony Blair's commitment to Africa was also an important factor. The context was therefore very political, with an emphasis on the practical and achievable.

Saint-Malo established the basis for strengthening cooperation and harmonising policies and the overall approach to Africa. This emphasis on the practical led to a focus on initiatives like cooperation between Heads of Mission in individual countries, secondments between ministries, and joint visits to raise the profile of the cooperation. Cook and his successor Jack Straw visited African states with Védrine in 1999 and 2002 respectively. Mutual suspicion was being overcome and trust had been strengthened by Cook and Védrine co-chairing the Rambouillet process, which in 1998/9 tried to solve the Kosovo issue. The bilateral summits of 2001 and 2004 gave a further impetus to cooperation.

In EU fora the two countries were putting forward joint initiatives and perceived to be of a common view on many issues, thus facilitating agreement to EU positions. Processes were pragmatic and evolutionary, moving policy forward and responding to circumstances and events, evoking often the spirit of Saint-Malo, and drawing in those responsible for International Development. There was no need to define particular structures, indeed to have tried to do so would have distracted from the substance and would have probably been much more difficult. Officials tried to solve the problems which needed resolution and could be solved, leaving until later the more difficult, or issues where agreement was not essential.

Gordon Cumming and Tony Chafer have researched this subject extensively, and evidently had excellent access to informed sources. Theirs is a comprehensive description of developments since Saint-Malo. Their account shows the considerable progress and achievements which have followed since December 1998. Of course there have been disagreements, and they set out the factors which inhibit as well as foster cooperation. More could certainly have been achieved but importantly, they set out clearly the starting points and constraints. In addition, today the UK has a wider appreciation of Francophone Africa, and France of Anglophone Africa, e.g. France is more understanding of the British approach to Zimbabwe.

I am not personally convinced that the absence of a tight institutional framework has been a serious impediment to cooperation. Political will, individual approaches to EU foreign policy, national interests, lack of resources and not just money but ministerial and official time, overstretch of military forces, and personal relations are more significant factors in my view.

This work provides a sound basis for debating achievement, and in particular for looking forward. The speculation about the future is very relevant to the continuing debate about EU foreign policy and the prospects for British/French cooperation. There is much material to support the view of those who believe that increased cooperation, especially in hard military issues, is even more important as we confront global challenges and economic realities. Policy-makers in both London and Paris would profit from paying close attention to the arguments, and profiting from the history and analysis which is set out.

Sir Emyr Jones-Parry
Formerly UK Permanent Representative on the North Atlantic Council, 2001–3,
UK Permanent Representative to the United Nations, 2003–7

Second Preface:
A French Perspective.
A Helping Partner at Hand:
Enough to Forget Old Rivalries?

Commitment to the Saint-Malo Declaration on cooperation in Africa remains weak in France, even among officials and politicians supposedly in charge of the matter. This strikes me as an inescapable and rather disappointing conclusion. This book as well as the articles and reports (for Chatham House and the Institut français des relations internationales) on related topics confirm my own rather sad personal assessment of the Saint-Malo Africa Declaration and do so with a wealth of broad-based evidence and a strong theoretical framework.

Why have there been so many shortfalls in terms of implementation, especially when we consider that joint Franco-British action is much needed on a continent where the combined efforts and experience of the two main former colonial powers should clearly be helpful? The answer would appear to lie at least partly in France's lack of intellectual appetite for British cooking, that is to say, for collaboration with the UK.

This book, sensibly in my view, takes a neo-classical realist approach to explaining Franco-British and for that matter other forms of bilateral cooperation in Africa. When dealing with Africa and other parts of the world traditionally neglected by International Relations, French academia seems still to be divided between, on the Left, a determinist socio-philosophical approach (*olim* Marxist turned to Weberian now) and, on the Right, a no less determinist and self-proclaimed 'geo-political' and realist school supported by an essentialist vision of world affairs. Not much room then for this 'third British way'. For French scholars, rejecting 'normative' approaches to the world order remains the dominant paradigm. In effect, this means giving *carte blanche* to the classic 'state-interest' view of international relations. This point is illustrated notably by the work of Jean-François Bayart who describes the 'democracy' phenomenon as simply the last layer of 'extraversion' (and a miserably crushing one) for African countries. Given these intellectual and cultural roots, how could France ever have made any positive contribution to such international trends as the brand of 'ethical' diplomacy promoted by New Labour in Britain or the 'evidence-based' and systemic assessment of human rights and state legitimacy propounded by the United States?

The above observations provide a French perspective on the backdrop to the Saint-Malo Africa Declaration. Yet what of the operational side? Since 1998 and notwithstanding political changes in France or Dr Kouchner's principled personal stand on the 'duty to protect', Paris has more or less remained mid-way between a G77 emphasis on state sovereignty as an unchallenged given and the standard Western interventionist view on the need to promote democratisation in Africa. This is the first point to bear in mind.

Secondly, there is a need to distinguish between short-term motivations for accepting a joint venture with Britain in Africa and longer-term constraints on implementing an agreement. At the start of the political process, what could have been the rationale for deciding, on 3 December 1998, to put a stop to centuries of bitter rivalry with the UK and develop a sort of understated partnership for dealing with Africa? It was not so much driven by any overriding desire to overcome the 'Fashoda syndrome' (the French fear of 'Anglo-Saxon' expansionism in Africa). Rather it was underpinned by opportunism, as a French Prime Minister, the Protestant-educated Jospin who had not the slightest attachment to Africa, seized the chance to escape from the deadly mangroves of 'Françafrique' by grabbing the hand of a former foe and new-found partner, the UK.

Thirdly, it is worth underscoring that the implementation of the Saint-Malo Declaration on Africa has been extremely patchy. As shown in this book, the relationship between French and British officials and politicians was rather positive on the military cooperation side, above average in strategic, foreign affairs matters, and very poor on development assistance issues. The low-point came during the disastrous Clare Short–Charles Josselin trip to Sierra Leone and Guinea in 2001. Old rivalries came back to the fore to destroy the whole joint visit. Similar situations arose at other points with a deep misunderstanding usually lying at the core of the failing process. These misunderstandings might also be related to structural divergences i.e. the national interest paradigm and the project-oriented French development approach as opposed to the deliberately global and programme-centred DfID way.

In short, it is indeed comforting to reconcile with old foes. But a new friendship will only survive if there are reciprocal benefits. As Napoleon once said: '*Les petits cadeaux entretiennent l'amitié*'. Such gifts have been few and far between in the context of the Saint-Malo Declaration on Africa.

François Gaulme
Agence Française de Développement
Formerly editor of *Afrique contemporaine*

Third Preface:
An African Perspective:
Divergent Views of
Anglo-French Cooperation

Because of their colonial past France and the UK are confronted with a myriad of perceptions in Africa. The latter are deeply rooted in the history of rivalry which characterised their relations on the continent for several centuries. Although the Saint-Malo process is mostly unknown to Africans – even to many of those dealing with broader security matters – these perceptions are not linear and therefore reflect a certain degree of complexity. Generally, African perceptions of French and British policies on the continent diverge substantially depending on the perspective of the observer but also of their function. In fact, there seems to be a wide gap between the perceptions of what can be called public opinion and those of a more informed category of decision-makers and other actors and experts of cooperation (FPAE 2008). Public opinion refers to the large public sphere where information is generated and shared through media (press, radio, television and increasingly the internet). On the other hand, officials from government, regional organisations, civil servants and civil society cadres constitute the category of informed decision-makers to whom we could add various experts (researchers, journalists and development cooperation actors). Another distinctive feature of African perceptions is the gap between French and English speakers. Whereas the majority of French speakers (from both public opinion and informed decision-makers) have no or just a vague idea about British Africa policy, most English speakers have an opinion about French Africa policy. This opinion is deeply rooted in a web of perceptions that mostly ignore recent major developments in French Africa policy. More importantly, this opinion seems also to be based on an ideological posture of 'defence of African identity' that France is perceived to pervert. Both the mutual ignorance and the ideological posture, characterised by suspicion of a neo-colonial agenda, are mostly found in Southern Africa, where the regional hegemon (South Africa) has clashed with France over the right approach to mediation on a certain number of conflicts, such as Côte d'Ivoire and Madagascar.

France is widely perceived in Africa as a country that supports authoritarian regimes (this perception has been exacerbated by the crises in Togo, Côte d'Ivoire and Madagascar); exploits African mineral resources to its unique advantage (oil in Central Africa and uranium in Niger); has difficulties breaking with a unilateral tradition of intervention in African internal affairs despite an increased Europeanisation of its instruments (Chad); and remains paternalistic towards African partners (Bourgi 2009).

It is recognised of course that there have been reforms to French African policy and that France now acknowledges the diminishing economic importance of Francophone African countries for France's external trade and the higher costs incurred in maintaining a strong security and financial presence in the former colonies. Former English colonies like Nigeria, South Africa and Kenya have a larger share of trade with France than traditional countries of the '*pré carré*' such as Côte d'Ivoire, Gabon and Cameroon (Gounin 2009).

France is perceived as having a neo-colonial agenda on the continent and as such, it is an easy scapegoat for all the problems of that part of the continent that it colonised (Ngoupande 2002). France therefore faces a deep image deficit that has been exacerbated by its own incapacity to substantially reform a policy widely considered domestically as inappropriate. The country's effort to 'Europeanise' its Africa policy is partly a response to this image deficit, as much as it is a reaction to a growing incapacity to fund past policies alone.

On the other hand, the UK does not face the same challenges in terms of image in Africa, despite a similar status as former colonial power. This is probably a function of both the marginal place that Africa occupies in British foreign policy as well as its instruments and policies on the continent. This appears clearly in what has been termed the intervention dilemma. Whereas France's military interventions in Africa are generally seen to be pursuing a neo-colonial agenda, the UK's few interventions (particularly those in Sierra Leone and Liberia) were considered as helpful in stabilising a deteriorating socio-political situation (Gaulme 2001). The UK is perceived as having moved from benign neglect towards giving pre-eminence to development and humanitarian aid. As set out in Alex Vines' contribution to this volume, the developmental (and in some instances humanitarian) turn in British Africa policy was championed by the New Labour government under Tony Blair (1997–2007) and continued by Gordon Brown until 2010. New Labour's proclaimed value-orientation in Africa policy was taken more seriously on the continent than François Mitterrand's speech at La Baule. This was for a number of reasons. Taking advantage of the domestic consensus on Africa, New Labour translated the vision of a moralistic Africa policy into institutional arrangements whose modus operandi appeared to be in line with stated objectives. In creating the Department for International Development (DfID) and providing it with substantial budget allocations the UK was able to position itself as a serious actor in the international fight against poverty. This widely shared perception among African development and security practitioners was at least partly made possible by the introduction of a results-based development approach. However, both the draconian DfID reporting requirements and the selective engagement of the UK in African crises remind African actors that the UK is much more than just the self-proclaimed altruistic partner that aims at 'healing the scar' (Gallagher 2009).

Despite differences in style and priorities in French and British Africa policies, collaboration between the two countries is generally welcomed by most African partners as it helps reduce transaction costs and reporting requirements. Given these contrasting perspectives on French and UK Africa policy, it is refreshing to read in this study that France and the UK have taken genuine, if somewhat faltering, steps towards closer coordination. It remains to be seen whether this cooperation will in the end benefit the UK and France more than Africa. The effort at coordination seems worthwhile nonetheless.

Paul-Simon Handy
Institute of Security Studies, Pretoria

Acknowledgements

We wish to express our thanks to those officials in the Foreign and Commonwealth Office, Department for International Development, Ministry of Defence, French Foreign Ministry, French Defence Ministry, Agence Française de Développement, European Commission, European Council, African Union and United Nations, who agreed to be interviewed. We would also like to thank all those working in US and European diplomatic missions in Africa who met with us and answered our many questions. Without their help, and the support of NGOs such as OXFAM and Médecins sans Frontières and pressure groups such as Human Rights Watch, the research on which this book is based would not have been possible.

We would equally like to thank Paul Brand and Odile Bomba Nkolo, who transcribed some of the 160 interviews we undertook during the preparation of this book, Joanna Warson for preparing the Bibliography and Index, and Natalja Mortensen at Ashgate for her support, patience and forbearance during the gestation of this work. A particular thank-you goes to Theresa Callan at University of Portsmouth for her invaluable contributions at various stages of this project. We also wish to thank the Centre for European and International Studies at the University of Portsmouth and the School of European Studies at Cardiff University for hosting the project. Finally, we would above all like to thank the British Academy for providing the large grant that was used to finance this important research and both Chatham House and the Institut français des relations internationales (Paris and Brussels) for hosting the seminars at which we presented our key findings.

List of Abbreviations

ACOTA	Africa Contingency Operations Training and Assistance
ACP	Africa, Caribbean and Pacific countries
ACRF	African Crisis Response Force
ACRI	African Crisis Response Initiative
AFD	Agence Française de Développement
AFDL	Alliance des Forces Démocratiques pour la Libération du Congo-Zaire
AFRICOM	Africa Command
AMIS	African Union Mission in Sudan
AMISOM	African Union Mission in Somalia
APSA	African Peace and Security Architecture
ASF	African Standby Force
AU	African Union
AUPG	African Union Partners Group
AWG	Africa Working Group
BMATT	British Military Advisory and Training Teams
BRIC	Brazil, Russia, India, China
C2D	Contrat de Désendettement et de Développement (Debt for Development scheme)
CAF	Country Assistance Framework
CAR	Central African Republic
CEWS	Continental Early Warning System
CFSP	(EU) Common Foreign and Security Policy
CINC	Commander-in-Chief
CNDP	Congrès National pour la Défense du Peuple
CODEV	Committee on Development Cooperation
CPA	Comprehensive Peace Agreement
CPP	Conflict Prevention Pool
DfID	Department for International Development
DG Relex	Directorate-General External Relations
DOD	(US) Department of Defense
DOS	(US) Department of State
DRC	Democratic Republic of Congo
DSCA	Defense Security Cooperation Agency
DSO	Departmental Strategic Objectives
EASBRIG	Eastern Africa Region Brigade

EC	European Commission
ECOMIL	ECOWAS Mission in Liberia
ECOWAS	Economic Community of West African States
EDF	European Development Fund
ESDP	European Security and Defence Policy
EU	European Union
EU NAVFOR	European Union Naval Force Somalia
EUFOR	European Union Force
EUMC	European Union Military Committee
EUMS	European Union Military Staff
EUPOL	EU Police Mission
EURORECAMP	European programme for African peacekeeping capacity-building (see RECAMP)
EUSEC	EU Advisory and Assistance Mission for Security Reform
EUSR	EU Special Representative
FCO	Foreign and Commonwealth Office
FDLR	Forces Démocratiques de Libération du Rwanda
FHI	Fuel Hubs Initiative
FPE	Foreign Policy Executive
FOCAC	Forum on China-Africa Cooperation
G7	Group of Seven industrialised nations
G8	Annual meeting of the heads of government of the G7 + Russia
G20	Group of Twenty Finance Ministers and Central Bank Governors of major industrialised and developing economies
GDP	Gross Domestic Product
GNI	Gross National Income
HIPC	Highly Indebted Poor Countries
IFFm	International Finance Facility for Immunisation
IGAD	Intergovernmental Authority on Development in East Africa
IPU	Integrated Police Unit
IR	International Relations
IMF	International Monetary Fund
LLDC	Least Developed Country
LRA	Lord's Resistance Army
MDGs	Millennium Development Goals
MFA	Ministry of Foreign Affairs (France)
MINURCAT	United Nations Mission in the Central African Republic and Chad
MoD	Ministry of Defence
MONUC	United Nations Mission in DRC

NATO	North Atlantic Treaty Organisation
NEPAD	New Partnership for Africa's Development
NGO	Non-Governmental Organisation
NHS	National Health Service
OAU	Organization of African Unity
ODA	Official Development Assistance
OECD	Organisation for Economic Cooperation and Development
P3	France, UK, US (informal grouping of three permanent members of the UNSC)
P5	The five permanent members of the UNSC
PAPU	(UK) Pan-Africa Policy Unit
PSA	Public Service Agreement
PSC	(AU) Peace and Security Council
PSC	(EU) Political and Security Committee
PSI	Pan Sahel Initiative
RECAMP	Renforcement des Capacités Africaines de Maintien de la Paix (Reinforcement of African Peacekeeping Capacities)
RPF	Rwandan Patriotic Front
SADC	Southern African Development Community
SHAPE	Supreme Headquarters of Allied Powers in Europe
SSA	Sub-Saharan Africa
SSR	Security Sector Reform
TFG	Transitional Federal Government (Somalia)
UNAMID	African Union/United Nations Hybrid Operation in Darfur
UNITAID	International facility for the purchase of drugs against HIV/AIDS
UNMIS	United Nations Mission in Sudan
UNSC	United Nations Security Council
USAFRICOM	US Africa Command
USAID	US Agency for International Development
USCENTCOM	US Central Command
USEUCOM	US European Command
USPACOM	US Pacific Command

PART I
Introduction and Theory

Introduction

Tony Chafer and Gordon Cumming

Throughout the early post-colonial decades, the challenges of Africa, whether in terms of poverty, conflict or human rights violations, were largely of peripheral concern to Western (or as they became known in the post-Cold War era 'Northern') states. While developed countries recognised the scale of these challenges,they tended to see the African continent primarily through the prism of their own geopolitical, economic and strategic interests (McKinlay and Little 1986) and they competed, among themselves and with the Soviet bloc, for the influence, prestige and resources that a foothold in Africa could offer (Martin 1985; Amin 1975). In line with this hard-nosed approach, most Western states engaged in unilateral initiatives and, less enthusiastically, in multilateral action to help solve Africa's problems. Britain's Military Assistance Training Teams, France's 30 high profile military interventions in Africa between 1960 and 1990 and the support by the United States to anti-Marxist forces in Southern Africa and the Horn are all examples of the former. The half-hearted commitment of developed countries to the North-South dialogue in the 1970s (Fitzgerald 1979; Brown 2002: 49) and the timidity of their multilateral debt reduction schemes in the 1980s (Brown 2002: 81) are illustrations of the latter point.

Over the last decade or so, and in particular since the UN Millennium Summit in 2000, Africa has been identified as a moral and strategic priority by the international community. Already in 1999 Madeleine Albright had labelled it 'a major battleground in the global fight against terror' (Albright 1999). Then, at the 2001 Labour Party conference, Tony Blair described Africa as a 'scar on the conscience of the world'. The scale of the African challenge has been used by some Northern governments to legitimise a new military and to some extent politico-economic interventionism. This new-found activism has not generally been translated into large-scale unilateral initiatives, which can be extremely costly and can lead in many cases to allegations of necolonialism. Instances of interventionism by individual donors can nonetheless be cited, including the French RECAMP peacekeeping project, the British military intervention in Sierra Leone and the American AFRICOM scheme. Instead, the more pronounced forms of interventionism have taken place at the multilateral level, where a plethora of initiatives – including the Highly Indebted Poor Countries (HIPC) debt cancellation scheme, the Paris Declaration and the Millennium Development Goals (MDGs) as well as some that overlap such as the New Partnership for

Africa's Development (NEPAD) and the Blair Commission – have been launched in a renewed effort to resolve the challenges of Africa.

Reflecting this new readiness to intervene, UN Secretary-General Boutros Boutros-Ghali stated in his *Agenda for Peace* (1992): 'The time of absolute and exclusive sovereignty ... has passed; its theory was never matched by reality. It is the task of leaders of States today to understand this and to find a balance between the needs of good internal governance and the requirements of an ever more interdependent world'. However, while this new interventionism helped to show that Northern donors were serious about tackling the problems of Africa, it has also been used to spread the blame more evenly for the developmental and political failures that Africa has suffered over the last half century.

This heightened activism on the part of Northern donors has, however, met with at best limited success in tackling African crises. A case in point is the poor performance of most of the African continent relative to the MDGs, not to mention the equally unimpressive performance of some donors in relation to aid pledges designed to facilitate Africa's achievement of those goals (OECD 2010). Another illustration might be the delays to the formation of an African Standby Force as an effective Africa-wide force with which Africa can peacekeep itself. There are many reasons for the limited success of such initiatives. They include the failure of African governments to stand by their own commitments to clean up corruption and practise sound forms of governance, the reluctance of many African regimes to divert money away from military expenditure towards poverty reduction, the failure on the part of the donor community to understand that the recipient governments with which they are dealing are often little more than a front for more powerful, even criminal elements to ply their trade. Other factors relate to the failure of Western governments to reform the international trading system, notably in agriculture, to enable African farmers to compete on a more level playing field, their frequent collusion with autocratic regimes in Africa despite a rhetorical commitment to good governance and human rights, the failure of donors to honour their aid pledges, their reluctance to work together and share the credit for their activities south of the Sahara, and the double standards of some donors who are unwilling to accept lessons from others. More sceptical commentators might also argue that many of the recent initiatives were predestined to failure because many of them are based on a technocratic set of targets which are meaningless to African governments that do not have the capacity or in many cases the will to achieve such goals.

It would be deeply unfair to attribute recent lack of progress on Africa's challenges entirely to the donor community. There is nonetheless clearly an element of truth in the claim that donors have continued with the traditional mindset of rivalry, exacerbated in some ways by the emergence of new and powerful players in Africa, such as China, India and Brazil (Lafargue 2008). Many of the recent grand initiatives such as the NEPAD and Blair's Commission for Africa have in effect involved leading Western or 'Northern' powers competing among themselves and seeking to portray themselves as Africa's champion, whether this be through the writing of reports by think tanks such as the Commission for Africa, the French President's invitation to African leaders to attend the 2003 meeting of the G8 or George W. Bush's launch of the Millennium Challenge Account.

Towards Bilateral Cooperation and Partnerships?

One 'new' approach that could make a difference and break free from or at least limit the impact of imperial and other rivalries involves bilateral and 'bi-multi' cooperation. In this volume we use the term 'bilateral cooperation' to refer to collaboration between two donor states, often two leading players in Africa working together towards common goals, sharing mutual interests and, in some cases, with some form of joint-decision making mechanism. In some cases this can be seen as a prelude to 'bi-multi' cooperation, meaning that efforts are then made to bring other members of the donor community on board.

It should be stressed that bilateral cooperation on and in Africa has of course taken place in the past. Indeed during the Cold War, there was an implicit, at times explicit, agreement between the United States and former colonial powers with continuing links to Africa that the ex-colonial power would be responsible for keeping its formal empire within the Western orbit. This coordination was, however, the product of necessity, a common fear of Soviet penetration and a desire to curry favour with the US Superpower. It was not an active form of cooperation or one that involved anything resembling partnership. A case in point was the crisis in the Congo in the early 1960s when the UK and France, out of concern for their own mineral interests, neither worked together nor gave their full support to the United States and the US-led mission, ONUC. Other instances of joint cooperation have tended to be on a case by case basis. To illustrate, France and Belgium worked together in response to incursions into Congo-Zaire in 1977 and 1978 (Chipman 1989: 133) while the French also relied on US support in Chad in 1983–8 (ibid.: 164–5).

Collaboration was therefore typically implicit and ad hoc rather than formally adopted as a matter of policy or practice, or for that matter as an effective means of tackling the problems of Africa. The most loudly trumpeted example of bilateral cooperation to emerge in recent years is between the two most important former colonial powers, Britain and France. Agreed at Saint-Malo in December 1998 and subsequently reaffirmed in 2001 and 2004, this initiative seeks to go beyond earlier unilateral and multilateral initiatives and establish a joint or 'bilateral' approach to African issues. Anglo-French cooperation will be central to the focus of this study but other bilateral arrangements between Northern powers will also be examined and used as a barometer for assessing whether there is anything exceptional about the Anglo-French 'partnership', whether such cooperation is a common phenomenon and the extent to which Anglo-French relations really do represent a partnership.

Aims

This book will evaluate the significance and strength of the Anglo-French partnership and will explore whether this and other forms of bilateral and 'bi-multi' cooperation serve as a valuable alternative or complement to traditional approaches to the challenges of Africa. As well as exploring how far the UK, France and other donors have moved away from rivalry to partnership, this volume will also seek to identify, with the help of a theoretical framework, the drivers behind, and constraints on, policy change.

The potential significance of these partnerships is widely recognised in most of the donor administrations and governments covered in this book. It is not of course universally acknowledged, with one senior official at the Department for International Development (DfID) going so far as to comment: 'Why do bilateral ... just go directly for the multilateral' (personal communication, 2009). *A priori* it might also be argued that such ties are anachronistic in a context of Europeanisation, globalisation and indeed of universal targets such as the MDGs. This scepticism is not, however, widely shared by officials or politicians in the donor countries examined in this book, whose policy-making elites overwhelmingly saw the benefits of closer cooperation with a key donor, in areas where views were shared or potentially compatible. The possibility of reducing duplication of effort, saving money, avoiding contradictory policies, practices and statements was seen as a goal worth pursuing and the scope for bringing others on board later (bi-multi cooperation) was also widely acknowledged. More broadly, there has, since the turn of the century, been increasing pressure on donors better to coordinate their support for Africa, as the costs of wasteful duplication of effort became increasingly clear to both donors and their African partners. It was clearly in the interest of donors to ensure a more efficient use of the resources they deployed in support of African development, as it was in the interest of African governments for donors to make less demands of their limited state capacities. Thus the 2005 Paris Declaration on aid effectiveness and donor harmonisation requires donors to work together in order to meet their commitment to coordinate their aid efforts. Meeting this target inevitably means more bilateral and bi-multi consultation and negotiation between donors than in the past. A good example of this is the creation of the African Union (AU) partners group in Addis. Moreover, at EU level, with the European Council rather than the Commission now taking the lead on EU Africa policy and with the Council also responsible for the European Security and Defence Policy and taking primary responsibility for implementation of the EU-Africa strategy, bilateral and bi-multi consultation between member states on Africa policy have become a necessity. Indeed, a measure of the importance with which this concept is treated in some UK government circles might be the fact the editors of this book have been invited to brief the Conservative Minister for Africa and the Liberal Democrat spokesman on African affairs on these questions.

Yet, despite the need for bilateral and bi-multi cooperation for improved donor policy coherence and for enhanced effectiveness in tackling African challenges such as unaccountable government, unrelenting poverty and chronic instability, this concept of closer working relations between two donor states – 'bilateral cooperation' – has mostly been overlooked in the literature. The focus of this literature has been on multilateral and unilateral donor approaches. There is inevitably some discussion of donor coherence at the multilateral level, partly in the context of the 2005 Paris Declaration, partly in relation to poverty reduction strategies (Craig and Porter 2003; OECD 2010) and partly in connection with ESDP missions (Olsen 2009; Howorth 2007). Equally, there have been surveys of donor cooperation in fragile states (Browne 2007) and in relation to debt reduction (Birdsall and Williamson 2002). There have also been numerous analyses of aid regimes (USAID 2004; Noël and Thérien 1995). Another set of studies has homed in on and compared the different approaches of different individual donors. These include works by Schraeder 2000; Crawford 2001; Cumming 2001; Gaulme 2003; Taylor and Williams 2004; Engel and Olsen 2005; Chafer and Cumming 2010.

It is worth emphasising two points about the above literature. Firstly, despite the acuity of the above analyses, very little of this work is underpinned by any meaningful theoretical framework with which to explain Northern state policies towards Africa or indeed towards other Northern donors. Indeed, Noël and Thérien (1995), with their focus on regime theory, and Engel and Olsen (2005), with their focus on Africa's place in IR theory, are exceptional in this regard. This dearth of theoretical analyses of relations between the North and Africa will be recognised here, and an attempt will be made to explain policy towards Africa with reference to neoclassical realism (discussed below and in Chapter 1). The second point worth noting is that none of this body of literature looks seriously at bilateral cooperation between donors or at the concept of partnerships. Clearly the bulk of writings on partnership are to be found in business (e.g. Roberts 2004) and there is also a growing literature on NGO-government (e.g. Owen 2000) and NGO-business (e.g. Heap 2000; Jamali and Keshishian 2009) partnerships. However, rather than draw on a literature which focuses on partnerships that are either entirely private or that involve one state and one non-state actor, it makes more sense here to take as one of the baselines for comparison two examples of actual partnerships between states: the Anglo-US special relationship and the Franco-German tandem. The former is instinctive, based primarily on security concerns but also draws on shared language, history and culture (Dumbrell 2009). The latter has economic concerns at its core but has also expanded into the cultural and security domain; it is more institutionalised and less 'natural' (Cole 2001).

Needless to say, it would be unfair to expect any of the 'partnerships' outlined in this book to approximate to the two special relationships outlined above. There has not been sufficient time for such a relationship to develop and there are less vital economic and strategic interests at stake in Africa for such a partnership to develop. That said, it might be reasonable to expect progress to be made towards greater two-way consultation, possibly even joint decision-making mechanisms, joint actions and a range of informal joint working practices. Have such forums, mechanisms as well as informal arrangements actually emerged? This will be a key question considered in this study and one which should shed light on whether such bilateral cooperation is extensive or marginal, or indeed whether partnerships actually exist at all in the context of Africa.

Scope

Before proceeding to address these questions, it is important to stress that the focus of this book is on donor state-to-state relations, particularly ties between elite officials and politicians. This approach is consistent with the theoretical approach adopted here, neoclassical realism, which homes in on elite officials and other policy-makers who act as the filter through which systemic pressures flow and whose perception of the national interest can have a determining influence over the foreign policy of a particular state. These comments should not, however, be taken to imply that this study will ignore the views of civil society, the donor public and the media, since these are incorporated into the neoclassical framework of analysis (see Chapter 1).

Second, this study focuses on states that have claimed to engage at some level in some kind of bilateral cooperation. The rationale for the choice of these case studies is set out below. This should not, however, be taken to signify that other states have not been involved in bilateral cooperation (e.g. the UK's DfID has a special agreement with the Australian Agency, AusAID). Nor will it be assumed that because the concept of partnership has been introduced into the discourse of these donor states that it has been implemented even to the most basic extent in practice.

Third, and linked to this, while we would argue that improved cooperation between donors, such as the UK and France, should enable them better to tackle the challenges of Africa, space constraints will not allow for an assessment of the impact of Anglo-French cooperation or indeed other bilateral collaboration between Northern countries on African issues in terms of policy outcomes. This is clearly an important question but it must be left to future researchers to identify and analyse the huge array of factors that determine the results of any such partnerships.

Finally, it should be emphasised that the focus here is Northern-centric. It is about cooperation between donors. To be sure, if Africa is taken as the object of proposed cooperation, this begs questions about African perceptions and about 'actor-ness'. Only a series of case studies of interactions between donor partnerships and African governments and multilateral organisations would make it possible to address these questions. It is nonetheless clear that, if, as might be inferred from Paul Simon-Handy's preface to this volume, cooperation between donors is seen by Africans as above all addressing donors' needs, rather than the needs of Africa, then the bilateral and 'bi-multi' partnerships examined here will not provide a new and sustainable means of supporting Africa.

Methodology

How then are we to answer the questions set out above? A number of methodological tools have been deployed towards this end. Thus contributors to this commissioned volume have been working to a clear but flexible set of guidelines. They have, where relevant, undertaken a review of the literature in respect of partnerships and looked, usually unsuccessfully, for precedents for this kind of arrangement.

Secondly, most contributors have carried out semi-structured interviews with elite officials. The editors for their part have, thanks to a large British Academy grant, conducted over 160 interviews with officials, politicians and practitioners in Paris, London, Brussels, Dakar, Abuja, Kinshasa, Khartoum, New York and Washington D.C.

Thirdly, the contributors of the empirical chapters have made use, explicitly or obliquely, of a single theoretical framework, namely neoclassical realism. As will be explained in detail in Chapter 1, this theoretical framework goes beyond classical realism and neo-realism by seeking to explain not the pattern of outcomes of state interactions but the behaviour of individual states. As Gideon Rose (1998) has observed, 'Neoclassical realism argues that the scope and ambition of a country's foreign policy is driven ... by the country's relative material power. Yet ... the impact of power capabilities on foreign policy is indirect and complex, because systemic pressures must be translated through intervening unit-level variables, such as decision-makers' perceptions and state structure'. Domestic governmental variables thus may be accommodated within foreign policy analysis. Neoclassical realism has mainly been used in the past to analyse Superpowers' behaviour. However, its integration of domestic political variables into foreign policy analysis is useful in the context of the issues addressed in the present volume as it can help us appreciate to why states sometimes cooperate in ways that are, on the face of it, not entirely self-interested.

This book is not primarily aimed at corroborating or refuting the validity of neoclassical realism as a theoretical tool. Rather, as a commissioned volume structured around the theme of cooperation and bilateral partnerships, its aim is to lay down a broad theoretical framework and examine whether it might have the potential to help us to understand better the complexity of foreign policy-making and the multitude of factors and actors driving and/or hampering recent joint approaches to the challenges of Africa and, in particular, the case of the British and French approaches to bilateral partnership on Africa. Thus it is argued here that bilateral cooperation cannot be understood without disaggregating the state and including a strong focus on the perceptions, interests and ideas of elite policy-makers, not to mention institutional constraints and other domestic variables. Nor can recent Anglo-French collaboration and other bilateral partnerships be fully explained in terms of the quest for power and influence; as various contributors to this volume show, ideas and values have also played a role. With this more limited objective in mind, a relatively non-prescriptive approach has been taken by the editors to the deployment of this theoretical framework. In effect, contributors have been free to make only limited use of this theoretical perspective if they deem it to be of limited value, with the result that some have inevitably made more extensive use of the theory than others. The findings of the contributors regarding the explanatory value of this theory in the context of donor cooperation will be examined in our conclusion.

The third methodological tool employed is case studies. The question arises as to which case studies to choose given the large number of donors that have bilateral and bi-multi relations with other donors. In this volume, two types of case study will be used to explore how bilateral cooperation has been used to address the challenges of Africa. The first will involve a direct comparison of Anglo-French cooperation with other bilateral relationships (Part III). These comparative case studies will serve as 'barometers' and better enable us to gauge the extent to which the Anglo-French partnership since Saint-Malo signals a new departure and a genuine partnership. They will at the same time extend our evaluation of the value of bilateral partnerships as a means of better addressing the problems of Africa. The first such study focuses on what is often assumed to be a natural partnership between the UK and the Nordics (given their strong mutual commitment to poverty reduction strategies) and a less fruitful alliance between France and the Scandinavian states (given the much lower priority France attaches to economic development and the MDGs). The next two studies concentrate on British and French cooperation with the same country, namely the United States. Once again, *a priori*, it might be expected that Britain and the US would have an instinctive, intuitive partnership backed up by shared histories, language and values, whereas France and the US would have much less in common in their approach to Africa. Yet are these assumptions borne out in practice, or is collaboration taking place in other sectors and/or in unexpected ways?

In Part IV a second type of case study of bilateral cooperation will examine examples of the actual practice of Anglo-French cooperation in relation, firstly, to a specific country and, secondly, to a particular organisation. The first of these looks at the Anglo-French partnership in one of Africa's crisis-ridden countries, the Democratic Republic of the Congo (DRC). The DRC has been chosen as it has been identified in statements by the British and French as a priority country for collaboration. The question addressed here is thus: have British and French commitments made at Saint-Malo and at subsequent Anglo-French summits been translated into a policy partnership in the DRC? The second case study is of Anglo-French cooperation vis-à-vis the African Union. This has been chosen as the UK and French governments committed themselves at Saint-Malo to move beyond their traditional spheres of influence in Anglophone and Francophone Africa and promised 'joint cooperation to promote sub-regional integration, in particular between networks of anglophone and francophone countries' (Saint-Malo Declaration 1998). The question to be addressed here is thus: what does this Anglo-French cooperation vis-à-vis the AU tell us about the success, or otherwise, of their efforts to move beyond their traditional spheres of influence and engage with the whole continent?

Finally, Part V examines a different type of cooperation involving a supranational actor, namely the EU. Marie Gibert examines implicit cooperation and explicit coordination between EU member states and institutions. By exploring the complex processes involved in the making of EU security policy and by homing in on bilateral and bi-multi cooperation within this supranational actor, she throws an interesting light on how these latter forms of cooperation can lead to what might best be described as 'messy multilateralism'. The question this raises is: how far can the forms of bilateral and bi-multi cooperation examined here actually serve as a model for a different, perhaps even a more relevant and hence more sustainable type of approach to supporting Africa? Or, since bilateral and bi-multi cooperation often take place within multilateral fora, are they best seen as a complement to, or simply a new dimension of, more traditional multilateral approaches? Finally, Ian Taylor looks at the partnership between China and Africa and its implications for the EU-Africa partnership. The EU and China are usually assumed to be in competition with each over resources such as oil and cobalt. Yet have they been in a constant state of conflict or have there been cases where they have managed to work together in ways that are beneficial to Africa? And what are the implications of Sino-African cooperation for leading European states such as Britain and France?

Overview of Book

This book, then, seeks to explore the question of bilateral and bi-multi cooperation in the context of Africa. The first chapter sets out the theoretical framework employed. Theresa Callan explains that neoclassical realism provides a valuable alternative or complement to theories concerned with liberal interventionism and other variants of realism. Callan demonstrates how neoclassical realism combines the rigour of neorealism with some detailed consideration of domestic political factors. She stresses the role of elites, officials and politicians in serving as an opaque filter through which systemic imperatives are filtered. Callan argues that neoclassical realism, despite some shortcomings, provides a rich explanation of the workings of and drivers behind foreign policy.

Part II then includes four chapters that provide an up-to-date analysis of the African policies of the two donor states that are at the heart of this book, namely the two leading European powers in Africa: the UK and France. Alex Vines concentrates on UK African policy, particularly the legacy of the New Labour governments (1997–2010). Daniel Bourmaud then explores the French case, looking in particular at the extent to which France has made the difficult transition from a unilateral to a multilateral approach. In Chapter 4, Gordon Cumming sets out a broad overview of Anglo-French cooperation, highlighting institutional and informal ties as well as examining cooperation on democracy promotion and poverty reduction. In Chapter 5, Tony Chafer then explores Anglo-French security cooperation, with particular emphasis on ESDP missions and the training of African peacekeepers.

As noted earlier, Part III provides a comparative dimension, examining other bilateral 'partnerships' both in their own right and as a barometer of the progress of the UK-French partnership south of the Sahara. In Chapter 6, Gorm Rye Olsen looks at the partnership that exists between Nordic donors and the extent to which the Nordics have sought to cooperate with the UK and, to as lesser extent, France. Olsen uses not only a neoclassical realist lens but also theories of small states in order to understand Anglo-Nordic and Franco-Nordic cooperation. The focus in Chapter 7 turns to the UK-US special relationship as it applies to Africa. Paul Williams examines the extent to which this relationship has been a privileged one and the significance of Anglo-US cooperation in Africa as a component of the wider Anglo-American 'special relationship'. In Chapter 8, attention turns to Franco-American relations. Niagalé Bagayoko examines these relations and asks how far France and the United States have been able to work together on African issues despite the tradition of 'Anglo-Saxon' rivalry on the continent.

Part IV contains case studies of the actual practice of partnership in relation, firstly, to a specific country (DRC) and, secondly, to the African Union. Chapter 9 by Gordon Cumming homes in on Anglo-French cooperation in the DRC, concentrating on collaboration in the areas of poverty reduction, democracy promotion and army/police reform. In Chapter 10 Tony Chafer then asks how far Anglo-French cooperation vis-à-vis the AU has been taken, particularly with reference to capacity building.

Finally, Part V provides a different angle on the issue of partnerships. Marie Gibert homes in on the 'messy multilateralism' of EU security cooperation in West Africa and looks at the role of the UK and France, as well as that of other actors, within this, while Ian Taylor asks whether the EU partnership with Africa is in competition with the Sino-African partnership or whether there are areas of common ground and potential synergies that could lead to implicit, if not explicit, cooperation.

It would of course be premature to propose a conclusion at this stage, before the theoretical framework has been established and the findings of individual contributors have been set out and synthesised. This will be the subject of Part VI. It should suffice to note here that there is sufficient evidence of the existence of bilateral cooperation and of attachment to the notion of partnership to suggest that these ideas do have resonance in the fields of international development, peacekeeping and democracy promotion in Africa. Furthermore, it is worth noting at this stage that the theoretical framework employed here is deemed by most of the contributors to have some explanatory value, even if some are more fully convinced of its value than others. We shall return to this theme in the final chapter.

Chapter 1

A Theoretical Perspective on Northern Cooperation in Africa

Theresa Callan

It is a commonplace to remark upon the relative under-theorisation of Northern state relations with Africa within International Relations (IR). This chapter introduces a theoretical framework which should help to shed light on these relations and which will be used, explicitly or more obliquely, within each chapter of this book. It identifies and critically discusses contending theories which purport to explain why states and non-state actors behave as they do on the international stage. Next, this chapter draws attention to the key debates between different theories of, and approaches to, International Relations so that the genesis of neoclassical realism may be understood. It then introduces and explains the key contentions and propositions of neoclassical realism. It places the latter within the realist tradition and explains how it is one of the more recent variants of realism to emerge. It distinguishes this form of realism from both its classical and structural antecedents, and focuses on the key arguments it makes concerning state behaviours in general and foreign policy-making in particular. It ends by using neoclassical realism to anticipate some of the book's later findings regarding Northern cooperation in Africa.

Contending Theories

Explaining why states, or more accurately, policy-makers within states act as they do is a contested area. Various theories give primacy to different actors and privilege different variables within and across states in their respective accounts. Theorists are drawn towards those accounts which best accommodate their own ontological and epistemological positions. There are no 'right' answers, of course, in the social sciences – but there are some that have greater explanatory utility than others. The competition to demonstrate this utility, often through a critique of the then dominant theory, constitutes the ground of IR. This ground then is replete with debates. The traditional fault-line in the discipline lies between Liberalism and Realism – with the latter rejecting the 'utopian', 'idealist' Liberals, such as Angell (1933) and Zimmern (1939) and their contentions that increased interaction between states and societies would lead to a safer and more peaceable world. Classical realists, such as Morgenthau (1948); Niebhur (1932);

Kennan (1951); and Carr (2001), held that in the anarchical international system, strong states would do as they chose, while weaker states would do as they must. Egotistical, atomistic and rational states prioritised their security and helped themselves to it, viewing other states as potential threats. Such mutual suspicion and the self-help approach to security gave rise to the security dilemma at the inter-state level. Conflict could not be eradicated but only managed – notably through the balance of power. International institutions, lauded by Liberals as fora for cooperation, dialogue, and the development of collective interest, were criticised for having no independent agency and for being rather less than the sum of their parts. The fate of the League of Nations seemed to attest to the validity of the Realist perspective of international affairs. The Realist approach was to remain the dominant discourse for decades to come, not least as it seemed the most explanatory of the Cold War environment, with its evident concern with the balance of power, a clear security dilemma and an obvious arms race.

A later inter-paradigm debate took place in the late 1970s into the 1980s between three perspectives – Realism, Liberalism (or more broadly, Pluralism) and Marxism (or more broadly, Radicalism). The latter two perspectives challenged the primacy that Realism accorded to the state, noting the presence of a host of non-state actors within international politics. They challenged too Realism's focus on a unitary state by 'unpacking' it to accommodate sub-state actors and interests, as well as other actors, processes and interests above the state, such as transnationalism, regionalism, and globalisation. The Realist emphasis on 'high' politics was criticised given the rising importance of 'low' politics, such as economic, environmental and human rights issues. In many ways, this 'debate' was 'not a debate to be won, but a pluralism to live with' (Waever 1996: 162).

The fault-line between Realism and Liberalism opened again with the 'neo-neo' debate between Neo-liberalism and Neo-realism. Neo-liberalism contended that the international system was characterised by 'complex interdependence' – multiple channels of communication and interaction within and across societies between a wide range of actors (Keohane and Nye 1977). Interactions took place over a similarly diverse range of issues, such as finance, communications, and commerce – none of which had more primacy than others. Interdependence was asymmetrical as some states had greater vulnerability than others in particular issue-areas. Neo-liberals accepted that states were rational and that the international system was anarchical but rejected the Realist consequences of both. Rational states, in the absence of a sovereign systemic power, would seek to uphold contracts and agreements to mitigate the effects of anarchy. International institutions would reduce the costs, transactional and otherwise, of collective action. States would be able to gain more information about one another's respective intentions and any state tempted to cheat on their contractual agreements would be deterred by the visible costs of such transgression. Institutions, according to the Neo-liberals, help shape state preferences and lock states into cooperative patterns of behaviour.

Neo-realism shared the rationalist underpinnings of Neo-liberalism but stressed the international system as the core causal variable of state behaviour (Waltz 1959:

1979). States were compelled to seek security because they existed in an anarchical environment. States were rational actors that were ever-watchful of the balance of power between them. It was this distribution of capabilities between the states that both defined the international system and accounted for its agency/impact on state behaviour. Cooperation could occur but it would be more limited than imagined by the Neo-liberals.

This focus on institutions developed within International Relations through regime theory. A regime constitutes an arrangement of 'implicit or explicit principles, norms, rules and decision-making procedures around which actors' expectations converge in a given area of international relations' (Krasner 1983: 2). Neo-liberals have a more optimistic view of the impact of institutions and regimes, formal and informal, on state behaviour. Inter-dependence and the cooperation it elicits are broadly interpreted. Different issues and different actors are accommodated within the framework. The policy-making milieu is complex, taking note of the values and beliefs of individual decision-makers, the bureaucratic context in which they work, their past experiences and understandings of previous policy trajectories, and viewing such factors as fundamental to the making of preferences and, eventually, interests. Neo-realists, such as Krasner, stress the anarchic nature of the system in which regimes operate. The structural systemic context tempers inter-state cooperation through regimes. Realists see regimes (and all else) through a power-based focus. Regimes help more powerful states to better manage interdependence and so preserve their dominant position within the system. Hegemons can use regimes to help provide stability and, of course, in so doing to safeguard and promote the interests of the hegemonic state (Ikenberry 2001). In Neo-realist accounts of regimes, however, states remain the most important actors, the agency of international institutions is constrained by the most powerful members within the international system (Mearsheimer 1994–5).

Neo-Realist approaches to IR clearly have held the balance of power central to their analyses. There has been a debate within structural realism, however, concerning exactly how the balance of power affects state behaviour. This debate involves offensive realists (Mearsheimer 2001) and defensive realists (Van Evera 1999; Walt 2002). Offensive realists have a 'more is never enough' approach to states and power. States are seen as ever-vigilant in the power competition and ready to grab any opportunity to increase their power. Their best outcome is to become the hegemon and have power over other states. Defensive realists reject such counsel. They advise that a state should not strive for hegemony as such attempts will simply set off opposition among other states. The other states will feel threatened and will band together to balance the would-be hegemon. The aspirant-hegemon's position is unlikely to triumph over those states as the defence-position tends to be stronger than that of offence. Any 'win' would be pyrrhic as the hegemon would find itself unable to meet the costs of holding the newly-acquired territory or best using its resources. In response offensive realists argue that defensive realists over-estimate both the willingness of other states to balance and assume the inherent costs and refute that the defensive hold necessarily is stronger than that of the offensive hold. Despite the clear differences between offensive and defensive realism over states as power maximisers, both are structural theories and focus on systemic variables. It is this exclusive focus on structural variables that Neo-classical realism seeks to offset – not by denying it but by reconciling it in some ways to the focus and counsel of classical realism.

Neo-classical realism [handwritten margin note]

Neoclassical Realism: Its Contentions and Propositions

The term 'Neoclassical realism' was coined by Gideon Rose (1998) as an appellation for those realist writers who seek to address the parsimony of structural realist accounts of state behaviour. Structural realism is regarded as too limited to explain the diversity of state behaviours due to its exclusive focus on systemic, or third image, variables. Neoclassical realists do not jettison structural realism but progress it – to the extent that their collective works have been termed 'the next generation of structural realists' (Rathbun 2008: 296). They continue to treat the international system as the primary independent variable when explaining state behaviours. Consequently then '[a]t their core, all neoclassical realists are structural realists as well. It is not what neoclassical realism is called but what it does. A rose by any other name is still a rose' (Rathbun 2008: 297). Neoclassical realists' inclusion of first-image and second-image variables (the individual and the state levels of analysis respectively), however, distinguishes them from structural realism. This unit differentiation and focus on the human agency of chief policy-makers denotes their common ground with the classical realist tradition. Neoclassical realists argue that state behaviours cannot be adequately explained unless actors and processes within states and societies are included. In this way 'neoclassical realism resuscitates the "political" element of political realism' (Kitchen 2010: 143), though such endogenous processes and practices remain subordinate to systemic pressures. Neoclassical realists privilege systemic variables but do not view them as exclusively deterministic of state behaviour. Structural accounts of state behaviour are seen as too limited in their explanatory utility because they fundamentally constitute theories of international politics rather than theories of foreign policy-making. The purpose of neoclassical realists is 'to explain variation in the foreign policies of the same state over time of across different states facing similar external constraints' (Taliaferro *et al.* 2009: 21). As theorists of foreign policy, such realists focus not on output but on the processes and behaviours and 'daily stuff' within the state and society which contribute to that output. Neoclassical realists thus deepen the explanatory dimension within the neorealist analytical framework:

> Actors are free to act as they wish, pursue any goals they desire, and to allow
> their interests and behaviors [sic] to be determined by the processes in which
> they are engaged. They are also free to die, but it is the choices they have made

vis-à-vis themselves and others that determine the outcome, not anarchy itself (Sterling-Folker 1997: 19).

Neoclassical realists argue that systemic constraints and opportunities pass through an opaque 'transmission belt' of unit-level variables. Key policy-makers must attempt to divine the systemic messaging through this channel of mediation. The policy-makers' own perceptions also play a role in this translation process. Anarchy then is 'a permissive condition, rather than an independent causal force' (Taliaferro *et al.* 2009: 7). It may not be entirely what statesmen make of it but its impact is mediated through their 'intentions, desires or perceptions' (Wohlforth 1993: 6) and 'their perceptions of shifts in power, rather than objective measures, are critical' (Zakaria 1998: 42). The policy-makers must cut their foreign/security policy cloth in line with their state's relative material power but they do get to choose the pattern – in conjunction with the wishes of the plethora of other influential actors within the domestic sphere.

Neoclassical realists argue that states do not make policy, governments do or rather specific parts of the governments do – notably the 'national security or foreign policy executive' (Kitchen 2010: 133), the FPE. The FPE comprises the principal governmental actors and the key personnel of the national security bureaucracies. The FPE interprets the national interest within this milieu of pluralistic politics, bargaining with other societal, sectoral elites. The neoclassical view of the state, however, is not liberal. It adopts a top-down approach, with the Janus-faced FPE standing at the apex, specifically 'at the intersection of the international, and the domestic' (Lobell 2009: 43). The FPE's autonomy from society differs in various contexts – its limited autonomy means that it must bargain and ally with other elites so that it can 'enact policy and extract resources to implement policy choices' (Taliaferro *et al.* 2009: 25). Nor is the FPE a unitary actor. Its internal balance of power shifts between the different government ministers and security service heads. Its choice of policies, therefore, will reflect bargaining within the FPE and between the FPE and other domestic stakeholders. The FPE will attempt to follow policies in the national interest but the pursuit of such policies will be affected by the other actors with influence who are 'motivated by personal, parochial or domestic political motivations' (Ripsman 2009: 172).

The FPE's ability to extract the resources essential for the implementation of policy thus is constrained by other stakeholders from different parts of the state – such as diplomats and generals – as well as the leaders of influential interest groups and other civil society organisations. The opinions and perceptions of such 'movers and shakers' influence the FPE's choice of policy course. These key stakeholders are not all equally influential, of course, and nor is their level of relative influence static. The FPE must heed especially those which constitute 'veto players' – namely those who are able 'to obstruct the government's programmatic goals, or those who can shape the definition of national interests' (Taliaferro *et al.* 2009: 37). When the government or regime is weak and faced with either an election or a more summary expulsion from office such as a coup or the FPE is so weakened or internally fragmented to the extent that there is little consensus over the policy to adopt, then 'can a domestic actor most effectively emerge as a policy entrepreneur and shape policy' (Ripsman 2009: 188). The FPE, however, should not be regarded as constantly at the mercy of the buffeting of other domestic actors. It stands at the intermestic intersection, and this position accords it privileged status in accessing information and feedback from systemic forces. It can and does manipulate the information it receives in order to shore up its position against the other domestic actors perhaps through the adoption of a tough foreign policy or initiating an inter-state conflict in order to:

> ... divert attention and create internal solidarity due to the 'rally-around-the-flag' effect, expand the power of the state over society, punish and thereby weaken internal opposition, or mobilise internal backing for costly grand strategies the population would not otherwise support (Lobell 2009: 52).

Nor need such manipulative behaviour be restricted to its home-state, as the FPE could via its choice of strategy signal to corollary elites in other states and so, in the longer term, produce a re-articulation of their politico-economic structures (ibid.: 52–3).

When policy drifts too far from the course it should take in accord with systemic pressures – either through the FPE manipulating policy for its own ends or diluting the policy it prefers in response to the demands of influential stakeholders – the systemic penalty is applied. According to Rathbun (2008: 296), 'The more the state comes to be captured by actors, and the more elites come to believe in alternative social constructions of reality different from the objective reality outlined by neorealism, the more severe the penalty'.

Ultimately, then, no one can buck the system but policy is affected by both endogenous and exogenous variables. The domestic political milieu can give rise to strategic shifts, as may external events. Dueck (2006: 12–13) distinguishes between two types of strategic shift. The former constitute 'a massive shift in the extent of strategic commitments' and may take the form of the emergence of a new threat or the upgrading of an existing threat – witness post-9/11 US strategic shift, for example. The second type is less dramatic and involves not a change in strategic goals but a change in the policy instruments used in pursuit of such goals. A state may choose perhaps to increase its diplomatic efforts or its foreign aid in order to attain a certain policy goal rather than increase its military spending or step-up its military manoeuvres.

The reaction of other states to strategic shifts within their counterparts is not systemically preordained either. The calculations by policy-makers which inform reactive behaviours are not based on instant, unequivocal information. Rather such 'feedback may be delayed and indirect' (Taliaferro *et al.* 2009: 29) leading policy-makers into debates and bargains with the other stakeholders on how to move forward. The FPE's preferred policy options will be informed not only by its interpretations of the messages from 'out there' but also by the domestic potential political costs of such options 'in here'. These potential domestic political costs will be paramount for the other endogenous actors too when they try to 'sell' their view of threat to the FPE:

> Societal leaders will seek to identify and brand states that have a component of power that harms their parochial interests as a national threat. The more their welfare depends on foreign threat identification, the harder societal elites will lobby the FPE. By getting the FPE to balance against the foreign state, the cost of balancing will be borne across the society as a whole while the benefits will be reaped by their narrow constituency (Lobell 2009: 60).

Explanations of strategic change – either of primary or secondary order – need to incorporate both internal and external variables. In addition to material dynamics, ideational factors also are important. Kitchen (2010) highlights how ideas affect state behaviour and which sorts of states are likely to be affected in which ways. He contends that very strong states are less constrained by the international system as their material and ideational strength 'largely defines' that very system. Relatively unfettered, such states are free to pursue policies more of choice than of circumstance, as he (2010: 141) notes: 'The question "what must we do?" is replaced by "what shall we do?"'. These strong states can follow auxiliary goals, optional extras as it were, rather than needs-based goals. As Kitchen (2010: 136) argues, 'Auxiliary goals may be expansionist in terms of territory or economic power; they may create interests for a state based on historic or cultural ties; they may seek to further ethical concerns or political ideas; they may be directed to "global" interests'.

In these states, where certain ideas are 'highly institutionalised and culturally embedded' in terms of thought and practice and constitute a shared elite discourse then '[t]hese ideas filter and limit options, ruling out policies that fail to resonate with the national political culture' (Kitchen 2010: 141). Ideas, identities and ideologies can be utilised by the FPE in its efforts to increase state power, that is, 'that portion of power the government can extract for its purposes and reflects the ease with which central decision-makers can achieve their ends' (Zakaria 1998: 525). The FPE can enhance state power via 'ideational factors such as ideology and nationalism' and so 'extract, mobilise and direct societal resources and cultivate support among its power base' (Taliaferro *et al.* 2009: 38).

This extractive capacity is illustrated in Dueck's thesis which explains the shift in US strategy from isolationism to internationalism with reference to the FPE's mobilisation of liberal internationalism and its attendant readings of threat and security (Dueck 2006). Taliaferro's work (2006) also explains that some states may not follow structural realist prescriptions on the emulation of successful states in the system because such 'disobedient' states differ in their internal capacity for mobilisation and extraction. His 'resource extraction model' explains whether or not states, in their search for national security, can emulate 'the successful military institutions, governing practices, and technologies of more powerful states' (Taliaferro 2006: 465). He contends that states differ in this extractive capacity because '[d]omestic variables … limit the efficiency with which states can respond to … systemic imperatives' (Taliaferro 2006: 467). Schweller (1998; 2004; 2006) offers an explanation for why states either do not balance at all or balance inadequately against a threat. Such behaviours confound structural realist strictures which hold that states will always try to offset threats either through increasing their own power, allying with other states, or doing both. Schweller's key argument is that 'underbalancing' is explainable only as consequential to 'a political act made by political actors' at the unit-level (2004: 164). Elites in the state are pivotal in deciding which course of action to take and their decisions will reflect their own perceptions and preferences and their analyses of 'the domestic political risks' of the choices available to them (2004: 169). In turn, these risks themselves are affected by four key variables: the degree of consensus within the elite; the degree of cohesion within the elite; the degree of societal cohesion; and the degree of government immunity to the loss of office. When all four degrees are ascendant, the domestic risks of balancing are correspondingly low and the elite will opt for a balancing strategy. It is assured in this climate that it can extract the necessary resources from society to implement balancing policies. Zakaria (1998) too explains US expansionist policy with reference to the increased extractive capacity of the federal government. As its power increased, so it could extract and mobilise resources for a more expansionist foreign policy. Greater influence abroad is desired and sought once 'central decision-makers perceive a relative increase in state power' (Zakaria 1998: 42).

A Recent Variant of Realism

State power may differ between states and, over time, within states thus helping to explain diversity of foreign policy-making. It is not synonymous with the relative capability of the state that is primary within structural realism. Neoclassical realism is distinct from more recent versions of structural realism – offensive and defensive realism respectively – in that both of them discount unit-level variables in their analyses. Neoclassical realists see anarchy as 'murky' rather than 'generally Hobbesian' as do the offensive realists or 'often more benign' as do the defensive realists (Rose 1998: 154, 149). These accounts are both limited in their explanations of foreign policy behaviours because neither accommodates how the perception and construction of threat by actors within the state are affected by those actors' perceptions of their relative material power.

Kitchen (2010: 118–19) has noted that '… to date "neoclassical realism" has referred more to works whose focus is essentially diplomatic history' and that the various authors within this approach have used different domestic variables in their respective analyses. This is a valid comment but clearly all neoclassical realist authors share a common stance:

> ... that over the long term the relative amount of material power resources countries possess will shape the magnitude and ambition ... of their foreign policies: as their relative power rises states will seek more influence abroad, and as it falls their actions and ambitions will be scaled back accordingly (Rose 1998: 152).

Different authors advance different theories within the neoclassical realist approach but their use of different variables does not weaken the explanatory value of the approach as neoclassical realism commonly accepts 'that different states will react to the international environment in different ways' due to their differently constituted domestic transmission belts (Kitchen 2010: 139):

> Because domestic processes are not identical, no group addresses the pressures of environment in quite the same way or emulates the processes of others in quite the same way. The interpretation of success itself is filtered through perceptual lenses colored [sic] by existing internal processes and their differences (Sterling-Folker 1997: 21).

It is the fusion by neoclassical realist theories of systemic pressures with subordinate unit-level variables that allows the approach to offer 'a richer portrait of foreign policy-making' (Ripsman 2009: 192). Its inclusion of a plethora of domestic variables may constitute 'thick description' but this should not detract from the explanatory power of neoclassical realism: 'For Neoclassical realism, to paraphrase Clausewitz, explaining foreign policy is usually very simple, but even the simplest explanation is difficult' (Rose 1998: 166).

Neoclassical Realism and Northern Cooperation in Africa

Having distinguished NCR from other theories and set out its key propositions, it is worth asking what light this theoretical perspective can shed on Northern cooperation, or the lack thereof, in Africa. To begin with, it is anticipated, from a neoclassical realist viewpoint, that the case studies within this book should attest to the influence of domestic political variables and strategic concerns on the making of foreign policy towards Africa. The second observation relates to the nature of Northern cooperation. The next dozen or so chapters all focus on instances of bilateral and 'bi-multi' cooperative action between states and non-state actors and advance rationales for such cooperation, its format, and its limits. Neoclassical realism anticipates that such cooperation should occur as and when it is perceived, by the FPE of the state(s) concerned, to be in the 'national interest', that is, it enhances the state's influence within international politics. The FPE is not, however, hermetically sealed from wider societal pressures and actors. The FPE's degree of autonomy will change in specific temporal and spatial contexts – and it is this autonomy that affects its capacity to mobilise support for new directions in policy.

Furthermore, the case-studies should demonstrate that the FPE is not a unitary actor but rather is disaggregated and subject to competition between its constituent parts, such as between different bureaucratic actors with contending visions of policy and its means of delivery. Changes in policy may reflect discernible strategic shifts as a reaction to exogenous or endogenous pressures, either material or ideational. The case studies then may be expected to identify policy change in response to changing perceptions of the systemic distribution of power, including re-calculations arising from governmental change or newly-emergent aspects of national political culture. These ideational variables would relate especially to the stronger states within the international system which seek to promote their perceived global interests. Smaller states would still be expected to try to expand their influence, working with similar-minded states – similar in terms of common values, norms, and expectations. States will be more likely to cooperate with such 'like-minded' states if other domestic stakeholders endorse the policy-makers' sense of similarity and common purpose.

The case studies then should demonstrate that policy-making within states is not systemically determined. Rather policy-makers act within a wider foreign policy-making milieu, where structural variables are transmuted through the 'transmission belt' of domestic politics. The impact of such domestic variables on policy output is not clean and linear but rather erratic and unpredictable as policy-makers' perceptions of their situation differ from case to case. The explanatory richness of neoclassical realism then should be reflected in the depth and breadth of the case study chapters.

PART II
The UK, France and Cooperation in Africa

Chapter 2
Africa and the United Kingdom: Labour's Legacy, May 1997–May 2010

Alex Vines[1]

It was only five years ago that Tony Blair as British Prime Minister in 2006 wrote that 'the world must judge us on Africa' (Blair 2006; Cumming 2004).[2] This moralistic statement followed on logically from his decision to make African development a key objective of Britain's presidency of the Group of Eight (G8) and European Union (EU) in 2005 and was consistent with the tone of British policy toward Africa during the 13 years of Labour government.

Tony Blair's personal interest in Africa should not be doubted and out of office he has continued to work on Africa through The Office of Tony Blair. In 2010, Blair insisted that:

> Africa has been at the top of my foreign policy for the last ten years. From the very beginning I wanted to forge a new partnership with African leaders and countries. I really believe that Africa is the next big opportunity for investors, it would not only be good for business but could transform the lives of Africans (Blair 2010).

This interview reflects a wider shift in UK thinking about Africa, namely a move away from a policy driven by a concern with counter-terrorism or by guilt over colonialism, humanitarian concerns and charity. So will there be a dramatic shift away from Labour policy as African affairs risk sliding down the agenda for Britain's foreign policy-makers? Such a scenario could certainly be envisaged under the new Conservative-Liberal Democrat coalition government that replaced Labour in Government in May 2010 and that has signalled a new focus on enlightened self-interest and a greater trade emphasis in UK-Africa relations.

The above question will be one of a number covered in this chapter which will begin by setting out some of the drivers behind UK Africa policy and relating these briefly to neoclassical realist theory. It will then examine the evolution of UK Africa policy under recent Labour governments, focusing specifically on two distinct but closely overlapping periods: the first phase (1997–2005) when

---

1   This chapter draws in part on Vines and Cargill (2006).

2   The British focus on Africa during a G8 presidency followed a trend started at Kananaskis in Canada in June 2002 and Evian, France in 2003.

increasing levels of priority were attached to Africa culminating in the anti-climax that was the Commission for Africa; and the second phase (2005–10) when cutbacks began to set in both for the Foreign and Commonwealth Office (FCO) and to a lesser extent the Department for International Development (DfID). Finally, an assessment will be made of the legacy left by Labour and of the ways in which the current Conservative-Liberal coalition might wish to respond to this legacy.

Interests and Values

While this chapter will not make extensive use of neoclassical realism, as this theoretical perspective is applied to UK Africa policy in subsequent chapters, it will nonetheless draw attention to two key elements of this theory: first its focus on the way that states pursue their own strategic interests and seek to enhance their relative power within the international hierarchy; and second, its inclusion of unit-level variables such as the perceptions, values and ideas of policy-makers, who execute government policy and, in so doing, take account of pressures from the domestic polity.

The basic tenet of neoclassical realism is that states are primarily driven by the quest to increase their relative power. While this claim should not be exaggerated in relation to UK Africa policy, there are some grounds for saying that Africa has been important in maintaining the UK's claim to be a global player. The UK has certainly been able to draw on its sphere of influence in Africa to help shore up its increasingly contested claim to a permanent seat on the UN Security Council, not to mention to enhance its status in Europe. The UK has also, at times, seen Africa as a continent on which it can take the lead internationally (as the later examination of the Commission for Africa demonstrates) and where it can demonstrate its military might (as per Sierra Leone) and its unrivalled capacity to promote international development (via the DfID).

The UK does also have tangible strategic and economic interests in Africa. The most obvious areas are immigration, crime and or counter-terrorism – particularly in relation to those countries from which the UK already has a large immigrant (and, until recently, emigrant) population such as Nigeria, Somalia and Zimbabwe. In 2008 Home Office figures show there were 7,165 applicants for British citizenship from Somali, 5,710 from Zimbabweans, 5,265 from South Africans, 4,530 from Nigerians and 3,135 from Ghanaians. This compares with 5,540 asylum applicants from Zimbabweans, 1,360 from Eritreans and 920 from Somali in 2009. African inmates in British prisons are also significant: 963 from Nigeria, 463 from Somalia and 209 from Zimbabwe and 154 from Ghana. These figures show that Africans from across the continent still find Britain an attractive country to live in. Despite emotive reports about crime, Africans represent a tiny proportion of jailed persons, although Nigerians come second after Jamaicans. Zimbabwe in 2009 remained one of the largest sources of asylum applicants to the UK.

The 2001 census found that sub-Saharan Africans constituted Britain's fastest-growing minority group during the 1990s, with 486,000 respondents recording their ethnicity as Black African, outnumbering Britain's Caribbean population. Yet illegal migration and related underreporting suggest this figure is a very significant underestimate. Many new British citizens are, moreover, of African origin.

As regards economic interests, these are meaningful but by no means vital. UNCTAD figures show UK exports to sub-Saharan Africa valued at $11.6bn in 2008 ($9.7bn in 2007) and imports to the UK from sub-Saharan Africa of $15.07bn in 2008 ($13.7bn in 2007) (UNCTAD 2009). Arguably, only South Africa plays a significant commercial role, as it was the UK's top export market in Africa in 2009 (and UK's 25th largest overseas market) with sales in goods alone totalling £2.14 billion. The UK is also the largest single investor there.[3] Nigeria is the UK second largest trading partner in Africa and its 33rd largest overseas market for goods. UK's exports of goods to Nigeria were worth £1.23 billion in 2009 and exports of services were worth £1.28 billion in 2008 (latest available figures). Aid rather than trade was the prime focus of British efforts in Africa under the Labour government but this has radically changed since May 2010, with the Conservative-Liberal Democrat Government insisting that trade needs to be prioritised.

Although the expression of UK interests in Africa remains something of a taboo, there was, towards the end of Labour's term of office, a growing readiness to make the UK's strategic interests more explicit. Of relevance here are public service agreements (PSAs) and the FCO's strategic priorities and its Strategic Framework. The UK's international strategic priorities were also set out in the FCO's 2006 White Paper, *Active Diplomacy for a Changing World.* In 2007, in an attempt to promote joined-up government, 30 PSAs were set for 2008–11, which included eight relevant to the FCO, with three of them relevant to Africa on migration, poverty reduction and conflict reduction (PSAs 3, 29, 30). Under David Miliband as Foreign Secretary in 2008 a new 'smarter and leaner' framework for foreign policy was introduced as eight Departmental Strategic Objectives (DSOs).

According to the DSOs, Africa of course would feature as it is an important focus of the UN Security Council and to a lesser extent the EU's common foreign and security policy (CFSP), largely because of armed conflict and increasingly because of counter-terrorism. Africa also represents a terrain in which the UK can, together with France, increase its relative power within the EU through strategically important, if selective, participation in ESDP civilian and security missions (discussed later and in Chapter 5).

It would, however, be wrong to overstate the extent to which relative power and strategic interests were driving UK Africa policy. A good example of this point might be the case of Zimbabwe where ideological and domestic pressures

---

3   351,000 South Africans visited the UK in 2006 and in 2007, 498,474 Britons visited South Africa. Some 700,000 Britons live in South Africa and some 350,000 South Africans reside in the UK. South Africa was the 21st largest importer of goods to the UK in 2009, worth £3.58 billion.

interact. From a purely strategic point of view what happens in Zimbabwe is of limited interest to the UK, yet domestic pressure forces engagement. Ironically this engagement has rarely been thoughtful or strategic, lacking as it does the framework of a broader awareness of interests and opportunities amongst many of Zimbabwe's neighbours (Cargill 2007).

The UK's interests in Africa under Labour, as from 2004, were upgraded by policy-makers for the first time since the end of decolonisation. These decision-makers were keen to emphasise the moral dimension of the UK approach and in the process engage younger voters. This approach was facilitated by the downgrading of the Foreign and Commonwealth Office and the upgrading of the DfID, with a near exclusive focus on development and poverty reduction. Labour politicians and government officials underscored the symbolic role Africa policy has come to fill in UK self-perceptions as a 'moral' power willing to do good and they were able to do so since they were operating in an arena where there is limited party political or media dissent (Gallagher 2009).[4] Indeed, surprisingly given Britain's finances, all the main political parties in the 2010 elections supported ring-fenced international development from future cuts and promised to maintain the UK's commitment to provide 0.7 per cent of national income for international development by 2013. This promise has been upheld by the Conservative-Liberal Democrat government which has pledged to enshrine it into law. Given the depth of public spending cuts in other areas, this commitment to development assistance and the new government's signalling that poverty reduction will remain core to Department for International Development (DfID) are remarkable.

An inevitable consequence of this stress on the value-driven nature of UK Africa policy was that the UK, under Labour, found it harder probably than any other country to identify or admit to selfish strategic interests. Indeed this lack of a proactive approach to strategic opportunities in Africa has meant that the UK has been least active amongst the major powers in building and securing political alliances and business engagements. Scandals during the Labour years in government surrounding some of those business engagements, such as around BAE's deals in South Africa and Tanzania, have further tarnished the reputation of British business engagements with African states. It will be an irony somewhat in keeping with UK tradition if other countries benefit from the stability and growth towards which UK development agencies (and the British taxpayer) have made a significant contribution. China is, for example, successfully increasing its commercial efforts in Sierra Leone thanks to British post-conflict stabilisation investments.

---

4   When Gordon Brown announced his resignation as Prime Minister following the May 2010 elections, the UK media speculated that like Tony Blair he could atone for his time in office by 'doing charity work in Africa'. This has proven correct, as Brown's first public appearance following his election defeat was at the AU summit in Uganda, campaigning for several charitable causes.

In a similar vein, the UK's employment of African health professionals in the National Health Service (NHS) has generated particular concern and publicity about Britain's African engagement. A survey suggests that almost a quarter of new overseas-trained physicians recruited into the NHS came from sub-Saharan Africa. In 2002 the government drew up a voluntary code to prevent poaching of nurses from Africa by the NHS (Styan 2007: 1180).[5]

This reluctance to pursue hard-nosed strategic and commercial interests in Africa was also no doubt at least partly a consequence of a growing appreciation on the part of policy-makers of the changing nature of domestic political and, indeed, electoral constituencies. Over 80 per cent of Africans live in Greater London, with significant concentrations in four of London's poorest boroughs: Southwark, Newham, Lambeth and Hackney. A second significant characteristic is the diversity of Britain's Africa population: it is no longer Anglophone West Africans but there is significant Francophone African settlement in addition to large inflows from the Horn of Africa, and expansion of the long-established Somali population (Styan 2007: 1186). It is not just in London that African communities prosper in Britain, there are concentrations of Angolans in Coventry and Manchester and a large Somali community in Cardiff, for example.

Just as the profile of Britain's African community has become diverse, so has the manner in which African migrants organise. An Institute for Public Policy Research (IPPR) study in 2007 showed that official Nigerian migrants were the second most successful immigrant group in Britain. South Africans, Ghanaians and Zimbabweans did well too, earning significantly above the British average (Sriskandarajah *et al.* 2007). Three new British members of parliament in the 2010 elections are of African origin and a number of others needed the African vote to maintain their seats. This makes understanding African issues more important, not only for British foreign policy but also for domestic politics. Africa will become increasingly important because significant communities of British of African origin care about it and lobby for attention.[6]

The Rise of Africa Policy Under New Labour (May 1997–May 2005)

For much of the 1990s Britain was largely uninterested in Africa, except as a destination for aid and managing post-colonial legacy disputes. This was to

---

5   The fragmentary official data available suggest that total remittances into sub-Saharan Africa were around $9 billion in 2006. While this represented barely 5 per cent of global remittances, it is significant to African economies, the Black and Minority Ethnic (BME) Remittance Survey found that black British Africans had the highest propensity to remit of any migrant population in the UK.

6   With devolved government, the Welsh Assembly has been developing its own aid projects in Lesotho and Somaliland. The Scottish Parliament has been doing likewise in Malawi.

change (Clapham 2002: 87). During the Labour Government's first term Blair authorised British troop support for UN and regional peacekeeping efforts in Sierra Leone in May 2000 (Ero 2001: 60; Leboeuf 2003). Blair started to promote Africa's cause(s) at international gatherings, starting with the G8 summit in Genoa in 2001 (Porteous 2005). By the beginning of Labour's second term in 2001 a discernible UK policy on Africa was emerging (Williams 2004). Blair at the Labour Party conference of September 2001 announced that Africa was a 'scar on the conscience of the world' that would become 'deeper and angrier' unless something was done to heal it. Blair announced that Africa would be a policy priority for his new government, although this agenda was distracted by the war on Iraq for much of 2004.[7] Although officials in the Prime Minister's Office were not surprised, Blair's speech on Africa caught the Africa specialists in the Foreign and Commonwealth Office (FCO) off guard. Blair reaffirmed his commitment towards Africa in February 2006 while in South Africa. He stated that:

> I think Africa is probably the great moral cause of our time, because of the ... millions of people who die unnecessarily through conflict, famine, or disease, and because ... in an interdependent world it makes no sense for us to leave ... Africa in the situation of being the only continent anywhere in the world over the past few decades that has gone backwards. And there is such vitality, and energy, and intelligence here, and it is a tragedy that it is not mobilised and used in the way that it should be. So I think we have a huge moral obligation in countries like mine, but also in the end I think in our self-interest to act (Blair, 11 February 2006).

The British general public supported the government's focus on Africa according to a 2005 survey by Chatham House (the Royal Institute of International Affairs- an independent London-based think tank) of people's views in Britain (Kaplan 2005). Climate change was also ranked highly as were concerns over migration. However, the real focus of UK Africa policy from 2001 was on reducing poverty through economic development, motivated by a mixture of moral imperative and a sense that Africa's problems could threaten western interests (Porteous 2005: 290). This approach was consistent with the first of the 'three key motifs' of British foreign policy since 1997 identified in a House of Commons report as being 'the pursuit of an activist philosophy of interventionism; maintaining a strong alliance with the US and a commitment to placing Britain at the heart of Europe'(Lunn *et al.* 2008). With the exception of the UK's operations in Sierra Leone, however, British engagement in Africa was more symbolic than physical. The UK's main contribution under Labour to Africa was as an aid donor rather than trading nation or investor in peace and security.

---

7   Although not 9/11 which convinced him that dealing with Africa's failing states was important for international security.

The increasing importance of Africa policy under Labour in these years is then most clearly reflected in the emergence and growth of DfID. The establishment in 1997 of a separate cabinet-level Ministerial department, the Department for International Development, under the control of the outspoken Clare Short, signalled a powerful and not entirely unwelcome shift on Africa given past Foreign Office priorities south of the Sahara (Kampfner 2004). During Labour's 13 years in government, international development became an area in which Britain punched well above its weight, as aid spending tripled in real terms and DfID enjoyed a reputation as a progressive, innovative and effective donor. It helped Britain have a strong voice on the Millennium Development Goals (MDGs), in the G8 and in international institutions. This was in stark contrast to the position in the mid-1980s when aid was the poor relation to foreign policy and used to support UK commercial interests.

By 2001 DfID had a larger budget than the Foreign Office and much more influence. Unlike the FCO, DfID has also under the Labour government had relative ministerial stability – Clare Short, Baroness Amos, Hilary Benn and Douglas Alexander. However, the shift went too far, downplaying the role of traditional diplomacy and politics and exaggerating the humanitarian and development agenda in Africa, an agenda with which politicians were more comfortable as it emphasised the role of aid and de-emphasised the need to understand politics, history and context. Although DfID did try to develop its own political analysis through its Drivers of Change work, this was downgraded following a turf war between Douglas Alexander and the Foreign Secretary, David Miliband.

In many ways in 1997 DfID took on the role of 'Ministry for sub-Saharan Africa' (Lunn *et al.* 2008). DfID's bilateral and regional programmes in sub-Saharan Africa increased from £300m in 1997–8 to £1.5bn in 2008–9. Nearly 90 per cent went to priority countries of which only two are not in the Commonwealth (Democratic Republic of Congo and Ethiopia – Rwanda and Mozambique are part of the Commonwealth but are not former British colonies). By 2005, DfID was channelling direct budget support to 17 African countries, which raised questions about whether these governments were committed to good governance and poverty reduction. Some of the most effective DfID aid programmes have involved broad-based interventions in support of national strategies such as construction of primary schools in Tanzania and supporting a food security strategy in Malawi.

The Commission for Africa: The Anti-climax of Labour's Africa Policy

It was in 2005 that the single most visible action of Labour on Africa was effected, namely the hosting of its Commission for Africa report for its presidency of the G8. The setting up, process and publication of the report revealed as much about Britain and its own politics and perceptions of Africa as it did about Africa itself. Then Prime Minister Blair was influenced by celebrity. Irish pop star campaigner

Bob Geldof at the Evian summit convinced Blair that he should create a commission to re-assess the causes of African poverty, and the Commission for Africa was duly established by Blair in February 2004 (Williams 2005; Brown 2006; Hurt 2007).

The aim of the Commission was to take a fresh look at Africa's past and present and the international role in the development of the continent; it was timed to seize on the political and symbolic opportunity that 2005 presented thanks to the UK's chairmanship of both the G8 and EU. 2005 also marked the holding of a summit to review the implementation of the UN MDGs and also the 20th anniversary of Live Aid and the 25th anniversary of the publication of the seminal Brandt Commission report 'North-South'.

The were 17 members of the Commission, nine of them African, including then South African Finance Minister Trevor Manuel, then Tanzanian President Benjamin Mkapa and Ethiopian Prime Minister Meles Zenawi, although all the Commissioners were officially working in their personal capacity. The composition of the Commission was flawed from the outset, allowing as it did individuals such as Ethiopia's Zenawi to sit on it. It is not surprising that human rights issues hardly featured in the Commission report. South Africa's Trevor Manuel sat on the Commission more as a gesture mandated by President Thabo Mbeki for repairing the damage to bilateral relations caused by the crises in Zimbabwe and Iraq, than as a signal of any real South African buy-in.

Bob Geldof and fellow Irish pop star Bono also joined forces to promote the Make Poverty History Campaign and arrange Live-8 pop concerts in G8 countries and in South Africa during the summer of 2005. Following increasing unpopularity inside the UK due to the Iraq war, Tony Blair appeared to find this alliance with pop stars very seductive, especially when he decided 2005 was to be an election year.

Unlike under the first Labour Government, increasingly key foreign policy decisions, including now on Africa, shifted to the Prime Minister's office, and the FCO was often not consulted. This was apparent in the choice of who was invited to serve on Blair's Commission for Africa, launched in mid-2004. The Commission was also adversely affected by the wider political contest between the UK's Chancellor (No. 11 Downing Street) Gordon Brown and the Prime Minister (No. 10 Downing Street). This competition thus impacted on its early effectiveness as both these offices competed for the heart of the initiative as part of an ongoing and increasingly bitter succession battle (Taylor 2005).

The ambiguity surrounding the Commission for Africa itself is central to this. There were questions being asked about the nature and purpose of the Commission. Its stated aim was to create a report and set of proposals containing 'new and radical thinking' on how to develop Africa, but to what extent this would be differentiated from official UK foreign policy was left open to question.

The Commission, and by extension the UK government, developed a reputation for being loftily out of touch, an image not helped when a key figure in the Commission reportedly claimed at a dinner for senior international diplomats that 2005 would be the year when 'Africa was discovered on the international agenda', by implication discounting recent initiatives by the Canadian, French and American governments. Such thinking was reflected again in Blair's February 2006 interview in South Africa where he claimed: 'I think the G8 last year was the first time Africa has come centre stage for the G8 Summit' (Blair, 11 February 2006).

The launch of the report took place at the British Museum in March 2005, and was dominated by the Prime Minister, Chancellor and Bob Geldof. Choosing a British charity event such as Comic Relief's Red Nose Day to launch the Commission for Africa report did not assist relationship-building with sceptical G8 partners and Africans who complained of British arrogance. *Our Common Interest* the Commission's 400-page report was a cogent summary of existing ideas on what is required to boost growth and good governance across Africa (Commission for Africa 2005). The launch event was carefully managed, but it was striking that although probably the most substantive efforts at consultation were by business there was no reference to the importance of business in Africa at the launch. This emphasised the vision at the time of Blair, Brown and Geldof that this was a charitable exercise. The emphasis was not on what Africa could do for itself but rather the West for Africa.

The blunders surrounding the Commission were widely noted and the House of Commons' International Development Committee in its December 2004 submission to the Commission for Africa emphasised the need for policy coherence (House of Commons International Development Committee 2004). The Commission itself dissolved at the end of September 2005. The report's recommendations were declared by Tony Blair to have been incorporated into UK foreign policy, but many of the key recommendations failed to have an impact. The UK's presidency of the EU from July to December 2005 did not see much progress although a new EU Strategy for Africa was agreed by the European Council on 15 December 2005.

A follow up report, *Still Our Common Interest*, marking the Commission's fifth anniversary, was launched at the British Museum in September 2010 by Myles Wickstead, the former head of the Commission's Secretariat (Wickstead and Hickson 2010). This time, the importance of private sector engagement in Africa was emphasised by all the key speakers, a dramatic contrast to the original launch: a sign of how in five years the debate has shifted.

A Degree of Retrenchment: UK Africa Policy from June 2005–May 2010

In the Labour government's third term the focus on Africa seemed to wane although Labour rushed through in nine weeks the arrangements for a South African President Jacob Zuma's state visit to Britain in March 2010, just ahead of the May elections. Then Foreign Minister Jack Straw in a keynote speech in Abuja on 14 February 2006 underlined that development, governance, conflict, terrorism, migration, crime and drugs, energy security, environment, Islam and China were the key pillars of UK engagement towards Africa (Straw 2006).

Straw's successor David Miliband insisted that 'By no stretch of the imagination is it possible to argue that the UK's influence in Africa is lower today than it was 10 years ago. In fact, it is massively enhanced' (Lunn *et al*. 2008). Miliband in practice, however, showed little interest in Africa except for Kenya's post-election crisis in December 2007, DRC and Zimbabwe. For his part, Gordon Brown as Prime Minister maintained an aid focus, even during the 2010 election campaign.

Despite an outward appearance of unchallenged continuity, British policy towards Africa was coming under closer scrutiny. The need for cost-cutting to compensate for the high costs of British engagement in Iraq as well as for a review of security of British diplomatic and aid missions abroad had been recognised and this was about to impact on the UK's capacity to deliver on Africa. It follows that during 2005 significant Whitehall restructuring was under way and that, while Africa was officially a government priority, there were dramatic contradictions behind this rhetoric. Government departments working on Africa entered 2005 being downsized. In the case of the FCO, this was by 20 per cent in personnel, with diplomatic missions being closed in Lesotho, Swaziland and Madagascar by the end of 2005.[8] A number of other embassies downsized, merged positions or were downgraded. The Consulate in Douala was also closed.

Africa at the FCO has not enjoyed stability of leadership under Labour. By the 2010 elections, eight Labour ministers had overseen Africa policy but had not had time to develop proper ministerial expertise.[9] The appointment of Chris Mullin in 2003 might even have been an afterthought because his appointment was made in a late and rushed manner. After Lord Malloch-Brown resigned in 2009 there was a gap of over six months before Baroness Kinnock took over. It was telling that at a meeting on Africa at No.10 Downing Street in 2004, the Prime Minister introduced his Africa team to a high-profile gathering – but forgot to mention his FCO minister – the one minister in government tasked specifically to cover Africa.

This rapid turnover of Africa ministers may have contributed to the vulnerability of the Africa departments to financial and personnel cuts – although other regions such as Latin America have also suffered. Ten positions in the Foreign and Commonwealth Office's Africa Command disappeared in 2005. Cutting government bureaucracy was an electoral issue, assisted by the post-9/11 cross-government emphasis on thematic rather than geographical expertise. Some FCO desk officers who before the cuts covered a few African countries now cover many, several of them complex and strategic to the UK. The expansion of the Pan-Africa Policy Unit (PAPU) and the creation of positions dealing with energy security in Africa in 2005 have not compensated for these cuts, and geographical desks

---

8   Tony Lloyd MP-1998; Peter Hain MP-2000; Bill Rammell-2001; Baroness Amos-2002; Chris Mullin MP-2003; Lord Triesman-2005; Lord Malloch-Brown-2007; Baroness Kinnock-2009.

9   Mali had already closed in 2003, thereby providing funds for a British diplomat to be stationed in Monrovia, but housed at the US Embassy. A number of DfID offices in Africa were also closed in 2005, such as Botswana.

complain of over-stretch and an inability to assess what the missions in Africa are reporting. Indeed this expansion of the FCO's PAPU was short-lived. It was further downsized in 2006. Due to the volume of work, desk officers have also been discouraged from attending off-site meetings that could expand their expertise. Under Labour the FCO was no longer tasked with housing expertise but rather with implementing policy although the state of play has been changing since May 2010. Lord Malloch-Brown (2010) following his resignation as minister observed:

> that the real crisis for the Foreign Office is whether it will be allowed to lead in its embassies and Whitehall, or will it be reduced to landlord and events organiser for other parts of government. Abroad, diplomats are usually outnumbered by trade, immigration and development officials with their own priorities. In Whitehall, impatient prime ministers often elbow the Foreign Office aside to run foreign policy. Whether from sofa or bunker, prime ministers have over-ruled the Foreign Office to play to the news cycle.

The result is that British capacity to develop a more subtle and differentiated understanding of Africa has been further eroded. Academic bodies, NGOs and think tanks will increasingly try and fill some of the gaps but there is no longer effective capacity inside government structures to assess quality and either commission or encourage innovative work. Increasingly country policy is decided by diplomatic missions on the ground, except where there are strategic interests such as energy security or a domestic angle, such as Zimbabwe or Sudan (which both had dedicated FCO-housed units).

The closure of High Commissions in Lesotho and Swaziland in 2005 did not result in much comment but do represent an emotional break with Britain's colonial past. The Prime Minister of Swaziland did complain that the timing was poor, as Swaziland was in a complicated transition. Swaziland and Lesotho are now covered from South Africa. Madagascar in fact raises greater questions about policy coherence. Following its change of government, Madagascar was in a democratic transition that in 2009 ended in crisis, and Britain had to redeploy a diplomat to be stationed in Antananarivo for over a year until May 2010. It is also globally strategic for bio-diversity and global warming and has just had significant inward British investment through Rio Tinto. A UK diplomatic mission in Antananarivo ticked a cluster of the key current UK strategic policy boxes and its closure is a contradiction except if based upon size.

At the same time, it should not be forgotten that the drive for personnel and expertise cuts inside DfID was equal to that of the FCO. DfID has suffered cuts and a number of its offices have been downsized and positions merged although, unlike the FCO, a number of programmes were also greatly expanded, as in Nigeria which due to its population size is seen correctly as strategic. Like the FCO, small programmes were vulnerable and DfID almost closed its Angola and Gambia offices during 2005 – the decision on Angola postponed until early 2009 following robust lobbying by the All Party Parliamentary Group on Angola. The

Gambia office closed in early 2010.[10] DfID's overall budget under Labour did not suffer, but cuts in personnel have resulted in increased outsourcing to think-tanks and NGOs, resulting in weaker project analysis and appraisal. The emphasis came to be increasingly on spending in order to reach targets; this made small DfID programmes, such as in Angola and Lesotho, increasingly unattractive for senior managers because of their high administrative costs.

The Legacy and Lessons of the Labour Years for UK Africa Policy

In terms of UK Africa policy, recent Labour governments have left an important legacy that can be built upon by the current Conservative-Liberal Democrat coalition. Labour has in concrete terms left behind, first the DfID; second, a closer working relationship with the EU on Africa; and third, a Conflict Prevention Pool. Each of these will be examined briefly in turn.

First, the DfID is undoubtedly Labour's main legacy in relation to Africa, and the new coalition government's commitment to maintain it as a separate cabinet-level-led ministry has been welcomed by the wider donor community. Britain's finances in 2010 provide an opportunity for clear thinking and less waste. Although William Hague admitted in September 2010 to the Foreign Affairs Committee that 'the reduction and withdrawal of this country's diplomatic presence – something that we know has taken place in large parts of Africa – is a mistake', there will be cuts in Africa. The future British diplomatic network will be more reliant on small posts and staff numbers in many posts have already been cut back in 2010. There is a commitment not to repeat 2005 and close further posts and in some African countries DfID and FCO will merge for efficiency's sake or the UK network will become DfID-led. A clear definition of interests and how to burden-share with allies and partners would also bring real benefits. For example, in 2010 DfID was housed in the Irish Embassy in Lesotho, DfID and FCO share office space in Tanzania and British diplomats operate from the US embassies in Côte d'Ivoire and Liberia and the Canadian embassy in Mali. Although the Comprehensive Spending Review of October 2010 resulted in the closure of DfID's Lesotho office most of the UK network in Africa has been retained, although staff numbers have been reduced, resulting in many more British diplomatic small posts. Fewer diplomats and aid workers will need clearer strategic objectives. In theory, the EU and its European External Action Service should be able to plug some of these gaps, but that is a long-term project.

---

10   DfID decided that obvious aid cuts during 2005 – the year of Africa would be too embarrassing but cuts did occur to middle-income countries like Botswana. All Party Parliamentary Groups (APPGs) are run by backbench MPs. In 2009 there were 14 APPGs on sub-Saharan African countries or topics (Africa, Angola, Botswana, Ethiopia, Ghana, Madagascar, Mozambique, Namibia, Nigeria, Somaliland, South Africa, Sudan, Tanzania, Zimbabwe and the Great Lakes and Genocide Prevention).

There is a strong case for saying that while the DfID still needs to be listened to, the FCO in particular needs a stronger voice in the making of Africa policy than it enjoyed under Labour. For this to happen, the FCO will need to understand more about international development and DfID more about business and politics. Counter-terrorism efforts in Africa could also usefully draw more on aid and political analysis. That would no doubt lead the newly formed National Security Council to avoid looking at Africa as just a threat but also as an opportunity from which potential benefits can be drawn in terms of trade growth, energy diversification and frontier markets. In line with this thinking, the British Embassy in Mali, which was re-opened in mid-2010, should not be exclusively security-driven in its mandate.

Second, a closer working relationship with the EU, particularly on human rights and ESDP missions is another element of Labour's legacy. Although under Labour the UK was supportive of the EU's common foreign and security policy (CFSP) and its expeditionary missions under the European security and defence policy (ESDP), its physical commitments have nonetheless been primarily to NATO in Iraq and Afghanistan, with the exception of its efforts to combat Somali piracy.

Given its finances, the UK will no doubt need to turn to the EU more often as a source of legitimisation and burden-sharing. In the past London used the Union when it could provide extra support for its policies such as the EU sanctions regime on Zimbabwe in 2002. The UK however, ignored the EU's mechanisms, when it believed they might prove cumbersome, as in the case of its Operation Palliser in Sierra Leone in 2000. Under Gordon Brown as Prime Minister, Britain saw the EU even more in economic terms rather than playing an important role in the military security sphere. There is a danger that this will continue under the Conservative-Liberal Democrat coalition government. For the UK, the EU is viewed as one option for crisis management but NATO is clearly the preference. In Africa, the UK has only deployed symbolic numbers of personnel to ESDP missions, although it encouraged Artemis in 2003 and sent a special operations unit to Bunia in order to demonstrate that it could develop a European capability (Vines and Middleton 2008). As Chapter 5 demonstrates, Britain initially showed interest in supporting Eufor/Chad in 2008, but London became uninterested when Britain's Ministry of Defence (MoD) refused to participate in the mission and initially blocked funding. The UK only sent staff officers following a direct intervention from President Sarkozy to Gordon Brown.

In October 2008, when French Foreign Minister Kouchner visited Eastern Democratic Republic of Congo with UK Foreign Secretary David Miliband during a crisis and advocated intervention, their militaries advised against. The MoD was clear in Whitehall that a UK deployment fell outside UK national interest, but the problem was that British politicians found this difficult to spell out clearly to their EU partners and the general public. The same was true in France (Vines 2010).

In contrast, despite initial reluctance from the FCO and MoD in London, the UK permanent delegation in Brussels successfully worked with the naval chief of staff to obtain authorisation for Britain to take the lead on Operation Atalanta against

Somali piracy. For the first time in an ESDP mission, and encouraged by France, Britain hosted the operational HQ at Northwood. Interestingly following France's return to NATO, the opportunities for Anglo-French defence cooperation have been enhanced, as illustrated by the Franco-British summit of November 2010.

Britain is also a thought-leader on international development, and its 0.7 per cent aid commitment will allow it to maintain a strong voice in multilateral efforts, such as the MDGs, global health and climate change debates.

Third, an important legacy from the Labour years in government was the establishment of the FCO/DfID/ MoD Africa Conflict Prevention Pool in 2001. In 2008 the Africa and Global Conflict Prevention Pools were merged into a single Conflict Prevention Pool, symbolic of Africa losing some of the status achieved during the Blair government. In 2009, emergency cuts due to Britain's finances, worsened by a poor exchange rate for the sterling, swept away some goodwill built up through Britain's investment in this field. The Conflict Prevention Pool and other innovations such as the Africa Conflict and Humanitarian Unit established in 2003 and a joint FCO/DfID/MoD Post-Conflict Reconstruction Unit established in 2004 and the DfID/FCO/MoD Sudan Unit and a similar effort on DRC all have merit. Many of the gravest national security threats originate not in strong states, but in states marked by poverty, fragility and weakness, as found in parts of Africa. The Conservative-Liberal Democrat coalition's commitment to build on this and 'create a new stabilisation and reconstruction force' is therefore not relevant only to Afghanistan but also for Africa. However, aligning aid to national security interests will confront government with new challenges, such as how to integrate poverty reduction and security within a framework for defence. With the creation of a new National Security Council, regional analysis – including on Africa – may well feature less.

Conclusion

This chapter has focused on the legacy of 13 years of Labour government for Britain's Africa policy and suggested that the UK began to attach increasing priority to Africa in Labour's first and above all second term. The rise of Africa policy arguably was aid-focused and culminated in the anti-climax of the Commission for Africa, with the third term of Labour government seeing a degree of retrenchment in Africa policy.

While space constraints have ruled out any detailed analysis in terms of neoclassical realist theory, it has nonetheless been suggested that Africa represents a means by which the UK can enhance its international ranking and a source of strategic and economic interests which are important, though not vital. It has further been argued that these interests have not disappeared but that they were masked by the approach taken by Labour ministers and government officials, which was to conceive of Africa as essentially a 'development'/humanitarian problem as well as a 'migration' issue. This in turn led them to shape policy in a particular way, giving prominence to the DfID, marginalising the FCO and preventing the UK from owning up to the fact that it has strategic interests there – or at the very least making owning up to them a 'taboo' subject. The shaping of policy in this way also no doubt reflected in the readiness of UK politicians to respond to UK NGOs, media and public opinion on Africa. It remains to be seen whether the current Conservative-dominated coalition government will be quite so prepared to take account of the sensitivities of societal actors or whether it will wish to take Africa policy in a radical new direction, with much more explicit emphasis on UK commercial and strategic interests.

Chapter 3

From Unilateralism to Multilateralism: The Decline of French Power in Africa

Daniel Bourmaud

France's Africa policy has never been in such turmoil or seemed so disoriented. From its beginnings, when the Fifth Republic was set up, it was thought to be unshakeable Indeed, until very recently, an outpouring of literature, which has included journalistic texts as well as academic writings, was 'celebrating' its remarkable continuity (Martin 1995) and noting how, even when the winds of change looked like blowing away everything before them, France's Africa policy stood firm. The end of the Cold War certainly did not shake this colossus, which was weakened, certainly, yet remained determined to resist.

However doubt has crept in today and is becoming more insistent. Against the backdrop of large-scale changes affecting Africa and international relations, some analysts have voiced dismay that France's Africa policy has continued to renew its practices and preserve its dubious legacy while other commentators who have already decreed that the days of such a policy are long gone and that it is dead. For the latter the Africa policy that Paris follows is now performing its swansong since France has definitively 'lost' Africa (Glaser and Smith 2005).

So what then is left of France's Africa policy? Does France still have an Africa policy and if so what is it? Can France still pursue a unilateral policy in sub-Saharan Africa as it did in the days of its former 'splendour' or is it not obliged to base its action in Africa on United Nations or more particularly on European Union multilateralism, even at the risk of banalising that action?

To answer these questions, there is a need for some kind of pre-existing methodology. Analyses of France's Africa policy very rarely explain their epistemological categories and their theoretical bases. They draw upon numerous elements which are often (but not always) well established and which lead indubitably to converging conclusions that may be summed up as follows: France's Africa policy, which was built up in the spirit of a mission of cooperation that was supposed to enhance France's international standing has been degraded by the connivance of networks and by covert practices. This policy resisted change because it encompassed a vast array of interests, and being a deeply conservative policy, it was thus condemned to failure. This has still not been recognised as such by different French governments which have persisted in preserving a legacy that is both illusory and harmful in that it acts as an obstacle to the necessary changes that Africa in particular is demanding and which are echoed in French society.

Obviously, there are nuances to be drawn here but they do not detract from the fact that there is general agreement on the outdated, retrograde and dangerous character of this policy. Even if commentators have not clearly spelt out the basic assumptions upon which their analyses are based, these assumptions can nonetheless be discerned. They are implicit or unconscious and they have a dual nature. Firstly, they are the preserve of Africa specialists who see Africa policy as a specific policy, closed in on itself, with no link to either the rest of foreign policy or to the international system. Secondly, they all spring from a moral approach in the sense that they are part of a prescriptive attitude where ideas of good and bad predominate.

This double tropism does not mean that the facts on which these analyses are based are wrong but the imprecise and unstated framework in which they are placed considerably limits the scope and the validity of any explanation. That is why it is imperative to break with these approaches and define at the outset the research method which will in our view enable us to explain France's Africa policy.

In adopting such an approach, there is clearly a need to to spell out what is meant by France's Africa policy as an object of analysis, even if this can only be done in summary fashion. In this context, two things have to be borne in mind:

- Africa policy is indissociable from foreign policy. It is an element of a larger whole and thus is linked to analytical instruments created for the field of international relations. It follows that Africa policy is indebted to the paradigms and theories that govern this discipline.
- Africa policy, in terms of its perimeter, encompasses a vast number of actors, institutions and sectors. It is not limited to the narrow perimeter of political leaders and state institutions responsible for links with Africa (the presidency of the Republic, ministers or secretaries of state). It encompasses a group of private actors (the media, NGOs, businesses etc.) who are involved in relations between France and Africa, in their conception and in their implementation. Thus it is that many of them who are self-proclaimed analysts of Africa policy actually take on the role of actors insofar as they play an active part in activities or lobbying in relation to this policy.

In light of these remarks, how then should France's Africa policy be viewed? In line with the theoretical perspective underpinning this edited volume, we will situate our reflection within a perspective which, while retaining a focus on the interests of various states, includes these interests in a conceptual framework where ideas and values also play an important role. This crossing over between interests and values is associated with the theoretical perspectives that are adopted by authors who claim to belong to realism as much as to neo-realism. In his classic work *Peace and War: A Theory of International Relations*, Raymond Aron insisted on the difficulty involved in defining national interests which were 'an abstraction drawn from within the regime and composed of the aspirations of the different classes, of the political ideals of the city' (Aron 2004). Aron added that 'ideas and feelings influence actors' decisions'. In this desire to take the influence of ideas into account, some have seen the premises of neoclassical realism, such as it was later to be found in writers like Gideon Rose, for whom the perceptions of decision-makers are part of the foreign policy process (Rose 1998). Certainly, the structure of the international system constrains actors and limits the deployment of state power. But the perceptions and the calculations of leaders also affect the way in which a state will pursue its interests within the field of international relations.

This approach, which focuses on interests, power, the shape of the international system and actors' perceptions, sheds light on the factors underpinning France's Africa policy. This policy is not the result of a mechanical power-game to which decision-makers are forced to submit. Certainly, the political situation of Africa at the time of independence gave France the opportunity to develop a policy of power which is in many ways exceptional. No other colonial power, beginning with the United Kingdom, has cemented with its former colonies such close relations in order to serve its interests and its power. But there was nothing inevitable about this. This policy owes in part its extraordinary specificity to the way in which French leaders, and French elites along with them, imagined the place that France could occupy in Africa. This project was set in a favourable environment, that of the Cold War. It fitted with the great power status that France reserved for itself, all the more since the logic of a bipolar world corresponded to the African dream of French leaders. However this project was not fixed. It has evolved, influenced by changes in the international system and in the cultural and ideological references of the elites.

Thus the question of change or continuity in French policy south of the Sahara, its coherences and incoherences, its delays and contradictions, can be seen in a different light. This policy, which is now over half a century old, has undergone substantial changes. For a long time, it was the very embodiment of perfect continuity. Since the end of the Cold War it has struggled to place itself within a new framework within which the axes of power can be easily identified. French Africa policy was long based on thinking that was strictly and jealously unilateral but since the end of the Cold War, and more especially since the beginning of the 21st century, it has cultivated cooperation and multilateralism. Yet the observer cannot but be struck by the different kinds of resistance which act as a brake on this evolution. One step forwards, one step backwards, a sense of hesitancy seems to be at the heart of the current policy. Why? The answer could be framed as follows. Multilateralism is contrary to History and to the tradition of France's Africa policy. Looking beyond their differences, French political elites on the whole accepted the conception of foreign policy and particularly of Africa policy imposed by General de Gaulle. That age of consensus has now given way to an era of dissension. Foreign policy is no longer unanimously supported. Vague multilateral desires have come up against the impossibility of producing a new consensus likely to give coherence back to a way of thinking which appears to become unravelled. This impossibility is not so much due to the shortcomings of multilateralism as to a failure to root multilateralism in a foreign policy framework where state power would have a role, find its place. Instead of appearing as the instrument of a new statement of self-confidence, multilateralism seems to belong more to a strategy of abandonment. It follows that multilateralism has a limited capacity to garner and mobilise support which in turn reinforces the impression that French Africa policy oscillates permanently between nostalgia for past practices and the attraction of a future that is ill-defined and uncertain.

The Culture of 'Grandeur' versus Multilateralism.

It is said that France's Africa policy was inseparable from its founder, General de Gaulle. The institutional characteristics of this policy are well known as well as its specificities. Every aspect of the policy-making architecture that was set up had something exceptional about it. But this extraordinary specificity is only the surface of a construction whose foundations have been laid at the very heart of Gaullist ideology, which is itself deeply rooted in French political culture. Gaullism only took off and became as successful as it did because it chimed in fully with core elements of French identity. If it is cut off from its cultural and ideological pillars, France's Africa policy simply cannot be understood.

The success of Gaullism is undoubtedly linked to particular circumstances: the aftermath of the Second World War, the colonial traumas of Indochina and Algeria and the shortcomings of the Fourth Republic, all of which created a context of crisis that was not only political but also cultural. The magic of Gaullism was that it grappled with the scale of expectations and that it looked beyond the simple question of which political regime was in power and endeavoured to supply a global response to a global crisis. If Gaullism has no equivalent anywhere else it is because it is the reflection of a culture of national politics which is itself unmatched anywhere else. The theme of grandeur, the obsession with rank, the jealous claims to unchallenged independence, the right and the duty to speak directly to the world are all so many elements which reveal not the pathology of a man in power but more the expression of a culture which has been built around the affirmation of French exceptionalism. Since the French Revolution, the identity of France has been based on a universalism which is that of the nation and of human rights, on a political model which is the Republic, on a social contract which has restricted the scope for religious activity within the political arena through an almost untranslatable concept, namely *laïcité*. So, it is based on a historic mission that has to be carried out at a universal level. We recall Victor Hugo's phrase which so well sums up French identity: 'Without the (rest of the) world, France feels alone'.

It was in this cultural and ideological ground that French foreign policy took root. The same is true of France's Africa policy. Through its diplomacy, its defence policies and its 'sphere of influence' in Africa, France gave substance to its claims to greatness and prestige. In asserting power in this way, France was viewing multilateral institutions with suspicion or disdain. Suspicion was reserved for NATO, the instrument of American domination, which France made a point of leaving in 1966. Disdain was what was felt for the UN, the 'thingummy', as De Gaulle used to call it. Gaullist France was rebellious and hostile to any idea of supranationality of which multilateralism is the expression. The erratic developments within the European Community are but one of the most obvious examples. For Gaullism, grandeur required unilateralism.

And what of Africa? As an integral part of France's quest for power, the role it played was not secondary but, rather, pivotal. Thanks to nuclear weapons France was a military power. As a permanent member of the UN Security Council, France was also a diplomatic power. With Africa, it was a regional power. The French hexagon, reduced to about half a million square kilometres after decolonisation, was rebuilding a space in keeping with its size. Despite the failure of the French Community, which collapsed in 1960, de Gaulle set about making an Africa where France could be present by adjusting post-independence sovereignties to the needs of its policies. In this context, the institutional mechanisms put in place are revealing: they infringe the principles of sovereignty *de facto* by linking the functioning of newly decolonised African states to that of the French state. The mechanisms of the CFA franc, the pre-positioning of troops stationed in French bases in Africa, the signing of defence agreements which made France the guarantor of the security of its former colonies are all elements that suggest a special relationship based on co-sovereignty. The African states in France's 'backyard' are of course independent but some of their sovereign powers, notably on monetary and security matters, are actually shared with the former colonial power. When President Georges Pompidou set up the Franco-African summits in 1973 with a view to bringing together all the heads of state concerned every two years, he helped to reinforce the highly specific bonds that linked Paris and the young nations of francophone Africa. In so doing, France carved out a field of action within its means where, in the words of Louis de Guiringaud, a former French Foreign Minister, France could 'change the course of history with 500 men'.[1] The nickname 'gendarme of Africa' which France then acquired was not unfounded. France became the guarantor of Western order in the region, finally getting the assent of the United States which, in spite of American reservations with regard to General de Gaulle's foreign policy, considered that Francophone Africa was thus protected from the communist threat. In those areas where trouble appeared, for example in Chad, which was under threat from Libya, or in Gabon where there were problems of internal unrest, France was keeping watch.

---

1 Louis de Guiringaud was Minister for Foreign Affairs from 1976 to 1978. The exact quotation is: 'Africa is very important to France because it is the only continent which can give France the feeling that it is still a great power. The only one where, with 500 men, it can still change the course of history'.

Africa was then built up as a 'multiplier of influence' for France, giving substance to its claims to be a great power. This view of Africa, forged by Gaullism and given concrete form in Africa by specific institutions, especially monetary and military mechanisms, drew its strength from its ability to win over and shape the thinking of policy-makers.

Françafrique, often denounced for its connivances and secret practices, was above all a cover for an ideological entente between French and African leaders locked in what was definitely an asymmetric relationship but one that was desired by both sides. Contrary to today's conventional thinking, Françafrique was founded on shared interests. Yet this fact disguises the key issue: the fact that the desire for closer relations with France was omnipresent in Africa's postcolonial elites while France's need of Africa was firmly anchored at the very heart of the French political elite. In this sense, we can refer to a hegemonic relationship, built on consent and assent, on both sides, in such a manner that France's policy of pursuing power in Africa had in some way built in its own control mechanisms. And it is because of this agreement, anchored in ideas, that France's unilateral power in Africa was able to be deployed with no real hindrance, at least during the Cold War. This notion of a common design and destiny grew all the stronger since it was able to rise above internal French political divisions. France's remarkable continuity in foreign affairs is ideological in nature. How else can we understand why the policy conceived by General de Gaulle managed for so long to resist political changes of all kinds or indeed why the General's successors at the Elysée have all claimed to be his heirs in this matter? Of all the heirs, the most surprising might be the socialist Left and the man who embodied it, in particular after his election to the French presidency, François Mitterrand. If truth be told, there was no need to force things in order to bring about this alignment. France's foreign policy and hence its Africa policy, as dreamt up by de Gaulle, chime so well with the cultural and historic heritage of France that the French Left did not have to make too much of an effort to adopt it. This discourse spoke volumes to Mitterrand since – given its roots, its references and its bases – it was also his own discourse. 'Mitterrand the African' (Marchesin 1995) was on familiar ground, not only on the continent itself, but also on the Gaullist ideological planet: rank, 'grandeur', universalism, the French language, the destiny of France … everything converged so that the opponents of the presidential election of 1965 were basically in agreement on the place of France in the world. The apparent desire to break with this at the time of François Mitterrand's election to the French presidency in 1981 was quickly buried. The most spectacular sign of this was the resignation of Jean-Pierre Cot, Minister for Cooperation and Development. But the most commonly advanced explanation for the Left's continuity in the conduct of African affairs is mistaken. The networks always evoked but rarely defined, the bureaucratic rivalries, the pressures from African leaders themselves are not just theoretical. If the Left's conversion to realpolitik in relation to Africa took place so rapidly it is because they were not ready to risk the loss of political clout gained from Africa and seen in terms of power for France. Renouncing the

Gaullist heritage in this area would have been tantamount to giving up their own image of France's place in the world.

Vague Multilateral Desires

The power of ideas allows us therefore to explain the extraordinary continuity in France's Africa policy as French political elites joined together in a shared conception of national interests in the name of grandeur and rank. The unilateralism that sprang from this is firmly rooted in questions of self-image. As a consequence, any evolution towards multilateralism implies a change of mindset not only in terms of Africa policy but also in terms of foreign policy. Yet such an evolution imposes a break with the idea that policy-makers have of France. It is for this reason that we can better understand why such a range of reservations are engendered by multilateral perspectives. However solid a concept might be, it cannot resist events. In its original version, Gaullism was in tune with the international system which gave France a rare opportunity. It was able to slip into the space between Soviet-American rivalry without betraying Western solidarity, and was also able to deploy its power, which was not only much-vaunted but also frequently exercised. The implosion of the USSR and, thus of the bipolar system, reconfigured the distribution of power. France no longer benefited from the dual superpower situation and could no longer get by in its role as the gendarme of Africa. The Soviet threat had vanished, while new forms of conflict called for responses other than those that had previously prevailed and that involved France's pre-positioned military bases. But change did not take place only in the field of security. The economic landscape had been re-ordered. After the first three decades of independence, African nations were in such a state of dilapidation that the word 'under-developed' hardly sufficed to summarise the seriousness of their situation. 'Cooperation', dreamt up just after independence, was obsolete. Its efforts to accompany development had been a failure. It therefore needed to be revised. As for African political regimes, they were shaken to their foundations following the collapse of the communist bloc. Single-party politics and authoritarianism had lost all credibility, leaving the monopoly of legitimate discourse to those who defended democratic ('good') governance. The speech made by President Mitterrand at the Franco-African summit at La Baule in 1990 made French support conditional on political reform of African powers/governments (Cumming 2001). It sounded less like a warning than a statement to the effect that France alone could not continue with its one-to-one support for its African 'backyard'. Finally, African and French societies had undergone shifts which had ended up contesting the hegemony which had been in place until then. In Africa protests increased against France's neo-colonial tactics, while in France a large number of state actors, especially in the judiciary, as well as non-state agents (NGOs and the press in particular) questioned the whole framework of *Françafrique* which was seen as flawed both in its substance as in its essence.

In short, the whole structure put in place by General de Gaulle and continued by his successors was in a state of crisis. The adjustments made by African societies and economies did not save France's Africa policy. This policy no longer had the steam to keep going on a unilateral basis and was obliged to adjust if it wanted to continue its existence south of the Sahara.

The new policy that was set up would rebuild the whole institutional edifice governing Franco-African relations. The famous reform of Cooperation that the Jospin government undertook from 1997 is the most enlightening illustration of this. But the first concessions to the new international political context were seen less in the institutional order than in the external theatre and more specifically in the field of multilateralism. The so-called 'Balladur doctrine' (and before that 'the Abidjan line') proclaimed by the French Prime Minister in 1993, broke with traditional unilateralism in economic affairs. From that point on, France would make its financial aid to Africa conditional on the signature of stabilisation agreements between the recipient countries and the International Monetary Fund (IMF). The change thus introduced was the follow-up to a development that had begun in the 1980s when the first plans for structural adjustment were set up. The countries which were subject to this tidying up of their public finances had to deal with the IMF since all the other lenders were obliged to align their own programmes to the IMF's six monthly evaluation of the finances of the countries concerned.[2]

France's adhesion to the policy of the IMF was not just technical. It also signalled an ideological acceptance, as France adopted the famous 'Washington consensus' which presided over the reorganisation of African economies along very neo-liberal lines. If we measure the Balladur doctrine in Gaullist terms, it is in fact a deviation in principle from the way that France intended to deal with its former colonies. This change was not just short-term. It was to inspire French policy in the long term in respect of reforming the public finances of African states. In 2001, in the very middle of the crisis in Ivory Coast, François Huwart, Secretary of State for Foreign Trade, recalled that France 'could not offer any particular or isolated solutions. The response must be global and must be channelled through the International Monetary fund and the European Union' (Conte year unknown). The notion that from that point on French Africa policy should follow the broad lines laid down by the forces of globalisation came up against the question of debt. The Heavily Indebted Poor Countries (HIPC) initiative was adopted in 1996 by the IMF and the World Bank and was backed by France. French unilateralism was clearly tempered by a bilateral initiative which complemented the HIPC Arrangements. The Debt for Development schemes (Contrats de Désendettement et de Développement), which were signed by Paris and a number of African countries (seven in 2006), were in fact presented as an additional dimension of the HIPC initiative. It remains the case though that this unilateral debt initiative differs

---

2   This explains the creation in 1986 of the SAF (Structural Adjustment Facility) then of the ESAF (Enhanced Structural Adjustment Facility) one year later.

from the Gaullist model: it is subordinated to the primary idea of a multilateralism which is symptomatic of the path travelled by French elites.

The feeling that it was no longer possible to have a unilateral policy progressively gained ground among all French institutions dealing with Africa. As a result, France's deference to a supranational order was not just limited to economic affairs. The military did not escape this general revision. During the genocide in Rwanda in 1994, France was already caught up in the contradictions of its policy of support for Habyarimana's regime, and got more bogged down in the multilateral issue which was brought to the fore by Operation Turquoise. Set up by the UN, officially the operation aimed at providing protection and safety for displaced persons.[3] Even if France was in charge of this UN operation the fact is that France's traditional approach could no longer be pursued. The 'gendarme of Africa' would increasingly incorporate its actions into a multilateral framework. The shield of multilateralism became all the more valuable as France became increasingly reluctant to undertake interventions, traumatised as it was by the accusations made against it following the Rwandan genocide. France was drawn into action in Ivory Coast, Chad, the Central African Republic and Congo and, as far as was possible, did this under the aegis of the UN or the EU flag. In Ivory Coast, French (Operation Licorne) troops operated under a UN mandate. In the Democratic Republic of the Congo (DRC) it was under cover of the EU that two successful operations were carried out, Artemis in 2003 and EUFOR in 2006 (see Chapter 5). These inaugurated the new Common Foreign and Security Policy (CFSP) which the European Union wanted (Loisel 2005; Banégas, Marchal and Meimon 2005). France then played a key role by ensuring in particular the control of operation Artemis. This French commitment at the heart of a European action clearly showed the limits that France placed upon its activity: in the front line, maybe, but alongside others. Some commentators state that multilateralism is the continuation of the same policy but by other means, as multilateralism is the shield behind which the same appetite for power is dissembled. As proof of this, the fact that the UN Security Council's Resolution 1484 which authorised the intervention in the DRC was followed by an urgent request by France to Secretary-General Kofi Annan to lead the operation.[4] A few years later, France had to intervene in Chad and in the Central African Republic with EUFOR (17 March 2008–15 March 2009). Once again it played a pivotal role since the headquarters of the operation were at Mont Valérien in Paris and out of a total of 3,700 men, France supplied 2000. Operation Atalanta (European Union Naval Force Somalia Operation) was

---

3   Operation Turquoise was decided by the UN Security Council (resolution no. 929). It was under the command of French General Jean-Claude Lafourcade.

4   This version however has not been corroborated in some French witness statements, which, on the contrary, stated firmly that France had been backed into a corner by the UN, anxious that the European Union should not leave the UN Mission alone to deal with the Congolese situation.

on a more modest scale. Set up in 2008 to deal with growing instability in Somalia, it included eight European countries including France.

The military multilateralism which these different operations reveal was not completely improvised. The doctrine itself was evolving. In 1998, at the same time that the reform of French 'cooperation' policy was at its height, France forged a new conceptual approach to military matters concerning Africa. Faced with the increasingly regional nature of conflicts, the unilateral framework was no longer adequate. The concept of RECAMP (Renforcement des Capacités Africaines de Maintien de la Paix/Reinforcement of African Peacekeeping Capacities) sought to involve African armies in conflict management, while France restricted its role to that of supplier of logistical support and help with training. This Franco-African multilateralism would spread to Europe with varying results. In 1998 in a spirit of friendly cooperation (known in France as the 'spirit of Saint-Malo', see Chapter 4) an attempt was made to bring together the two great ex-colonial powers to help in the resolution of African conflicts. The assumption was that this 'spirit' would then help to prompt the EU into similar forms of cooperative engagement.

In 2008 the concept of RECAMP disappeared, to be replaced by a larger concept, that of EURORECAMP. This Europeanisation of this mechanism gave official status to a form of cooperation that had become increasingly visible since 2000, several European countries having joined the RECAMP cycle as, over time, this became of more consequence. The process set up by France was therefore seen as a model since it extended equally to African institutions. The African Union had built up its defence structure on a regional basis (as laid out by RECAMP) by setting up the African Standby Force. Thus, this multilateral logic seems to draw France further and further away from its unilateral tradition in favour of active multilateralism. But these changes were not without contradictions.

The Paradoxes of French-style Multilateralism: The Refusal of Power

How can we understand the different ways in which multilateral operations have been undertaken? Their scope and their meaning are a reflection of the place they occupy in the way the political elite think of France. Bearing this in mind, the conclusion is relatively simple. There is no paradigm around today which could possibly be substituted for the old Gaullist paradigm of unilateralism. To be fair, since the end of the Cold War France's foreign policy and thus its Africa policy, suffered from an absence of hegemony. Multilateralism is just not a new doctrine which could impose itself progressively on policy-making elites in such a way as to give rise to a new consensus. Multilateralism is a practice that is often imposed by circumstances and it is sometimes 'cobbled together'. It is not, however, capable of sustaining a shared vision of the relationship that France should have with Africa. As for the Gaullist paradigm, although it has been in decline, it has not totally disappeared. It resurfaces regularly and, in the eyes of its opponents, it reinforces the theme of the permanence of *Françafrique*. Yet for all that, this group has not managed to impose a substitute doctrine and thus it seems that France's political practice is often akin to improvisation. The consensus which structured France's Africa policy has been followed by discord which is often the source of inconsistencies.

The obsolescence of the Gaullist paradigm became clear with the end of the Cold War. Different reforms took place during the 1990–2000 decade – the Balladur doctrine, the Jospin reform of cooperation and also the devaluation of the CFA franc – bringing into conflict two camps of policy-making elites: those for whom it was important to turn the page of Africa policy once and for all because it no longer made sense and even constituted an obstacle to an effective foreign policy, and those for whom it was important to follow the policy fixed at the time of independence and which had been followed thus far by all French presidents.

The split which opposed the *anciens* and the *modernes* is complex (Bourmaud 1996). It is not a split along Right-Left lines but on the contrary it crosses through the heart of both blocs. There are anciens on the Right and Left. The same goes for *les modernes*. These two camps squared off against each other amidst a certain amount of confusion under Chirac's presidency from 1995 onwards, exacerbated by the victory of the socialists in the general election of 1997 and the appointment of Lionel Jospin as Prime Minister. The *modernes*, who wanted a break with the old model, seemed to be the winners. The famous 'reform' of cooperation illustrates very clearly the desire to promote an Africa policy which would be rid of its encumbering embarrassments: clientelism, waste, support for personal power and compromising links to authoritarian regimes. That is why, *les modernes* reasoned, it was necessary to rationalise the institutions which dealt with Africa and to put an end to the French-speaking francophone African sphere of influence by diluting it into a larger whole which would be made up of almost every African state, including the English-speaking and Portuguese-speaking ones, as well as a few Asian and Caribbean states.[5] In short, there had to be an end to the privileged and corrupt tête-à-tête which is summed up in *Françafrique*.

The attempt to impose this resolutely reformist stance came up against serious inconsistencies. In particular, the French development assistance budget literally collapsed, which contradicted the reform's stated aims which required a strong increase in funding (Bourmaud 2005). In reality, the new policy seemed to be more of a kind of renunciation or normalisation. The refusal to intervene in critical situations such as that affecting Congo-Brazzaville, which was torn apart by warring militias, in the name of a policy of non-interference, gave credence to the idea that France was abandoning Africa. Hardly had it been announced than the new policy faded away, the victim of its internal contradictions and of the lingering unilateral old-style tropism. The networks were still in place, ready to act in the corridors of the Elysée, and to get involved in affairs in the Comoros, in Madagascar, etc.

---

5   This is the ZSP, Zone de Solidarité Prioritaire/Priority Area of Solidarity, which includes all the countries likely to benefit from French development aid.

However, with Jacque Chirac's re-election in 2002, it seemed as if coherence would be imposed with the official declaration of a 'route map' for Africa which, until that point, had been cruelly lacking.

Driven on by Dominique de Villepin, France finally tackled the question of making its Africa policy more transparent by integrating it into its overall foreign policy. The new policy was presented as a synthesis of tradition and modernity. On the side of tradition, France continued with the Gaullist ideal of a France which made Africa a key element of its foreign policy. At a time of globalisation, more than ever France needed to be active south of the Sahara. It was by way of Africa that France could shine. It could find the space that it needed for its language and culture, avoid marginalisation and thus remain a presence/force that counted in world affairs.[6] On the side of modernity, France took up the idea of multilateralism. France needed to make alliances everywhere, to be integrated into UN or European actions in order to inspire them better, to build coalitions which included France at their very core. That way France would benefit from the 'multiplier of influence' effect which would, once again, give it great power status. In the thinking of Chirac and de Villepin, multilateralism did not lead to a diluting of French power. On the contrary, it promoted it. This seductive neo-Gaullist myth crashed into the Ivory Coast crisis. France was obliged to intervene in a civil war in a 'backyard' country. For those who opposed France's Africa policy, the UN flag was not sufficient to hide the return of the French gendarme. This criticism is not quite justified because, as it happened, France was the only one capable of halting a conflict which threatened to spread to the whole West African region. But the suspicion was there, expressed not only within France but also in part of Africa. The new policy that was supposed to create a consensus was dead. De Villepin had tried to draw the two strands together and failed.

The split at the heart of the French elite has not healed. The two trends observed since the 1990s are still present. Those who cling to the old ways still find comfort in nostalgia for the original unilateralism which served France's grandeur. Those who believe in the modernist line, and who have a high profile in media and intellectual circles as well as in parts of the political class, are more heterogeneous. Within this group two elements cohabit: the idealists who believe in an essentially moral approach to African politics and the liberals for whom African politics belongs in the museum and should disappear in order to allow France to take part in the vast movement of economic globalisation. This moral-liberal alliance is dominant whilst advocates of the traditional line are in decline. But even though it is dominant, it cannot fully impose itself because international relations is not seen as a context in which power plays a key role. The two concepts do not come together in practice. Neither of them is hegemonic and so they are mixed up together and they produce a policy that is confused and contradictory.

---

6   The Africa policy advocated by de Villepin was part of the extension of French policy at the time of the Iraq war. By opposing the United States France became *de facto* the leader of those who refused the war that President Bush desired.

The presidency of Nicolas Sarkozy seems emblematic in this regard. During the 2007 election campaign, the discourse was one of a rupture with the past and this had already been set out a year earlier when Nicolas Sarkozy was Interior Minister.[7] The Head of State wanted to be decidedly modern. French foreign policy should abandon the idea of being exceptional. France should embrace the rules governing economic and political globalisation. France's return to NATO's integrated high-command structure was one of the clearest signs of this.[8] In Africa, the end of French exceptionalism was illustrated by the appointment of Jean-Marie Bockel as Secretary of State for Cooperation, for he explicitly demanded a break with the past.

However, the handing out of posts within administrations responsible for Africa and the retention of official advisers also mollified the keepers of the Gaullist temple.[9] And the connivance between the French political establishment and 'historic' heads of state in Africa, such as Omar Bongo, soon took precedence over the commitment to break with past practices. The price of this was the sacking of the Secretary of State for Cooperation who, unfortunately for him, did not please African leaders (Hugueux 2010). By replacing Bockel with Alain Joyandet, the French president continued with a policy that would not have displeased his predecessors (Gounin 2009). At the Elysée palace, the concentration of decision-making in Africa policy around the secretary-general Claude Guéant and a background adviser Robert Bourgi, a direct heir of Foccartism, illustrates the difficulties with making a break and with introducing the 'modernisation' so trumpeted by the French head of state.

Thus France's African policy is buffeted between the tropisms of yester-year and the temptation to make a break with them. Real multilateralism goes hand in hand with continued unilateralism. The impression of disorder arises less from an incompatibility of principle between the two trends than from an inability to express them in a coherent plan. This deficit in Africa policy results in a wider deficit that permeates all of France's foreign policy. Unable to be hegemonic, the '*modernes*' nevertheless dominate in terms of thinking: their inability to accept the constraints put upon France's power has led to foreign policy devoid of any clear strategy and one where opposites sit together in a general state of disorder.

---

7   During an official visit to Bamako in May 2006, Nicolas Sarkozy declared that it was time 'to drive out the old demons of paternalism, clientelism and handouts' and 'to turn the page on networks from a former era, of unofficial advisers, of back offices, of shadowy emissaries'. See *L'Express* 25 February 2010.

8   It is not insignificant to note that at the head of France's foreign policy were two politicians considered to be the most representative of the Atlanticist or pro-American trend, Nicolas Sarkozy, President of the Republic and Bernard Kouchner, until 2010 Minister of Foreign Affairs. During the Iraq war they each in their own way embodied opposition to France's official line against the war.

9   Robert Bourgi incarnates, better than anyone else, the permanent nature of shadowy advisers in the conduct of African affairs. See *L'Express* 7 September 2009.

These specific characteristics of France's Africa policy act as a kind of sounding board for France's difficulties in articulating what she wants to be and what she wants to do.

Chapter 4

Britain and France in Africa since Saint-Malo: Towards an Uneasy Partnership?

Gordon Cumming

At the December 1998 Saint-Malo summit, the British and French governments sought to draw a line under 'the history of rivalry, the misunderstandings and pointless competition' which had long hampered Anglo-French cooperation in Africa (French Embassy, UK, n.d.). The UK and France signed the Saint-Malo II agreement which committed them to set aside past rivalries and work together to tackle the challenges of Africa. This joint undertaking, which was less reported upon than the Saint-Malo I declaration on Anglo-French defence collaboration, committed Britain and France to engage in joint actions on Africa. It did not, however, set out clearly the terms and scope of this proposed cooperation. Was the aim to develop a relationship like the Franco-German tandem, which is characterised by a high 'degree of institutionalisation of communications and exchanges' (Webber 1999: 2) between the two governments? Or was it their intention to build a partnership akin to the Anglo-American 'special relationship' which, although interest-driven, is also more 'natural' and rooted in a shared culture and history (Baylis 1997: 155)?

Surprisingly, given the potential importance of this initiative for Africa and for the European Union's Common Foreign and Security Policy (CFSP), there has been no attempt to study this evolving UK-French 'partnership' on Africa. This chapter plugs this gap. It sets out the history of rivalry marking Anglo-French relations from colonial times to the early post-Cold War era. It demonstrates how closer linkages have developed between the UK and French administrations and how some degree of collaboration has taken place on shared objectives such as poverty reduction and the promotion of political reforms, with cooperation in the field of peace and security being discussed in the next chapter (French Embassy, UK 2001b). Finally, it explains the evolution of Anglo-French relations in terms of neoclassical realism. As noted in Chapter 1, theorists in this tradition focus upon the relative power of states, while also including within their analysis unit-level material and ideational variables, such as key political actors' perceptions of the national interest, state structures and other domestic constraints.[1]

---

1   The importance of the ideational dimension is recognised by numerous neoclassical realists, notably Kitchen (2010).

Before proceeding, it is important to sharpen our focus. First, this chapter does not look at the impact of partnership in terms of policy outcomes; this would be problematic given the multiplicity of factors that affect the success or failure of any joint UK-French action. Second, it does not assume that the British and French states should systematically cooperate. Such an assumption would require normative judgements on the basis of imperfect information and would overlook the complexity of foreign policy-making. Third, space constraints do not allow for a detailed analysis of relations between non-state actors, although new links have for example developed, with official encouragement, between the UK and French foreign policy research centres, Chatham House and the Institut Français des Relations Internationales.[2] The focus here is on state-to-state relations, with emphasis on linkages between government ministers and senior officials. It is this 'foreign policy executive' (FPE) or policy-making elite, whose perceptions and ideas are deemed by neoclassical realists to play a key role in interpreting systemic imperatives and choosing between foreign policy options.[3] Thus, as Gideon Rose (1998: 147) observes: 'Foreign policy choices are made by actual political leaders and elites, and so it is their perceptions of relative power that matter, not simply relative quantities of physical resources or forces in being'. Finally, this chapter does not cover areas of policy where the Anglo-French 'partnership' has been more virtual than real. The fight against international crime is one such area. Here, despite the UK-French Action Plan on transnational crime agreed at the November 2004 Anglo-French summit, 'cooperation on the ground has remained patchy' (personal communication, FCO, 2008).

Fashoda and Beyond

Rivalry had been a feature of Anglo-French relations in Africa since the 19th century and the 1898 Fashoda incident when the French were compelled by British forces to beat a humiliating retreat from Sudan. Anglo-French rivalry persisted during the early post-colonial decades, as Britain and France pursued realpolitik objectives and failed to work together on the challenges of Africa. Poverty reduction was not a priority for the UK, which typically tied around two-fifths of its aid to the purchase of British goods.[4] Successive French administrations tied an even larger proportion of assistance to French products and gave less aid to least developed

---

2   This exchange has led to seminars involving Foreign Ministry staff on Sudan and the Sahel. However, Chatham House's efforts to host a 'Saint-Malo ten years on' seminar elicited little official interest (personal communication, Whitehall insider, 2009).

3   This 'executive' is composed of 'high-ranking bureaucrats' and elected representatives 'charged with the overall conduct of foreign affairs' (Kitchen 2010: 133).

4   The UK tied 44.1 per cent of assistance in 1974–5 and 41.3 per cent in 1982–3; see Cumming (2001: 90).

countries (LLDCs) than to upper middle-income African states.[5] The UK and France also adopted a semi-competitive approach towards democracy promotion. They bequeathed their own models of government then turned a blind eye as their former colonies became one-party states.

A similar lack of Anglo-French cooperation was apparent over the early post-Cold War period (1990–97). Thus, while the UK and France both increased support to the poorest African countries (cancelling debt, untying and targeting assistance), they did not cooperate on poverty reduction. Britain remained primarily concerned with promoting neoliberal reform while France continued to provide hard loans and to allocate a fifth of its aid to promoting French cultural concerns. Similarly, while both London and Paris announced, in June 1990, that they were linking their bilateral assistance to political progress in developing countries, they remained reluctant to suspend aid, as the cases of Uganda and Togo illustrated (Cumming 2001).

The competitive nature of relations was nonetheless attenuated by three factors. The first was the Cold War context in which the UK and France were required to work alongside one another to keep ex-colonies in the Western orbit. The second was Britain's benign neglect of Africa (Styan 1996), which prompted one French official to comment: 'We did not really get the impression that the British were rivals, since they were not particularly present [in Africa] before the creation of the Department for International Development (DfID)' (personal communication, French Foreign Ministry, 2008). The third was the emergence of forums in which the UK and France could exchange views on Africa. The UN Security Council (UNSC) in New York was one such forum, but cooperation was limited here by Britain's tendency to side with the US and France's pretention to a 'non aligned' policy. The European Community provided another channel after the UK joined in 1973, but real differences soon emerged over the Lomé Convention (Europe's aid and trade agreement with its former African, Caribbean and Pacific colonies). The annual Anglo-French summit, which first met in 1978, was the most important forum for bilateral exchanges but was not used to discuss Africa.

Saint-Malo: Laying the Groundwork for a New Partnership?

The UK and French governments signed two important agreements in December 1998. The first was Saint-Malo, which paved the way for ESDP missions to be conducted autonomously of NATO. The second, Saint-Malo II, was a pledge to 'seek to harmonise their policies towards Africa'. While scant details were provided, it was stated that the UK and France would 'pursue close cooperation on the ground in Africa', intensify information exchange, explore the scope for co-location of French/British embassies in Africa and engage in joint ship visits.

---

5   France tied 67.5 per cent of aid in 1974–5 and 46.1 per cent in 1982–3; Cumming (2001: 90, 64).

Such statements were repeated and refined at subsequent summits, notably in 2001, 2004 and 2008.

Saint-Malo I and II served as the catalyst for the development of closer formal and informal or *ad hoc* ties between policy-making elites within the two FPEs. The formalisation of these linkages can be seen in the inclusion of a distinct 'Africa chapter' at Anglo-French summits as well as in the greatly increased ministerial presence (e.g. 10 ministers plus the Prime Minister and President in 2006) at these gatherings. There are, moreover, now six-monthly meetings between staff from the UK and French Foreign Ministry Africa Directorates. Similarly, meetings are scheduled three to four times a year at a senior level between the DfID and French Ministry of Foreign Affairs (MFA) officials working on international development.[6] Equally, there is an exchange programme involving officials from, on the UK side, the Africa Directorates of the Foreign and Commonwealth Office (FCO) and the DfID and, on the French side, from the Africa and Globalisation Directorates of the MFA.

Turning to the informal or *ad hoc* links, these have been event-, issue- or personality-driven. They include occasional but symbolically important joint ministerial visits, the first of which involved a trip in March 1999 to Ghana and Côte d'Ivoire by the then UK and French foreign ministers, Robin Cook and Hubert Védrine, and the most recent of which was by the former British and French Foreign Ministers, David Miliband and Bernard Kouchner, to the DRC in November 2008. Equally, there have been joint ministerial statements by, for example, the former UK Prime Minister Gordon Brown and the current French President Nicolas Sarkozy on Sudan/ Darfur (*The Independent*, 3 September 2007).[7] There is, moreover, now a tendency for newly appointed British and French ambassadors to visit Paris and London respectively before beginning their African postings. There have also been invitations to specific events, with Bernard Kouchner coming as a special guest to the FCO's annual ambassadors' conference in London in March 2009 (personal communication, FCO official, 2009).

Many of the above linkages have been possible partly because particular UK and French ministers and senior officials have perceived such ties as being consistent with the two countries' interests and values and partly because these elite policy-makers have actually 'got on'. This was the case with Cook and Védrine and with Miliband and Kouchner. Similarly Lord Malloch-Brown, as UK Minister for Africa, Asia and the UN, also established excellent relations with Bernard Kouchner, his special adviser Eric Chevallier, and Africa advisers in the Elysée. Other close links were forged between successive heads of the UK and French Foreign Ministry Africa Directorates (e.g. James Bevan and Bruno Joubert) as well as between Africa advisers in Downing Street and the Elysée.

6　Attendance by the Agence Française de Développement (AFD) is sporadic, due to a turf war with the MFA (personal communication, DfID, 2009).

7　After the visit Brown and Sarkozy also wrote a joint article published in *The Times* and *Le Monde*, 31 August 2007.

These informal ties have also become a more important feature of Anglo-French relations within multilateral forums. To illustrate, senior UK and French officials, usually from the DfID and the Elysée respectively, have engaged in regular bilateral exchanges in their capacity as G8 Africa special representatives – a grouping established in 2002 and reinvigorated ahead of the G8 summit in 2005. These meetings, coupled with strong political will at the highest level, have helped the UK and France not only to keep Africa high up the G8 agenda, despite America's lack of enthusiasm, but also to ensure strong African representation at G8 summits, notably in Evian (2003) and Gleneagles (2005).[8]

Within the EU, the UK and France have long engaged in informal exchanges between meetings and more formal dialogue within forums such as the Committee on Development Cooperation (CODEV), the Africa Working Group (AWG) and the General Affairs and External Relations Council. Their scope for such consultation has increased over recent years as some meetings have become more frequent (e.g. the AWG has been convened weekly rather than monthly since July 2009) and as new forums have emerged. The latter include the ambassador-level Political and Security Committee or PSC, which has, since its creation in 2000, focused, among other things, on ESDP missions; the *ad hoc* working group on the EU-Africa strategy (set up with strong UK-French backing); and the eight panels (the most important of which are led by the UK or France) established to implement the priority actions agreed in the 2007 Africa-EU Strategic Partnership.[9]

Informal and institutional links between the UK and France are most closely intertwined at the UN. As two of the permanent five members of the UNSC, Britain and France are invited – at permanent representative level – to attend informal lunches hosted by the Secretary General (personal communication, FCO official, 2009). Furthermore, Britain, France and the US make up the P3, an informal mechanism, launched in late 1997, which facilitates consultation on UNSC matters. According to one UK official,

> Within the P3, we sometimes speak first to the French and other times we speak to the US first. At other times all three speak simultaneously. Sometimes this is purely by chance … sometimes it is tactical, notably where Britain and France are more closely aligned with each other than either is with the US (personal communication, FCO official, 2009).

With two-thirds of UNSC business relating to Africa in recent years, the P3 has been an important arena for Anglo-French cooperation, particularly when the French and British ambassadors to the UN have enjoyed a good relationship.

---

8   African leaders were instrumental in placing Africa on the G8 agenda as from the 2002 Kananaskis summit (Vines 2005).

9   Britain leads on the MDGs and France on Climate Change. While headed up by the EU, the Peace and Security panel is chaired by a French general and heavily influenced by the UK.

This was the case, at least prior to the Iraq crisis, with Sir Jeremy Greenstock (1998–2003) and Jean-David Levitte (1999–2002), who had been Chirac's diplomatic adviser at Saint-Malo and who favoured cooperation 'in the spirit of Saint-Malo' (personal communication, former UK official, New York, 2008). It was equally true of relations between Sir Emyr Jones Parry (2003–07) and French Permanent Representative, Jean-Marc de la Sablière (2002–07). Thus, when Jones-Parry led UNSC missions to seven West African countries in June 2004 and to Sudan/Chad in June 2006, he allowed his French counterpart to take the lead in the francophone states visited. This rapport between the UK and French Permanent Representatives was no doubt facilitated by the fact that neither man enjoyed good relations with the truculent US Ambassador, John Bolton (personal communication, former UK official, New York, 2008). It was indeed regularly the case during the Bush presidency that the P3 initiative would see Anglo-French talks to coordinate positions as a prelude to trying to bring the US on board, for example when the British and French agreed not to invoke Article 16 of the Rome Statute, which would have deferred President Bashir's referral to the International Criminal Court for a year (personal communications, UK and French officials, New York and Paris, 2008–9; see also Chapter 5).

There have, however, been clear limits to Anglo-French efforts to coordinate their positions within existing forums and to build new institutional bridges. There is in fact a near-total absence of 'institutional mechanisms that bring ministers, officials and institutions together' (personal communication, FCO official, 2008). In this context, it is worth noting that the main bilateral forum has remained the Franco-British summit, whose existence predated Saint-Malo by over a decade. It has also taken over 10 years for the DfID and the Agence Française de Développement (AFD) to sign, in December 2009, an overarching agreement that focuses mainly on non-contentious sectors, such as health and education. There has, moreover, been no staff exchange between the DfID and the AFD. Furthermore, despite a growing culture of evaluation within the British and French foreign policy establishments, there are still no mechanisms for ensuring that lessons learned by exchange staff are formally recorded. Significantly too, there have also been no joint ship visits and there is no evidence of co-location of French and British embassies in Africa. In fact, in Abidjan, where the UK mission has been closed April 2005, British officials are more comfortable in the US than in the French embassy (personal communication, Whitehall insider, 2009).

Clearly this lack of institutional architecture does not mean that no cooperation is taking place. However, it suggests that 'there is nothing to fall back on' and makes collaboration dependent upon officials and ministers actually 'getting on' or at least sharing a common appreciation of the benefits of cooperation (personal communication, FCO, London, 2009). This has often not been the case. Relations were, for example, difficult between the UK Secretary of State for International

Development, Clare Short, and French 'Development Minister', Charles Josselin.[10] In personal communications with the authors, Ms Short commented that she was 'not aware' of any cooperation between the UK and France, while Josselin complained that during their joint visit to Sierra Leone and Guinea in April 2001, Ms Short asked to see Guinean President Lansana Conté ahead of him and seemed to undermine the French position by welcoming, rather than condemning, Guinean attacks on Sierra Leonean rebels (personal communications with Claire Short via email, 2008, and with Charles Josselin in Paris, 2009).

In other instances, the 'partnership' does not work because of a lack of awareness of its existence. This phenomenon is less common in international organisations, but there have been a number of occasions when policy-makers have proven unable to square UK and French positions. Thus while the French did sign up to major aid and debt cancellation commitments at Gleneagles, they were unhappy about the UK's attempt to use this 2005 summit to sideline the recommendations of the New Partnership for Africa's Development and impose instead the findings of the Blair Commission (Vines and Cargill 2006). More generally, within the EU, the UK does not see France as an obvious partner on African development and is usually closer to the 'likeminded countries' (the Nordics and the Dutch). Indeed, on the CODEV, one of Britain's concerns appears to be to ensure that France and Germany do not exercise their 'blocking minority vote'.[11] In the UN too, divergent interests have sometimes been hard to conceal, notably at the time of the 2003 Iraq War when Anglo-French relations were particularly strained.

Working Together in Practice

Having demonstrated that there is now a clearer framework for Anglo-French coordination, we will now examine whether Britain and France have collaborated on two of their core priorities for Africa: tackling poverty and promoting democracy.

Common Efforts to Reduce Poverty?

The UK and France have taken tentative steps towards closer cooperation on poverty reduction. They have supported each other's high-profile poverty-reducing

---

10   Despite the merger of the French Cooperation Ministry into the Foreign Ministry in 1999, the post of 'Development Minister' was retained or rather a similar position was created, namely the 'Minister of state within the Foreign Ministry responsible for Development and *La Francophonie*'.

11   Most decisions are by qualified majority voting, with votes being a function of contributions to the EDF. France, Germany and Britain used to contribute 24.3 per cent, 23.4 per cent and 12.7 per cent respectively (*European Report*, 23 February 2005).

initiatives. On health, the UK backed France's UNITAID proposal, which was formally launched in 2006 and aimed at financing vaccinations through a tax on international flights.[12] By the same token, Paris supported the International Finance Facility for Immunisation, a scheme proposed initially by London in January 2003 and subsequently by Britain and France in 2006 as a means of raising capital to support the programmes of the Global Alliance for Vaccination and Immunisation (OECD 2008: 40). Anglo-French cooperation on health was then taken further when, in September 2008, the UK and France helped form a High Level Task Force for innovative financing of healthcare.[13]

Similarly, on education, the UK and France made a joint statement in March 2008, with Gordon Brown and Nicolas Sarkozy promising to help get 16 million children into school in Africa by 2010 and every child by 2015 (*The Guardian*, 27 March 2008). They also undertook to work with others to train an additional 3.8 million teachers; and, in the context of the 2010 World Cup in South Africa, pledged support to the One Goal programme to highlight the need for universal education.

Alongside these strategic policy announcements, London and Paris have engaged in a three-way dialogue with the African Development Bank and agreed to coordinate their support to this organisation, notably on the issue of debt sustainability (personal communication, DfID official, 2008). Equally, Britain and France have collaborated at the programmatic level, with for example a 'silent partnership' (where one donor funds and another agency implements a programme) on education. This scheme arose partly out of the joint visit to Niger and Zambia by UK Secretary of State for Development, Hilary Benn, and French Development Minister, Xavier Darcos, in February 2005 and partly out of talks held in London a few months later between the heads of DfID African offices and a team from the French Foreign Ministry's Development Directorate. With no diplomatic representation in Niger, the DfID provided 7 million euros to the AFD to promote primary education through the Fast Track Initiative.

Ultimately, however, Anglo-French collaboration on poverty reduction has remained limited. Thus, although London and Paris both espouse the Millennium Development Goals (MDGs), they do not attach the same priority to these goals. While the DfID appears at the time of writing to be moving away from a more-or-less exclusive focus on the MDGs towards a more growth- and results-oriented approach, it has, since 1997, consistently made poverty reduction central to its aid programme, enshrining it in legislation (International Development Act, 2002) and

---

12   Initially conceived by the French and Brazilian Presidents in 2003, UNITAID was subsequently launched by France, Britain, Brazil, Chile and Norway. It now enjoys support from 29 countries. Retrieved 15 May 2011 from www.unitaid.eu/en/supporters-mainmenu-64/donors-mainmenu-122.html.

13   This culminated in a UN conference at which the UK contributed £400 million to a US$5.3 billion pool to improve global health care (*M2 PressWIRE*, 23 September 2009).

White Papers, providing unprecedented levels of aid (all untied), and channelling a high percentage of assistance to LLDCs (OECD 2006).

By contrast, the French government was not initially on the (UK-led) European panel on the MDGs that arose out of the 2007 EU-Africa Strategic Partnership (personal communication, Brussels, 2008). The French administration has, moreover, remained sceptical about poverty reduction targets which it sees as unrealistic, overly technocratic and, at best, only part of the solution. French policy-makers contend that donors, by promoting trade and growth, will create the conditions in which African countries can fund their own social programmes (personal communications, MFA, Paris, 2008). In line with this thinking or, more precisely, with France's longstanding pursuit of its own economic and strategic interests, the French administration has retained policies that sit uncomfortably with the MDGs, not least aid tying (OECD 2008: 15). The French Foreign Ministry has also continued to prioritise French cultural projects, while the AFD, which has taken over many of the Foreign Ministry's aid-related functions, has retained a banking culture and a strong emphasis on loans, investments and the productive sector.

Against this backdrop, it is unsurprising that joint initiatives on poverty reduction have not always been followed up. Thus, while the UK backed France's UNITAID proposal, it did not introduce this tax itself but confined its support to a budgetary contribution. Furthermore, while France promised to match Britain's commitment on school places, it has only provided £50 million for one year compared to the DfID's commitment of £500 million over three years (personal communications, MFA and DfID officials, 2009). Anglo-French cooperation has also remained weak at the programmatic level: the UK contribution to the education scheme in Niger is paltry when it is considered how large the DfID's total budget is (£5.7 billion in 2008–9) and how much scope there is for a cash-rich agency such as the DfID to use the French aid administration in silent partnerships (DfID 2009: 9). That this has not happened comes down to an issue of trust. UK officials had initially expected the French to follow up on the UK's funding of the Niger scheme by stumping up the cash for a DfID-run education project in Rwanda. But this fell through when the French ambassador was expelled from Kigali in November 2006. France was then invited to suggest an alternative country yet failed to do so. This has created suspicion in the DfID that the French are seeking to take credit for UK aid monies and that they do not live up to their rhetoric. There is, equally, concern in France that the UK might expose its failure to deliver on aid promises.[14]

---

14   France promised, at the 2002 Monterrey Conference, to increase aid to 0.5 per cent of GNP in 2007 and 0.7 per cent by 2012. However, France did not meet its 2007 target and has postponed the 0.7 per cent commitment to 2015 (OECD 2008: 39).

A Concerted Push for Political Reform?

Over the last decade or so, the UK and France have also taken hesitant steps towards closer cooperation on the promotion of democracy and human rights. The key forum for Anglo-French exchanges has been the EU, particularly through the work of the AWG, the CODEV and more recently the Africa-EU Panel on Democratic Governance and Human Rights, on which Britain and France are both represented. In line with the EU Common Position of 25 May 1998 on human rights, democratic principles, the rule of law and good governance, the British and French have cooperated on a number of African cases. In Kenya, for example, there was 'good, close cooperation' between Britain and France in the aftermath of the troubled elections of 27 December 2007. Standing in as the EU Presidency on behalf of Slovenia, which had no representation in Nairobi, the French were able to ensure that the UK channelled its response to the Kenyan crisis through the EU rather than adopting a more unilateral stance or collaborating solely with the US (personal communications, FCO, 2009, and MFA, 2008). The UK and France have also liaised regularly on Zimbabwe, particularly since 2004 when London and Paris effectively struck a deal whereby France backs UK efforts on Zimbabwe, particularly within the EU, while the British support France on Côte d'Ivoire, particularly in the UNSC. This arrangement has made it easier for Britain to have EU-wide sanctions, which began in February 2002, rolled over annually. French support has been essential for several reasons. First, several EU member states have harboured reservations about the harshness of the position propounded by London (personal communication, FCO, 2009). Second, British influence over Mugabe has been virtually non-existent ever since UK ministers stepped up their rhetoric and allowed the Zimbabwean leader to portray the dispute to other Africans as 'a post-colonial struggle over land' (Porteous 2005: 293). Finally, UK leverage within the Commonwealth and Southern African Development Community (SADC) has been reduced by 'the reluctance of African elites to take a hard line against a ... veteran of the struggle for independence' (ibid.).

Alongside policy coordination within the EU, there has also been Anglo-French cooperation at a programmatic level. The clearest example is a four-year silent partnership ('Media for Democracy and Good Governance') in the DRC (2007–11) aimed at promoting political freedom via the media (see Chapter 9). Yet although UK and French discourse on democracy promotion was certainly more closely aligned while the 'very human rights-oriented' Bernard Kouchner was Foreign Minister (2007–10), the fact remains that active collaboration on democracy and human rights has generally been patchy (personal communication, MFA official, 2009). To illustrate, in 1999–2000, the UK was pushing for EU aid sanctions against Liberia, whose president, Charles Taylor, was supplying arms to Sierra Leonean rebels (the Revolutionary United Front) in their civil war against Tejan Kabbah's democratically elected government. However, France – perhaps influenced by forestry interests in Liberia – ignored UK demands and only gave support when Taylor subsequently supported rebel forces in Côte d'Ivoire and began destabilising France's wider sphere of influence in West Africa (personal communication, former UK official in New York, 2009). Subsequently, in February 2003, the limits of Anglo-French coordination on Zimbabwe were laid bare. France invited Mugabe to a Franco-African summit on the day European sanctions expired against this dictator. The UK, which had been lobbying for tougher measures, had to acquiesce in exchange for a promise of French support to prolong European sanctions after the summit. In February 2007, the French did not invite Mugabe to the Franco-African summit in Cannes, but the trade-off was, allegedly, that Tony Blair agreed not to block the Zimbabwean leader's attendance at the May 2007 Africa-EU summit in Lisbon. This pledge was later honoured by Gordon Brown, thereby satisfying the demands of some African leaders that Mugabe should be invited and enabling the summit to go ahead. It was noticeable nonetheless that France was not one of the four European countries (Netherlands, Sweden, Denmark and Germany) to speak out publicly against the Zimbabwean regime at Lisbon (*European Report*, 11 December 2007).

More recently, differences have arisen over the response to be taken to military or 'constitutional' coups in francophone countries such as Mauritania in 2008; Niger, Guinea, and Madagascar in 2009; and Niger again in 2010. While the UK has been openly critical of such insurgencies, the French have taken a more softly-softly approach. The case of Madagascar is particularly revealing. Here the UK adopted a robust stance, with Lord Malloch-Brown the only European minister publicly to condemn the coup from the outset. Yet Britain had closed its embassy in 2005 and was thus at a disadvantage compared to the French who had retained their diplomatic presence there and 'initially took an even softer line than the African Union (AU)' (personal communication, former UK Minister, 2009).

There are many reasons for this relative absence of Anglo-French cooperation. These include divergent national interests (discussed later); the fact that UK-French coordination within the EU has to take into account the views of 25 other countries plus the European Commission; as well as the fact that the UK and France have different discourses concerning key concepts such as human rights and governance. Thus, while the British have emphasised civil and political liberties and have stressed the importance of women's rights generally, the French have given primacy in their discourse to the economic and social rights of *all* citizens. Furthermore, the UK has seen governance in economic and technical terms as a way of ensuring a streamlined, financially well-managed central state, whereas the French have viewed this concept in political and juridicial terms as a means of promoting robust local and central state structures that are legitimate and that provide an effective legal framework (an *Etat de droit*). A further factor relates to internal wrangling. In Britain, competition between the DfID and FCO has led to parallel African policies: allegations by the DfID that the FCO is prioritising strategic and commercial interests over developmental needs, and accusations by the FCO that the DfID prioritises economic development over questions of political freedom (Porteous 2005: 286).[15] In France, there have also been divisions, with the Elysée typically being less forthright on human rights than the Foreign Ministry. This distinction was much less clear when Bruno Joubert was second in command in the Elysée Africa cell and when the French 'Development Minister' Jean-Marie Bockel was leading the charge on human rights. However, the moving of André Parant into Joubert's role and the sacking of Bockel (whose focus on human rights had led to protests by Omar Bongo, President of oil-rich Gabon) would seem to point to a downgrading of human rights concerns (personal communication, MFA, Paris, 2009).

The final reason relates again to a question of trust. Thus, the UK remains wary that it is only dealing with the more enlightened parts of the French political establishment, whilst other French actors are still acting in ways that are underhand (cf. the recent Angolagate arms-for-oil scandal). This is an important concern as it suggests that the British are unconvinced by French 'paradiplomacy', that is, France's readiness to talk up African democratisation whilst continuing to pursue practices (such as collusion with autocratic African leaders) that directly contradict official discourse. The French, equally, are aware of double standards on the part of the British who have taken a less forthright stance on political freedom in countries that are allies in the war on terror (e.g. Ethiopia).[16]

A Neoclassical Realist Framework

It follows that there has been relatively little Anglo-French collaboration on 'soft' policy issues, such as poverty reduction and democracy promotion. How then are we to explain this comparatively limited evolution in UK-French relations in Africa in terms of neoclassical realism? As Theresa Callan has demonstrated in Chapter 1, neoclassical realist theorists contend that states are driven by systemic imperatives, notably a concern over their relative power within the international system. But they also go beyond neo-realism by assuming that states have some capacity for choice and that policy elites act as an 'opaque filter' between systemic imperatives and the actual implementation of foreign policy (Sterling-Folker 1997: 19).

This theoretical framework is well suited to accounting for France's overtly realist African policy. It appears, on the face of it, to ignore claims by the UK's new Labour government to be pursuing a value-driven and ethically aware approach towards the world's poorest continent. In reality, however, neoclassical realism does take account of this 'idealism' and sees it as a useful means of

---

15　The FCO feels that DfID can wash its hands of 'dirty politics' as it does not have to deal with unsavoury regimes (personal communication, FCO official, 2009).

16　Soon after the 2005 election-related violence in Ethiopia, 'much UK aid was in practice soon being spent in much the same way'; see Youngs (2008: 8).

mobilising public support behind a policy (such as aid rises in the midst of global recession) that might not seem intrinsically appealing; a way of garnering votes from a younger and more engaged public; and a mechanism for demonstrating the capacity of the British state to get things done in Africa (Gallagher 2009).

Drivers behind Enhanced Cooperation

So what drivers were pushing the UK and France to cooperate on Africa in the late 1990s? In Britain's case, the election of a reformist Labour government and its creation of the DfID in 1997 signalled a new readiness to engage with Africa. British policy-makers soon realised, however, that they could only help to make progress on the MDGs – and indeed on Tony Blair's promise to make Britain 'a leading partner in Europe' – if they became more active in Francophone Africa and engaged more effectively with France, as the only other European power with the ability and will to intervene south of the Sahara (speech by Tony Blair, Lord Mayor's Banquet, 1 November 1997). At the same time, France, under the modernising socialist government of Lionel Jospin (1997–2002), was anxious to scale down its presence, at least in some Francophone African countries, and keen to realign its diplomatic and strategic interests to its key commercial interests, which were increasingly in Anglophone African countries, such as South Africa and Nigeria (its largest trading partners).

The UK and France also had a number of common interests that were pushing them to cooperate. As middle-ranking powers, they had become increasingly aware of their inability to cope with the scale of Africa's crises and were facing growing challenges to their privileged positions within the UNSC, IMF and World Bank. By working together, they could secure a number of mutual benefits. They could, for example, garner a majority of the votes on the Security Council simply by drawing on 'a set of contacts and influences globally which were very complementary' (personal communication, former UK official, New York, 2008).[17] Second, by cooperating within the EU, the UK and France could swing votes within forums such as the AWG. Third, by presenting a united front, Britain and France could restrict the capacity of African regimes to play them off against each other; avoid tripping each other up in their attempts to resolve crises in former colonies such as Zimbabwe and Côte d'Ivoire; and cut down on reporting. According to a UK official, formerly in the UK mission in New York, failure to agree with the French leads to a requirement to write to London to explain. This lowering of transaction costs is particularly important in the case of the FCO, which has suffered over recent years from the closure of a number of African embassies, the loss of 20 per cent of its staff working on Africa and the fact that all

---

17   The threat to their P5 status is longstanding. More recently, China pressed at the G20 (Pittsburgh) to have UK and French voting rights on the IMF Board reduced; see *Lettre du Continent*, no. 1429, 23 October 2009. Unlike the UK, France's status is also at risk within the World Bank.

desk officers in London now deal with several African countries (*The Observer*, 9 January 2005). It is also useful for the French administration, which lost African expertise when the Development Ministry was absorbed by the MFA (1999) and when the Development Directorate was subsequently merged into a Directorate for Global Affairs (2009). Fourth, by joining forces, Paris and London can – significantly in an age of satellite media broadcasting – better respond to African crises. Finally, they can better camouflage their continuing loss of influence over a continent that is now being wooed assiduously by the world's fasting growing economies. According to a former UK Minister: 'If we use our history cleverly, one plus one equals three. But that is still in a world where you need ten to score on a lot of problems' (personal communication, former UK Minister, 2009).

The comparative advantages of closer Anglo-French cooperation south of the Sahara have come to the fore particularly at moments of crisis. Thus, for example, at the time of the 2003 Iraq War, UK and French leaders and officials were keen to find common ground in Africa as a way of overcoming the deep divisions caused by this conflict. French President Chirac's comment, at the February 2003 Franco-British summit, that there was 'complete consensus' on Africa should be viewed in this light (FCO 2003a). More recently still, amidst the current global economic crisis, the financial benefits of collaboration and burden-sharing have not been lost on British and French policy-makers.

Obstacles to Cooperation

While systemic imperatives appear to have been pushing the UK and France to work together, these pressures have not always translated into actual collaboration. The explanation would appear to lie in the fact that British and French leaders have taken account of key unit-level variables, namely the perception by decision-makers within the FPE of divergent national interests; institutional constraints; and the limited capacity of the UK and French states to act.

To begin with *decision-makers' perceptions*, it is clear that there is no 'elite consensus' in either the UK or France on the necessity of prioritising cooperation in Africa. A major divergence has arisen over the different relative importance that policy-making elites in London and Paris attach to Africa, which, in turn, affects their readiness to collaborate on African policy. For France, Africa plays a crucial role in enhancing its rank in the international pecking order, while for the UK, Africa is much more centrally a development issue. Alongside these core differences, there have also been instances where UK and French policy-makers have simply decided to go it alone and pose as the sole champion of Africa's interests. In this context, the Blair government launched the publication of the Commission for Africa report on Red Nose Day (a nationwide UK-specific event), then sought to impose its recommendations on the G8 at Gleneagles (Vines and Cargill 2006: 135). In a similar vein, the French President announced in January 2009 the 'Sarkozy Plan' for the DRC/Rwanda (discussed in Chapter 9). On other occasions, policy-makers have given priority to preserving British or French interests in a specific African country, particularly former colonies, where the African country concerned is a major source of trading opportunities (e.g. South Africa), oil (e.g. Nigeria), or minerals, such as uranium (e.g. Niger). This trend towards shoring up interests is particularly clear across Francophone Africa where France feels, according to Hubert Védrine, that there is 'a need to preserve French influence' (personal communication, Paris, 2009) and where there is anxiety that Britain's new interest in Africa has come at a time when France is said by some commentators to have 'lost Africa' (Glaser and Smith 2005).

Alongside divergent interests, there have been *institutional constraints* (or, more specifically, different bureaucratic set-ups, 'national policy styles' and institutional approaches) on closer Anglo-French cooperation. There is, for example, no exact counterpart of a Foreign Office Minister for Africa in France, and there is a greater tendency for the MFA to be left out of the loop by the Elysée than there is for the FCO to be excluded, at least on African policy, by Downing Street. The greatest problem is for the DfID which, with a cabinet seat and a massive aid budget, does not have any clear counterpart in France. Indeed, there is no longer a French Development Ministry or even a Development Directorate within the MFA, and the AFD feels closer to the German aid agencies, GTZ and KfW, than to the DfID (personal communication, AFD, Paris, 2009).

These problems have been exacerbated by different 'national policy styles'. Differences were particularly marked in the late 2000s. Thus, policy-making elites within the Foreign Office, with its deliberate approach to decision-making, were anxious not be dragged into unplanned initiatives proposed by France's spontaneous and energetic Foreign Minister, Bernard Kouchner (personal communication, former UK Minister, 2009). Similarly the French FPE was keen not to be sucked into the quantitative, announcement-driven approach used by Downing Street and DfID, particularly during the premiership of Gordon Brown (2007–10), lest it should be locked into commitments that it could not afford. Equally, there have long been, as discussed earlier, issues of trust, with the UK in particular remaining sceptical about France's readiness to deliver on its rhetorical promises and break with neo-colonial practices. Bearing in mind that the UK and France have both promised to set aside past rivalries and work together, the fact that one state is perceived as not keeping its side of the bargain might suggest that it is trying to increase its ranking in the international hierarchy at the expense of, rather than in conjunction with, the other state.

There have, moreover, been differences in institutional approaches, particularly on the development front. According to a senior DfID official:

> One [problem] is that we are in different countries and a lot of what we do is at
> country level. So we just don't bump into each other that much. And DfID has
> a much tighter focus: France have 55 focus countries; we have about 20. Where
> we have our big offices, our countries are mainly anglophone, except Rwanda,
> DRC and Mozambique. We aren't involved directly in francophone countries.

They are involved in anglophone countries, though usually have small [aid] programmes (as in Zambia).

On top of the above, the UK and France tend to prioritise different sectors. Thus, Britain's emphasis on primary education and budgetary aid are not matched in France, which attaches greater importance to tertiary education and prefers more visible project work.[18] In addition, France's focus on infrastructure and cultural promotion finds little or no echo in the DfID. Furthermore, although it has a large bilateral aid programme, the DfID likes to think of itself as having a multilateralist outlook and a strong strategic focus, which facilitates cooperation with the 'like-minded countries'. By contrast, the French aid administration lacks strategic direction and is more oriented towards bilateral assistance.

Turning to the final constraint on cooperation, *extractive capacity*, this refers to the ability of states, or rather of policy-making elites, to mobilise, often in consultation with societal and other domestic actors, the resources required to execute foreign policy. While UK policy-makers find it hard to mobilise troops for ESDP missions (see Chapter 5), British officials have, since 1997, had little difficulty securing high levels of aid, including three-year budget allocations from the Treasury, given strong public, cross-party and NGO support for the state's developmental and humanitarian efforts. This does not, however, usually translate into cooperation with the French since UK government departments must meet Public Service Agreement targets and must be satisfied that assistance will be delivered effectively by partners such as France. This is by no means guaranteed, since despite recent improvements in the effectiveness of French aid through the introduction of results-based management tools and the reinforcement of evaluation units, France is not as focused on economic development as the UK and does not take its commitments to the Paris Declaration on aid effectiveness and donor harmonisation as seriously as the DfID. This is a constraint, as is the fact that the French government has difficulty freeing up enough bilateral aid to be a credible partner on development. The French state's extractive capacity has clearly been limited by membership of the 1997 European Stability Pact, by internal spending cuts agreed under the 2001 Loi organique relative aux Lois de Finances, by commitments to the European Development Fund (EDF) and by the current eurozone crisis.

Conclusion: Less Rivalry but Still No Partnership

This chapter has shown how Britain and France have, since Saint-Malo, increased their collaboration on Africa, albeit only to a very limited extent in soft policy areas such as poverty reduction and democracy promotion. The UK and France have

---

18   To illustrate, in 2006, France allocated US$151 million to basic schooling compared to US$1.2 billion for tertiary education; OECD (2008: 15).

developed more constructive (formal and informal) ties and have wherever possible sought to 'deconflictualise' their stances – an approach which can often be achieved without setting up common structures or engaging in joint actions. But Britain and France cannot lay claim to a new partnership on Africa. Their relationship falls well short of the instinctive rapport enjoyed by the UK and US. It is, moreover, less firmly rooted or institutionalised than the Franco-German tandem. Significantly too, it is not underpinned by the same security interests as the 'special relationship' or the same key economic considerations as the Franco-German alliance.

It follows that the UK-French connection, even when account is taken of the closer security ties identified in Chapter 5, is a long way from the 'entente formidable' or even the 'entente amicale' that Gordon Brown and Nicolas Sarkozy, respectively, hailed in March 2008 (*Federal News Service*, 27 March 2008). It is instead a pragmatic arrangement whereby, according to one FCO official, 'We cooperate with the French on Africa where it is useful to do so. It is a loose framework and one of many we work in'. The relationship is said to be 'uneven, often very personality-driven and event- and political interest-driven', with cooperation being most likely on high profile issues and major crises, particularly in parts of Africa where the UK and France have few interests or historical ties (personal communication, former UK Minister, 2009).

As noted in our concluding chapter, the future of Anglo-French relations in Africa is hard to predict. Clearly the current governments in both countries are facing tight fiscal and financial constraints, which may push them towards increased burden-sharing in certain situations. Moreover, the creation of the European External Action Service will increase pressure for policy coordination as its role increases and member states seek to cut the costs of individual diplomatic missions. These issues aside, and notwithstanding the announcement of enhanced Anglo-French cooperation in the defence field in November 2010 (Cameron and Sarkozy 2010) and close collaboration over Libya in 2011, there are reasons for thinking that the UK and France may not develop significantly closer relations on Africa. First, the prospects of any enhanced collaboration are reduced by the fact the UK does not view Africa as geopolitically significant, while France's policy-making elites remain divided on the strategic importance attached to Africa. In this context, it is worth recalling that Saint-Malo was always less about the strategic value or, for that matter, the needs of Africa *per se* and more about bringing the UK and France closer, helping them to punch at least in line with their combined weight in the international arena and, at the same time, enabling them to exert more decisive influence over European African policy. Second, the decision to collaborate on Africa was ultimately taken by default and in the absence of other credible alternative partners. Thus Britain's preferred ally in most foreign policy situations, the United States, was too 'unpredictable' on Africa and too uninterested in its developmental needs (Porteous 2005: 293). Similarly, France's ideal partner, Germany, was too reluctant to intervene militarily and too quick to block funding for European initiatives south of the Sahara. Third, the recently elected UK Conservative-led government is unlikely, given that party's anti-European credentials and its longstanding Atlanticist tendencies, to be attracted to a strong partnership with France on Black African issues, particularly if this is going to mean an increase in the number of autonomous ESDP missions.[19] If, as a result, the Anglo-French motor behind Europe's African policy should run out of steam, the Africa-EU Strategic Partnership, in which the British and French are key players, could become more about words than deeds and, both the UK and France will lose out in Africa, in the face of unrelenting competition from G20 states.

---

19   The Conservative Party was said by Kouchner to be ready to collaborate bilaterally with the French but less inclined to cooperate within a European framework (*Agence France-Presse*, 7 April 2010).

Chapter 5

Anglo-French Security Cooperation in Africa since Saint-Malo

Tony Chafer

Given the burgeoning literature both on the European Security and Defence Policy (ESDP) and on Africa's security challenges (see for example Howorth 2007; Franke 2009), it is surprising that there has been no attempt to explore in detail Anglo-French security collaboration in Africa. This chapter begins by showing the lack of any meaningful UK-French cooperation from the colonial era to the immediate post-Cold War period. It then demonstrates how, in the wake of the 1998 Saint-Malo summit, collaboration has begun to take place in terms of the institutionalisation of the security relationship, peacekeeping missions and military training activities in Africa. Finally, recent developments in Anglo-French security relations are explained by reference to neoclassical realism. This theory usefully goes beyond neorealism's focus on recurrent patterns of inter-state interactions in the international system by introducing as variables in the making of foreign policy both policy-makers' perceptions of the state's relative material power and the degree of state autonomy.

Before proceeding, it should be emphasised that this chapter does not cover the security challenges of Africa in general or indeed explore the outcomes (or lack thereof) of Anglo-French security collaboration. Second, cooperation between the French and British defence industries is not the subject of this analysis, although joint procurement and moves to integrate Europe's defence industries are now realities that cannot be ignored (UK-France Summit 2010). Third, it does not attempt to cover intelligence sharing due to the difficulty of obtaining reliable data – although there are indications that the UK and France enjoy a semi-hostile relationship in this area. Under the '3Is' arrangement information and intelligence are shared only with Canada and the US, while '5Is' extends this arrangement to Australia and New Zealand. In each case France is excluded. Fourth, lack of space precludes treatment of the civilian dimension of security cooperation, such as police and security sector reform (SSR). As Chapter 9 of this volume demonstrates, there is some evidence of limited Anglo-French cooperation – or at least of avoidance of duplication of effort – in this field in the Democratic Republic of Congo (DRC), where the UK has given funding and the French have provided 'boots on the ground' and where there have also been attempts to fuse missions such as EUPOL (police) and EUSEC (security sector). In Guinea-Bissau, too, there has been some coordination of effort on

SSR. It should, however, also be noted that there is some ambiguity regarding the civilian and military dimensions of SSR. This ambiguity can be discerned in the different perspectives that traditionally mark the thinking of the European Commission ('soft' civilian SSR) and that of the European Council (a 'harder' military/security perspective). In this chapter the emphasis will be on the latter.

History of Rivalry

Anglo-French military rivalry was a feature of the colonial period in Africa. The late 19th-century scramble for Africa frequently pitted the French against the British, and this rivalry came to a head, bringing the two countries to the brink of war when the forces of Britain's Lord Kitchener squared up against those of France's Captain Marchand at Fashoda in 1898. Marchand ultimately was ordered to withdraw, and as a result the term 'Fashoda syndrome' entered the French language and became short-hand for Anglo-French rivalry, and more specifically British perfidy, in Africa. Such rivalry was attenuated by the Entente Cordiale in 1904, by cooperation during the First World War against Germany's colonies in Africa and by the ill-fated Anglo-French Suez expedition in 1956. But for a century after Fashoda, Anglo-French relations south of the Sahara were essentially characterised by competition rather than cooperation.

This rivalry continued during the Cold War and early post-colonial period. France adopted a 'voluntarist', unilateral military approach with pre-positioned forces in former colonies, advisers working closely with African governments, and military personnel embedded with African forces under the terms of French defence and military cooperation agreements with African states. The UK, in contrast, had no bases and undertook virtually no interventions (except Kenya 1963–4), although it did have British Military Advisory and Training Teams (BMATTs) working with the armed forces in ex-colonies. Furthermore, military academies in the UK, like their counterparts in France, took African soldiers from the former empire for training. All of this took place in a spirit of competition, occasionally even hostility, with Britain and France actually finding themselves on opposite sides over the Nigerian civil war in Biafra (1967–70). Indeed, these differences of approach were not confined to Africa, but reflected a wider lack of security cooperation at a European level and within NATO, particularly after France's withdrawal from NATO's integrated military command in 1966.

This lack of cooperation continued into the early post-Cold War era (1990–97). In this new context, Britain and France initially seemed quite prepared for multilateral militaro-humanitarian interventions, as the issue of sovereignty became less predominant, but events in Somalia in 1992 discouraged most Europeans as well as the US from undertaking such interventions. This reluctance was most clearly seen at the time of the 1994 genocide in Rwanda when the UK and US led the international community in its refusal to intervene and, subsequently, used the UN Security Council (UNSC) to limit the scope of France's Operation Turquoise, which was launched when the killing in Rwanda had largely stopped in June 1994 (Fenton 2004: 140). A similar scenario occurred in late 1996 when Britain and the US were instrumental in blocking French efforts to raise a multinational force to intervene in Zaire (now the DRC).

Throughout this entire period, Anglo-French divergences on security questions were compounded by the absence of a meaningful institutional framework in which Britain and France could work at a bilateral or bi-multi level. Franco-British summits provided a forum for wide-ranging discussions but did not focus specifically or even primarily on security issues. NATO was of limited use, even though from 1995 French President Jacques Chirac did begin to make overtures towards it. The Organisation of African Unity (OAU) also failed to offer a forum within which security cooperation could be taken forward. The UNSC did provide a mechanism but could just as easily be used to block as to advance proposals, as the aforementioned examples of Rwanda and Zaire have illustrated. The same is true of the EU where the UK hampered France's attempts to link up with the Germans within the purview of the Western European Union and through the creation of the Eurocorps in 1995 (Loisel 2004: 44).

Saint-Malo: A New Departure

The pivotal moment which brought about a shift towards greater cooperation was the 1998 Saint-Malo summit. The Saint-Malo I declaration is mainly noted for its role in laying the foundation stone of the ESDP (Howorth 2004: 4). In particular, it stated that the European Council 'must be able to take decisions on an intergovernmental basis, covering the whole range of activity set out in Title V of the Treaty of European Union' and that 'the Union must have the capacity for *autonomous* action, backed up by credible military forces ... in order to respond to international crises' (Howorth 2004: 4, 34, my emphasis). The word 'autonomous' marked a crucial breakthrough, as it made it possible for the first time for the EU to intervene militarily outside the framework of NATO. This was a key French foreign policy priority. Saint-Malo II – the declaration on cooperation in Africa – actually made no mention of security cooperation but simply committed the two governments to 'harmonise policies towards Africa and pursue close cooperation on the ground; promote the EU common position on human rights, democratic principles, the rule of law and good governance in Africa; [and] contribute to the stability of the continent' by focusing on debt issues and development assistance. The intention to cooperate on defence and security was only made explicit at the Cahors Franco-British summit in February 2001.[1]

The Saint-Malo summit also served as the catalyst for efforts to create a more meaningful institutional framework within which the French and British, often alongside other Northern states, could engage in bilateral or 'bi-multi' cooperation.

---

1   Document obtained from the FCO, 2 April 2001.

Since Saint-Malo, the French and British have developed more specifically bilateral links. Thus, the Franco-British summits now always include a section on Africa and the presence of both defence ministers at the 2001 Cahors summit symbolised the new spirit of cooperation in security matters. There have been joint statements by UK and French defence ministers and joint visits by foreign ministers Miliband and Kouchner to crisis-ridden countries such as the DRC in November 2008. Crucially too, institutional bridges have been built through Anglo-French secondments of personnel that are designed to improve the two countries' mutual understanding of each other's *modus operandi* in the peace and security field. Thus, the French and British ministries of defence exchanged *chargés de mission* from 2005–8, stationed reciprocally in the central policy-making departments of each ministry. The French attach considerable importance to these exchanges. However, the British abolished the post in 2008, which left one French official in London with no British counterpart in Paris. The UK also sends a British officer to Paris as deputy director of EURORECAMP (discussed later). In addition, a French officer is embedded with British forces in Nairobi and a British officer was seconded to French forces in Dakar until 2009, when British government cutbacks put an end to the arrangement.

Significantly too, Saint-Malo was the trigger for the creation of a number of fora in which cooperation and dialogue were possible at EU level, such as the Political and Security Committee (PSC) and the Military Committee. Anglo-French cooperation within the PSC has been a *sine qua non* for the approval of the ESDP missions (discussed below) and for a range of other initiatives on which joint actions or statements have been agreed, such as on Darfur and Chad for example (*New York Times*, 20 July 2007).

Another significant attempt by Britain and France to develop closer ties between themselves and with the United States in the security field has been the P3 initiative at the UNSC. While this informal mechanism for consultation between three of the five permanent Security Council members was announced in late 1997, it was not until after Saint-Malo that the P3 became effective as a forum for harmonising British, French and American policies on peacekeeping, capacity-building and other security challenges in Africa and beyond. With some 70 per cent of the UNSC's business relating to Africa in recent years, the P3 has been an important arena for Anglo-French security cooperation, particularly when the French and British ambassadors to the UN in New York have enjoyed a good personal relationship and even more so when relations between the UK and US Ambassadors have been strained, as they were between Sir Emyr Jones Parry and John Bolton (personal communications, former UK officials, New York and London, 2008).

During the Bush presidency, the P3 initiative would sometimes involve Anglo-French talks to coordinate their positions as a prelude to trying to get the US on board; for example, the Qatar initiative to get the Darfur rebels to join peace talks with the Sudanese government was initiated by the French with support from the UK and subsequently the US came on board. The Anglo-French initiative, launched in late 2008, to improve UN peacekeeping mandates is also a good example of bi-multi cooperation, with the US now increasingly involved in the discussions along with the other P5 members.[2]

It should of course be noted that the P3 and EU are multilateral mechanisms, and the UK and France do not always share the same analysis within these fora. London and Paris therefore need wider support in these arenas in order to take certain initiatives forward. This is not always forthcoming, particularly in instances where the UK or France is deemed to be instrumentalising the UNSC or ESDP to serve their national interests. Britain's stance on the 2003 Iraq War and France's promotion of the EUFOR Chad mission might be cited in this context. Nevertheless, the fact that both the UK and France are permanent members of the UNSC, key players in Europe and major actors in the peace and security arena in Africa does offer unrivalled scope for working together in areas of mutual interest before bringing others on board (personal communications, former UK officials, London and New York, 2008–9).

The UK, France and the ESDP in Africa

There have been two main forms of Anglo-French security cooperation since Saint-Malo, namely peacekeeping missions and training African peacekeepers. We shall begin by focusing on the former, specifically ESDP military missions, of which there have been four in Africa: Operation Artemis, DRC, June–September 2003; EUFOR DRC, July–November 2006; EUFOR Chad/Central African Republic (CAR), January 2008–March 2009; and EU NAVFOR Operation Atalanta, December 2008–ongoing.[3]

Peacekeeping Missions in Africa

Artemis was the first 'autonomous' EU military operation (that is, conducted without recourse to NATO assets) and the first ESDP operation outside Europe. France was the 'framework nation' for the operation and provided the operational headquarters and the majority – 90 per cent – of the 1,400-strong force on the ground, although the UK sent a special operations unit, which played a crucial role in resurfacing the runway at Bunia, as all supplies had to be flown in. The UK also provided invaluable support by persuading a reluctant Ugandan government to offer airport facilities at Entebbe (Bagayoko 2004: 103). The

---

2   This initiative now extends to the C34 Special Committee on peacekeeping, which includes around 120 members; communications with British officials, New York, 2009.

3   There have also been other civilian/military missions in Africa: EUSSR Guinea-Bissau, 12 February 2008–31 May 2009; EUPOL DRC, 1 July 2007–30 June 2009; and EUSEC DRC, 8 June 2005–30 September 2010. These operations will not concern us, as this chapter focuses on military missions.

operation was limited in time (four months) and had a mandate to protect civilian life and stabilise the humanitarian situation in Bunia (eastern DRC) following the withdrawal of Ugandan forces and the inability of the UN force, MONUC, to prevent renewed violence. In the aftermath of European divisions over the Anglo-American invasion of Iraq, 'France badly wanted a mission to show the EU was capable of acting alone, where NATO would not be involved' (Gegout 2005: 437), while London's go-ahead was mainly to prove that the UK was still interested in developing a European defence capability (personal communication, former UK official, New York, 2008). In this case Anglo-French cooperation was clearly the product of convergent agendas that were themselves the result, in the British case at least, of changing domestic policy preferences. This textbook operation was widely acclaimed and demonstrated that the EU could undertake a peacekeeping mission far from Europe's borders (Helly 2009: 183–5).

Like Artemis, EUFOR DRC was a time-limited and targeted operation. Its mission was to support the UN force, MONUC, in supervising the 2006 election process in DRC. Germany provided the operational HQ; the largest troop contributors were France and Germany; and the largest bilateral contributor to the elections (£35m) was the UK, although it sent no combat troops. Here, in order to appreciate how France, without any offer of manpower from the UK, was able to ensure the launch of such an operation, we need to look more closely at the wider European context. Needless to say, France, and for that matter Belgium, had a strong national interest in using the EU 'as an instrument to take care of their concerns for the DRC's stability' (Olsen 2009: 18). Paris also brought other states, notably a reluctant Germany, on board, despite German anxiety about potential troop losses, thanks to the prevailing political situation in Europe. There was, in particular, a perceived need to reassert the credibility of the EU following the rejection of the Constitutional Treaty by Ireland, France and the Netherlands. In effect, EUFOR DRC was 'more about European form than African substance', with the 'actual reality on the ground in Congo [constituting] only a secondary factor' (*International Herald Tribune*, 13 June 2006). The EUFOR operation also needs to be understood against the backdrop of the adoption of the EU Strategy for Africa in 2005: the mission was seen by the operation's French commander, Major-General Damay, as a test case for the strategy and a 'laboratory' for the ESDP (quoted in *The EU's Africa Strategy* 2007: 5). More generally, there was a consensus between member states and the European Commission (EC) that the EU should contribute to conflict prevention and peacekeeping in the DRC, and EUFOR DRC also provided the opportunity 'to get some good coverage for the EU' (Howorth 2007: 239). For the UK, the stability of the DRC was of paramount concern: it was a significant contributor to SSR and, through the work of the Department for International Development (DfID), was one of the country's largest donors.[4] French and British agendas in the DRC thus converged,

---

4   In 2007, the UK was the third largest bilateral donor providing 121.3 M€, behind Belgium (153.1 M€) and the US (132.4 M€) but well ahead of France (52.1 M€),

with Britain keen to ensure the success of the elections and France concerned to stabilise the country and to demonstrate once again the EU's capacity for military action.

EUFOR Chad/CAR was authorised by UNSC Resolution 1778. Described as 'a multi-dimensional mission to help create the security conditions necessary for reconstruction' in Chad and the CAR, it was mandated to 'protect civilians, facilitate delivery of humanitarian aid and ensure the safety of UN personnel'. Its scope was thus very limited, as it had no mandate to address the underlying political problem in Chad, which is the refusal of President Deby even to talk to the opposition. Indeed, EUSR officials were specifically instructed not to talk to the Chadian rebels (personal communication, EU official, Addis Ababa, 2009). France was the largest contributor to the operation (2,500 out of 3,700 troops) and the operational HQ was in Paris, although the force commander was an Irish lieutenant-general, Pat Nash. Like its forerunners, it was a time-limited operation and was presented as a bridging mission that would stabilise the humanitarian situation while a UN force was put together. EUFOR Chad/CAR handed over to a UN force, MINURCAT II, in March 2009.

France's support for this mission was based primarily on its concern for the stability of two of its key allies in central Africa, Chad and CAR (personal communication, French official, Addis Ababa, 2009). It also saw the operation as a way of further demonstrating the autonomous military capability of the EU (Olsen 2009: 18) and of involving other European powers more fully in burden-sharing in the region. For the UK, however, the focus was more narrowly on Darfur and on the danger that events there could spark a truly regional crisis. The Foreign Office (FCO) began planning for this eventuality ahead of any mission and, with help from the British High Commission in Cameroon, it developed Whitehall's understanding of the Chad/Sudan situation and held a joint meeting with France on both countries. Yet Britain's Ministry of Defence (MoD) remained cautious, refusing to participate in the mission and initially blocking funding for it. It was only after a high-level exchange between President Sarkozy and Prime Minister Gordon Brown that the UK sent two staff officers to operational HQ in Paris and two to the field HQ in Chad, as well as later unblocking the money and even co-sponsoring the UN resolution that authorised the EU deployment (personal communication, UK official, London, 2009). This latter decision was no doubt prompted by the fact that the British public and the US administration were so exercised over the situation in Sudan/Darfur, that the killings in Darfur were being so widely reported in the UK media and that British NGOs were pressing for 'humanitarian intervention'.

The above account does not, however, explain how the two countries succeeded in getting the agreement of other member states to the ESDP mission; Germany, in particular, suspected France of using the international community to shore up its own African sphere of influence, or *chasse gardee*, a concern also shared

---

OECD 2009: 122.

by the UK. In the end, EU support was forthcoming, primarily because both the UK and France supported the mission and thanks also to widely shared concerns about the refugee crisis and the possibility that genocide might be occurring in Darfur, which gave rise to a diffuse sense that the EU needed to be seen to be 'doing something'. From the limited perspective of Anglo-French cooperation the authorisation of EUFOR Chad/CAR was a success.

Finally, Operation Atalanta broke new ground for the EU as it was the first ESDP naval operation. The UN passed a declaration, co-sponsored by France and the US, which authorised nations to enter Somali territorial waters with the agreement of the transitional Somali government. This opened the door to Operation Atalanta, the objective of which is to 'contribute to the deterrence, prevention and repression of acts of piracy and armed robbery off the Somali coast', with stakeholders including the UN, NATO and nine other countries, Atalanta involves 1,200 personnel and 16 ships, not all from EU member states (Gya and Herz 2009: 2). Crucially, it is the first ESDP mission to be led by the UK.

While there was widespread concern among EU member states about piracy off the Somali coast, this alone does not explain the EU's involvement or the specific configuration of the operation. From the French perspective, Atalanta offered another opportunity, in a new arena, to demonstrate the military capability of the EU. However, although France was instrumental in securing UNSC authorisation, it had played a key role in each of the three other ESDP missions in Africa and was keen – for political reasons and also due to cuts in its defence budget – not to take the lead on this occasion. This coincided with concerns within the UK permanent delegation in Brussels that Britain, having participated in just one ESDP military mission, might be criticised for showing insufficient commitment to ESDP or to peacekeeping in Africa. Despite initial reluctance from the FCO and MoD in London, the naval chief of staff was keen for the UK to be involved and France was happy for Britain to take the lead. Northwood thus emerged as the command HQ for the operation (personal communications, UK and French officials, Brussels; former UK naval officer, 2009). Again this appears to be a successful example of Anglo-French cooperation. But it would be wrong to explain the UK's involvement primarily in terms of support for ESDP; it was, rather, a response to lobbying by private sector actors keen to maintain London's status as the city that hosts the International Maritime Organisation and a major international hub for commercial shipping.

So what conclusions can we draw from these missions? The willingness to deploy European troops in peacekeeping and conflict management operations is a new feature of EU African policy since Saint-Malo. This willingness derives from the fact that the European Council, rather than the Commission, is increasingly playing the lead role in EU African policy, as it is the Council that has been tasked with the planning, launching and conduct of ESDP missions. Within this intergovernmental context, France in particular has played a key role in pressing for EU military interventions. It has been successful thanks largely to British support, or at least acquiescence, within the European Council. There is a sense in

London, Paris and Brussels that, when Britain and France agree, initiatives make progress. There are clearly synergies between the French and British positions, and from the UK perspective it is in Africa that there is most to be gained from these synergies. Nevertheless, cooperation remains far from automatic, and it is worth remembering that the UK intervention in Sierra Leone and French operations in Côte d'Ivoire were both largely unilateral, despite coming after Saint-Malo and being only partly driven by interests.[5]

Training Peacekeepers

Apart from cooperation to launch ESDP operations, the UK and France have been involved in training African peacekeepers. There are two closely linked aspects to this training: actions taken under RECAMP (Renforcement des Capacités Africaines de Maintien de la Paix) and related initiatives, and support for the peacekeeping efforts of African sub-regional organisations and of the African Union (AU). The focus here will be on the first of these aspects, as support for the AU's peacekeeping efforts is covered in Chapter 10, although brief mention will also be made of the back-up given to African sub-regional organisations.

By the mid-1990s, African states were increasingly sceptical about French military interventions and Northern governments were – following their experiences in Somalia, Rwanda and Liberia – ever more reluctant to intervene directly in Africa. Against this backdrop, France, Britain and, indeed, the US, all came to recognise the importance of Africans taking greater responsibility for peacekeeping on the continent. They also acknowledged that African forces could not be expected to contain instability on their own. Initially, they launched separate programmes: RECAMP (France), the UK's African Peacekeeping Training Support Programme and ACRI (US: African Crisis Response Initiative). However, the three countries quickly realised the need to coordinate their programmes and in late 1997 announced the 'P3 initiative' (discussed above), in an effort to harmonise their capacity-building programmes in Africa and also to get other actors involved (Franke 2009: 78). Subsequently, in 2001, the UK's training programme was subsumed into a much larger initiative, the Conflict Prevention Pool (CPP), which included one fund specifically for Africa and another for conflicts arising elsewhere in the world. Under both the Africa and the Global CPP programmes, the FCO, DfID and MoD pooled their budgets for promoting conflict prevention and peace, with the Cabinet Office providing coordination at ministerial level. This was an example of 'joined-up thinking' by Tony Blair's New Labour Administration.

The Africa CPP's priorities were laid out in a jointly agreed UK sub-Saharan Africa Strategy for Conflict Prevention, with activities being programmed and agreed annually. Its budget for 2005–6 was £60 million. This was a modest

---

5   France nonetheless offered diplomatic support to the UK intervention in Sierra Leone. The UK also backed France's request for UN peacekeepers in Côte d'Ivoire and financed a Ghanaian contingent subsequently deployed under UN auspices, Loisel 2004: 52.

sum in the context of overall DfID spending, but the Pool was principally seen as a 'catalyst to ensure coherence and effectiveness of UK intervention' (ACPP 2004). However, while the programme reflected much greater commitment to training and military exercises than was evident under the previous Conservative administration, the Pool has essentially functioned as a bilateral mechanism providing peace support in selected priority countries, such as Sierra Leone, and no formal mechanisms have been created for cooperation with other powers in the area of conflict management.

As for RECAMP, this represented a greater refocusing of France's security policy, away from its traditional unilateral approach towards a more multilateral approach designed to develop the capability of African armed forces to conduct their own peacekeeping operations. RECAMP sought to contribute to this objective in three ways: through support for military training schools involved in peacekeeping training for African soldiers; through peacekeeping training for African units in sub-regional training exercises; and through equipment and logistical support for units engaged in peacekeeping.

With respect to the training of African peacekeepers, the UK and France took steps, in the context of RECAMP and in conjunction with the US, to coordinate their provision in West Africa by establishing a regional network of training centres that would complement each other and reduce duplication. Thus, the focus of the Kofi Annan International Peacekeeping Training Centre in Accra, which was initially UK-funded, is on operational level training; the Ecole de Maintien de la Paix in Bamako undertakes tactical-level training (the UK is represented on the School board) and receives support from the EU and several member states, as well as from the US, Canada and a number of other donors; and the National Defence College in Abuja undertakes strategic-level training.

The work of these centres is complemented by the efforts of a network of regional military training schools, established by the French in 1997 to provide training that meets 'the needs of African army officers [and is] equal in quality to that provided in France while being adapted to local realities and resources' (Les Ecoles Nationales à Vocation Régionale n.d.). There are 15 such schools in eight francophone African countries. Some have been designated ECOWAS (Economic Community of West African States) centres of excellence and so now are eligible for EU funding. Like the three schools mentioned above, they are run by the hosting nations and recruit, in principle, throughout the region. However, all are situated in Francophone Africa, French is normally the language of instruction and their recruitment comes largely from francophone countries. This francophone bias has led critics to argue that RECAMP actually deepened 'the Francophone-Anglophone divide that is endemic in West Africa' and even undermined the sub-region's security efforts (Kabia 2008: 185).

These criticisms are less easily levelled against RECAMP's successor, EURORECAMP. This latter initiative emerged in the wake of the December 2007 EU Summit in Lisbon during which agreement was reached on the Africa-EU Strategic Partnership, one of the four key aims of which was 'to strengthen and promote peace, security, democratic governance and human rights ... and regional and continental integration in Africa' (the Africa-EU Strategic Partnership 2007: 2). It was in this post-Lisbon context that France and the UK took the lead in transforming RECAMP, which was originally a national initiative, into an EU programme, EURORECAMP. Based in Paris, as France is the 'framework nation' designated by the EU, EURORECAMP has a French general as its director and a British officer as its deputy director. Like RECAMP, it aims to strengthen African peacekeeping capacity through education and training. Unlike its predecessor, however, it is 'guided by the principle of African ownership', and its focus is much more explicitly on the AU and Africa's regional organisations to enable them to contribute more effectively to regional security (the Africa-EU Strategic Partnership 2007: 5). A good example of this new focus by EURORECAMP is the 2008 launch of its first training cycle, Amani Africa, ('Amani' means 'peace' in Swahili), which is discussed in Chapter 10.

The UK and France have also been keen to bolster the peacekeeping capacity of African regional organisations, such as ECOWAS and the Intergovernmental Authority on Development in East Africa (IGAD). As mentioned above, the French and British first began to collaborate on African regional military exercises within the framework of RECAMP. For example the UK contributed equipment to the RECAMP exercise Tanzanite in 2001 and France took part in the UK-led map exercise, Blue Pelican, at the ECOWAS Executive Secretariat in November 2000. Subsequently, between 2002 and 2006, the UK, alongside some other EU member states, provided *ad hoc* support to RECAMP military exercises. This was mainly in the form of logistical support, but was not on a large scale, was not linked to any institutional partnership and was largely symbolic. The UK nonetheless did provide more substantial support to a Franco-ECOWAS military training exercise in December 2007, which was funded 50 per cent by the French and 25 per cent by Britain (personal communication, UK official, Abuja, 2009). However, since 2009 a combination of budgetary constraints and a FCO strategic review of priorities have led to cuts in spending on peace and security in Africa, including a reduction in support for ECOWAS – for example, the UK has withdrawn support for the Kofi Annan International Peacekeeping Training Centre in Accra.

The UK and France have undoubtedly helped ECOWAS to develop its peacekeeping capability. The two countries have often collaborated particularly effectively at the operational level, when it is a question of immediate problem-solving on the ground such as ensuring that a training exercise is able to go ahead. However, Anglo-French cooperation has been far from systematic at the political or strategic level. A case in point is their different approaches to the East African brigade (EASBRIG) of the ASF. The UK initially took the lead in supporting EASBRIG but, in so doing, ran into problems with the French, who have generally been reluctant to acknowledge UK leadership. In 2007, for instance, France provided a secure LAN for EASBRIG without discussing it with the UK. Such problems arise because, once again, there is no formal mechanism for deciding what the two countries can or should do together.

Finally, French and British interest in providing support to Africa-wide peacekeeping efforts was heightened when, in 2002, the AU replaced the OAU and moved away from a stance based on absolute respect for national sovereignty, to one which took greater account of the responsibility to protect (Mwanasali 2009: 42–4). The UK, France and other EU member states backed AU efforts to develop a framework for crisis management on the African continent, namely the African Peace and Security Architecture (APSA) although this backing was limited to conflict prevention work and not well targeted prior to the adoption of the EU Strategy for Africa in 2005 and its successor, the joint Africa-EU Strategy, in 2007. One of the key objectives of this joint strategy is to strengthen African capacities, not least in the security field (Assessment Report 2009) and it was with this objective in view that the Amani Africa training cycle was launched, in November 2008 (see Chapter 10 for fuller treatment of Anglo-French cooperation in support of APSA and Amani Africa). The UK is the largest financial contributor to Amani Africa while France takes the lead role in agenda-setting and implementation as the framework nation for the EURORECAMP programme (Elowson 2009: 62–3). In practice, however, both continue to provide a significant proportion of their support for the APSA on a bilateral basis. French and, to some extent, British reluctance to give up or share sovereignty over African policy or to lose autonomy over spheres of influence and a more general lack of willingness on the part of EU member states to pass on information about what they are doing bilaterally with the AU remain significant obstacles to more effective cooperation in the security field. Overcoming these obstacles is again often down to individual personalities.

Neoclassical Realism, Policy Drivers and Constraints

As indicated earlier, neoclassical realism focuses on interests, preferences and power, as well as incorporating domestic political variables within foreign policy analysis. In other words, the systemic structure is not determinative, and states, through policy processes, do have some capacity for choice. Nonetheless, the key point to stress is that neoclassical realism builds on the neo-realist assumption that both the UK and France are ultimately driven by concern over their relative power within the international system. Within this analytical framework, how then are we to account for this significant yet ultimately limited Anglo-French security cooperation? In order to answer this question we will examine first the drivers towards cooperation, then the constraints on enhanced cooperation.

A key factor, under the reformist government of Lionel Jospin, was France's wish to shed its reputation as the 'gendarme of Africa'. After the debacle of its involvement in Rwanda and former Zaire in the mid-1990s, France was keen both to restore its image in Africa and to draw down discreetly from its costly African bases. Both these objectives pointed to the need for a more multilateral approach. Thus, French military policy in Africa sought to shift the risk of intervention by obtaining prior UN or EU approval and through burden-sharing with its allies, notably in ESDP and other peacekeeping operations. Finally, on the security front, France was becoming disillusioned with the UN's peacekeeping efforts and looking to the EU – and indeed NATO – to play a greater role (Utley 2006: 65–7).

On the UK side, the drivers were quite different. The New Labour government of Tony Blair was beginning its move towards a policy of re-engagement with Africa. However, given the regional, and often continent-wide, nature of the security challenges facing Africa, the UK could not effectively re-engage without having a relationship with Francophone Africa, and this indicated a need to cooperate with France. Secondly, the creation of DfID, much of the work of which is focused on Africa, helped to keep Africa centre-stage in policy terms, notably within the Cabinet, in a way that had not previously been the case. Finally and crucially, Prime Minister Blair needed to deliver on his promise to 'put the UK at the heart of Europe'. Following Britain's failure to join the euro, cooperation on African policy – particularly in the security field – provided an arena in which the UK could play a central role within the EU (Porteous 2008: 5–15). That this was a propitious domain for cooperation had already been demonstrated by the understanding that developed between the two armed forces during the crisis in Bosnia (personal communication, former British naval officer, Portsmouth, 2008).

Thus the Saint-Malo process was launched at a key moment, when both the UK and France were anxious about their continuing status as permanent members of the UNSC and about their relative loss of influence, the former particularly in Europe and the latter in Africa. As a result, the two countries had complementary interests pushing them towards closer and mutually beneficial cooperation. Clearly by working together in the security domain, these two middle-ranking powers, with similar defence expenditures, could increase their influence over European security, a fact of no small significance at a time of heightened British fears and nascent French concerns about US abandonment. By coordinating their positions, the UK and France could generally sway the PSC and other military committees in the EU as well as have an impact at the global level, notably within the P3.[6] By collaborating, they could help to keep the Africa-EU Strategic Partnership on track and ensure that European Development Fund monies continue to be earmarked to support European peacekeeping initiatives in Africa. By working together, they could also – importantly in an age of rapid international media coverage – better respond to the often trans-sovereign security-related threats arising from Africa, be they from illegal immigration, the spread of AIDS, drugs trafficking, money laundering, international criminal activity or indeed the risk of genocide in fragile states such as the DRC and Sudan.

By the early 2000s, other factors and events were also pushing the UK and France to collaborate. The first of these was the Al-Qaeda attacks of 11 September 2001, which gave a boost to the idea of security and defence cooperation

---

6   The UK and France are expected under Article 19 of the Amsterdam Treaty to brief the other member states on UNSC proceedings and to represent the positions of the EU at the Council.

and contributed to the growing emphasis that has been placed on security in EU African policy since 2001. The second was the emergence of seemingly intractable crises in countries such as Côte d'Ivoire and Zimbabwe. As the former colonial powers, the UK and France had to deal with these crises and needed the other's political support so as, at the very least, to avoid tripping each other up. The third catalyst was the Iraq War, which initially led to deep divisions within Europe and at the UNSC, where the UK and France competed aggressively for the votes of African Security Council members (Angola, Cameroon, Guinea) in relation to the proposed second UN Resolution. In the end, however, the invasion of Iraq actually encouraged the UK and France to look for areas for cooperation in other parts of the world, not least Africa (personal communications, former UK officials at the UN, New York, 2008; see also Loisel 2004: 55). Indeed, the Franco-British summit declaration of November 2003 laid considerable emphasis on the two governments' commitment to cooperation in Africa and 'to the continued development of the EU's capacity to take decisions and act in crisis management' (Franco-British Summit Declaration 2003). A final factor has been the emergence of new partners that are playing an ever greater role in Africa (China, India, Japan and the Middle East countries). The UK and France have, in recent years, become an increasingly less significant part of Africa's foreign relations, with the result that their power to do things in Africa and their leverage over African leaders have declined. This has put further pressure on British and French governments to pool their efforts in order to maintain their relative influence.[7]

However, given these pressures to cooperate and the benefits that both countries derive from enhanced collaboration, it is perhaps surprising that Anglo-French cooperation has not been taken further. The explanation would appear to lie in the fact that French and British leaders have had to take account of other variables, not least their perceived divergent national interests, the capacity of their states to act and the views of the wider domestic polity on state preferences. On the first of these variables, it is important to underline that Paris and London attach different relative importance to Africa and this, in turn, affects both their readiness to collaborate on African policy and the areas (often outside the former French and British empires) in which they seek to cooperate. For France, Africa plays a crucial role in enhancing its rank in the international pecking order, while for the UK Africa is much more centrally a development issue. There is also a key difference between them over NATO. While neither country would deny the existence of a 'spatial differentiation' between ESDP and NATO missions, whereby Europe operates in sub-Saharan Africa whilst NATO is active in more geo-strategically important zones (Dyson 2008), the fact remains that France sees cooperation ultimately as a way of affirming an autonomous European

---

7   However, French concerns about Chinese economic penetration apparently outweigh those of the UK, which in 2009 provided $250,000 to support the China-Africa Business Council. Retrieved 18 March 2010 from www.crid.asso.fr/spip.php?breve58 and www.number10.gov.uk/Page18214.

security identity (beyond even 'Berlin Plus'), whereas the UK sees the ESDP as complementary to NATO.

Furthermore, neoclassical realists would argue that the level of cooperation depends ultimately on the 'extractive capacity' of the two states. In France, the state's capacity has been limited by its membership of the European Monetary Union and by internal spending cuts. The UK government has also faced budgetary restrictions, particularly since the 2008–9 global financial crisis. Moreover, its long-term commitment to SSR is in doubt: in August 2008, the UK's two conflict prevention pools were combined, and, in March 2009, the conflict prevention budget, which had never allocated more than £65m per year to Africa, was merged with the Stabilisation Aid Fund and the peacekeeping budget (which pays for the UK's peacekeeping responsibilities at the UN). In the process, the overall amount of funding for these activities was cut and the budget for Africa reduced to £43 million (Hansard 2009, 25 March). Significantly too, parliamentary and civil society constraints mean that the British government has more difficulty getting military missions approved than is the case in France, where the French president finds this comparatively easy. Other domestic constraints relate, especially in the UK, to the small size of available armed forces due to commitments elsewhere. The rise to prominence of DfID, which has no equivalent in France, is another factor of which the British government has to take account in decisions about security cooperation in Africa. While DfID potentially offers new opportunities through the creation of the Africa CPP, this is not primarily intended for 'hard' operations of the type that France is particularly well placed to undertake thanks to its pre-positioned forces in Africa.

Conclusion

This chapter has demonstrated how Britain and France have, since Saint-Malo, built new institutional bridges and cooperated more freely in ESDP missions and the training of African peacekeepers. It has also shown that there have been clear limits to this collaboration between Europe's leading military powers and that cooperation has often been a function of individual personalities. Clearly, the P3 initiative has enabled Britain and France to cooperate more at the level of the UNSC. The creation of the PSC has facilitated cooperation in Europe, as has the fact that the UK and France, as well as regularly holding the EU Presidency, have increasingly been called upon to chair European Council meetings in African capitals in which European member states and incoming Council Presidents, such as Slovenia and the Czech Republic, are not represented.

At the same time, there has been a convergence in understanding of the problems confronting Africa and of the link between security and development. Against the background of globalisation, the emergence of major new actors in Africa and the heightened perception of the economic and strategic threats posed by the African continent, Britain and France have felt the need to align their agendas, either bilaterally, as has happened to a limited extent in the DRC, or bi-multilaterally, as was the case with the development of the Africa-EU strategy in advance of the Lisbon summit (Elowson 2009: 27). However, there remains a strong sense of 'division of labour' between the two countries with France operating in Francophone Africa and Britain in Anglophone Africa. Cooperation has taken place on particular issues, thanks to a shared understanding of challenges and a shared interest in addressing them, or an acknowledgment of the 'comparative advantage' of the other country. But it has not been systematic. Nor has it been accompanied by the degree of institutionalisation that might be implied by the term 'partnership'.

The signs are that cooperation will continue to be patchy for the foreseeable future. There is, for example, evidence to suggest that the French are increasingly interested in developing a stronger security relationship with the US in Africa, notably in the Sahel.[8] On the British side, following the election of a Conservative-led coalition government in 2010, the UK may well play a much less constructive role in future ESDP missions. Furthermore, almost any future British administration is likely to consider with trepidation the idea, propounded by France, that such missions, given their sheer number and complexity, require the establishment of a separate European HQ operating autonomously from NATO. At the same time, however, future governments in both countries will be under pressure to make savings, which may push them towards increased burden-sharing in certain situations. Moreover, the creation of the European External Action Service, post-Lisbon, will increase pressure for policy coordination, not least in the security field where the two countries clearly have shared interests.

---

8   Hitherto, this relationship seems to have been an exclusive one, although in 2009 the UK government announced its intention to re-open an embassy in Mali in response to the execution of a British national and the wider threat of terrorism, migration and organised crime.

PART III
Other Bilateral 'Partnerships'

Chapter 6

Scandinavian Africa Policies:
Value-based Foreign Policies between
British Affinity, French National Interests
and EU Norms

Gorm Rye Olsen

During the Cold War years, the Scandinavian countries were known to have a special position in international affairs. The idea of Nordic 'exceptionalism' was crucial in this context, implying that these countries were different from or even morally better than others. The exceptionalism was assumed to reflect the particular experiences, the norms and the values of the Scandinavian countries and moreover, it was assumed that they could serve as a model to be copied by others (Browning 2007). The first element in the exceptionalism was the idea that the Nordics represented a 'peace-driven' approach to international relations. It was the official position that the resort to military means should be rejected in all but the most exceptional circumstances and if possible, international problems should be resolved through diplomacy and recourse to UN/international law (Browning 2007: 32f).

The second element in the Nordic exceptionalism was described as 'international solidarism' reflecting the attempts to play a role in overcoming the North-South divide by speaking on behalf of the world's poorest and most excluded. This third world solidarity expressed a feeling of moral duty to help those less fortunate than oneself. It was done with a strong leaning towards multilateralism and for many years, the UN became one of the most important vehicles of the Nordics' morally driven foreign policy. International cooperation through international organisations, active international diplomacy and participation in peace-keeping missions are often mentioned as core characteristics of this special brand of internationalism (Kuisma 2007: 13f).

However, the end of the Cold War meant a strong push for the three Scandinavian countries to start reflecting on the unexpected possibilities which opened with the new international system that was emerging (Archer 2005). At a first glance, it appears that Denmark, Sweden and Norway have developed their foreign policies in different directions during the past 20 years. These changes mean that it has become less clear what is so exceptional about the foreign policies of the Nordic countries as they seem to find it difficult to continue to adhere to special 'Nordic norms' and they even appear to have lost interest in selling a Nordic brand. Moreover, since the mid-1990s, the European Union (EU) has developed into being the most important multilateral forum for the formulation and implementation of the foreign and security policies of both Denmark and Sweden, but not necessarily of Norway which is not a member of the EU. In this context, it is remarkable to what extent elements of Nordic practices as well as of the Nordic model have become Europeanised. This 'Nordicisation' of the EU seems to contribute to further undermining a distinct Nordic profile in international affairs (Browning 2007: 44; Jacobsen 2009; Larsen 2009).

It is the aim of this chapter to look at Danish, Swedish and Norwegian policies towards Africa and ask whether new patterns of collaboration or conflict with the two most prominent external powers on the continent, the UK and France, can be identified. The analysis is based on two fundamental assumptions: one is the Nordics are small states and the second is the decision-makers in all three countries are fully aware of this fact. It is the hypothesis of this chapter that it is difficult to talk about one special or one exceptional Nordic policy towards Africa in the current century. First, this manifests itself in a trend where the three countries have been prepared to act unilaterally if that has been considered most appropriate in relation to the overall goal of optimising their particular national influence on the continent. Second, based on their historical heritage, the Nordics still have a strong inclination towards multilateral cooperation. Third, because of the basic foreign policy values of Denmark, Sweden and Norway, they find it much easier to cooperate with the UK, whereas France is considered a difficult partner due to its strong insistence on its national priorities and interests.

Before embarking on the analysis, the following section briefly presents the analytical framework of the paper. The empirical analysis is divided into four parts. First, collaboration and conflicts within the field of development assistance are scrutinised. Second, collaboration and conflicts within the area of foreign and security policy are looked into. Third, collaboration between Denmark, France and the UK on Africa in the Security Council is analysed during the years 2005–6 when Denmark was a member of the Council. Finally, Nordic policies and the pattern of collaboration related to the African Union are scrutinised. The focus throughout these four parts of the empirical analysis is on explaining the policies of the three Nordics and why they may lead to cooperation or conflict with the two former colonial powers. The chapter uses the terminology the Nordics and the Scandinavian countries in either case referring only to Denmark, Norway and Sweden.

The Analytical Framework

This chapter applies a theoretical framework developed with a view to analysing the foreign policy of small (European/Scandinavian) states (Petersen 2000). This particular approach is located within the broader context of a framework of neoclassical realism (Taliaferro 2009; Rose 1998). It is assumed that the two different theoretical approaches can be combined and moreover that they can cross-fertilise each other. First, they are in agreement on the independent variable, namely the significance of the relative material power capabilities. At the same time, they are both open to the potential significance of soft power. Second, they agree on the need to incorporate internal or domestic circumstances as intervening variables in the study of a country's foreign policy. In particular, the two approaches emphasise the role of the foreign policy bureaucracies. Third, the two approaches agree that coalition making is a crucial foreign policy instrument even though small state theory stresses this element as being particularly important (Kitchen 2010: 141f; Thorhallsson and Wivel 2006: 658ff; Jacobsen 2009).

Neoclassical realism departs from neorealist theories as it does not assume a direct logical connection between the nature of the system and the way states behave. Instead, the approach assumes the existence of intervening ideational variables which link the nature and the power of the international system and the specific foreign policy behaviour of the state (Kitchen 2010). It is a characteristic of neoclassical realism to place the impact of ideas alongside the imperatives of material power in the making of foreign policy. Thus, this approach rejects the notion that either ideas or material factors are the most fundamental and therefore deserve a particular analytical focus at the expense of the other (Kitchen 2010). Neoclassical realism stresses the importance of the quality of the state bureaucracy. As foreign policy choices are made by political leaders and civil servants, their perceptions of the relative power of their own country are important (Rose 1998: 147ff). The quality of the bureaucracy in combination with ideational factors can play an instrumental role in helping the political leaders to extract and mobilise support from the domestic power base, thereby adding to the totality of the country's power resources (Taliaferro 2009: 32ff; Rose 1998: 257ff).

Thus, ideas within nations may influence decision-making on foreign policy. Ideas, norms and values within nations may influence decision-making where they can be carried or promoted by both individuals, institutions in which they may become embedded and through the broader culture of the states (Kitchen 139ff). Nicholas Kitchen distinguishes between different types of ideas. 'Intentional ideas are of particular relevance for this paper as they are normative suggestions that seek to establish goals for foreign policy. Such ideas become translated into policy because it is considered as the right thing to do by the foreign policy decision-makers' (Kitchen 2010: 129).

Based upon their possession of material power, the three Scandinavian countries obviously have to be described as small states, defined by the fact that they are basically unable to change the contours of their international context. However, if the focus is not solely on the possession of power but also on the exercise of power, another picture of small states emerges. When it is no longer only a question of material power resources, possession of 'soft power' becomes crucial. It means that the understanding of the foreign policy elites and of the general public of the proper role of the state in global and regional politics becomes an important power asset for the small state (Thorhallsson and Wivel 2006: 664). To be precise, the possession of soft power is the key to understanding Nordic internationalism or Nordic 'normative internationalism', which refers to the 'shared history as social democratic welfare states in which the values of solidarity, egalitarianism and social justice have loomed large by Western standards' (Lawler 2007: 102, 104ff; Stokke 1989). If the relational definition of small states is applied, it implies that a small state may be weak in one relation but powerful in another context. Concretely, a small state may be powerful in Africa policy and in development policy where soft and normative values may be supposed to dominate, whereas it may be weak in trade policy where much more hard core interests are at stake.

Applying small state theory in combination with neoclassical realism means domestic actors, not least civil servants and domestic political values and norms, come into the focus of the study of the foreign policy of small states. On the other hand, the emphasis on ideational factors and domestic institutions does not lead to the neglect of the significance of material power resources. On the contrary, it only shows the special characteristics of, in this case, the three small Scandinavian states, which is that they can punch above their weight in a self-sustaining way by taking on the role of 'norm entrepreneurs' and by working in international coalitions and in international organisations such as the EU and the United Nations (UN). Unlike small state theory, neoclassical realism suggests that small states only temporarily can punch above their weight as they ultimately are bound by their relative lack of material and security power.

By working in international organisations, the Nordics are able to contribute to shaping them and also to forming their policies. For the analysis in this chapter, the European Union is of particular importance both to Sweden and Denmark as members of the Union and also because the EU is an important actor in relation to Africa. Within the EU, the Nordic countries including non-member Norway are supposed to act as norm entrepreneurs exporting values and norms to the other member states. The norm export has led to claims that the Union has become Nordicised i.e. the Union has taken over Nordic values and norms, typically within 'soft' policy areas like development aid and policy towards Africa (Lawler 2007: 104; Stokke 1989). On the other hand, it can just as well be argued that elements of Nordic practices and the Nordic model have become Europeanised (Browning 2007: 44).

Summing up, it is assumed that it is possible for small states to exert significant international influence as their power resources not only include material resources but also values, norms and ideas. For values and ideas to become effective means as power resources they have to be communicated clearly, both domestically and internationally. It is also a crucial precondition that these states are able to build international coalitions in order to influence international politics (Thorhallsson and Wivel 2006: 659ff). Often, this has been possible because international organisations represent a structural framework for exchanging information between small and big states. Active participation in international cooperation combining soft power variables like prestige, diplomatic ingenuity, reputation and resolve are extremely important instruments for buttressing a small state's influential capability (Petersen 2000: 79ff). The latter elements presuppose the presence of a highly qualified foreign policy bureaucracy which is particularly important for small states.

Data and Method

The academic sources concerning Danish, Swedish and Norwegian Africa policy are extremely limited. When the focus is narrowed down even further to the pattern of cooperation and conflict with France and the UK in the current century, the number of sources is even smaller. Therefore, a considerable part of the information presented in this chapter comes from interviews undertaken by the author. The interviewees work in the Danish Ministry of Foreign Affairs, the Swedish Ministry of Foreign Affairs and the Norwegian Ministry of Foreign Affairs. It has to be stressed that the number of persons interviewed is limited. Therefore, it is necessary to secure their anonymity. When reference is made to critical or particularly important information obtained via the interviews, it is marked with 'confidential interview'. The information on the Swedish and Norwegian Africa policy is obtained via telephone interviews with staff employed in the two Foreign Ministries. A standard questionnaire was sent to the individuals in advance and it was followed up through the telephone interviews. A second source of information comes from the author's participation in seminars, even though the seminars were not directly related to the Nordic countries' relations to France and the UK in Africa. Third, some of the information presented here is collected by scrutinising reports, homepages and evaluation reports.

The strong reliance on information obtained from civil servants involved in the actual policy-making and implementation of the Africa policies can be argued to be an advantage as it is precisely this group of individuals that is emphasised by the theoretical framework as a very important intervening variable. On the other hand, for obvious reasons, this type of source is a challenge concerning the reliability of the information, as the interviewees can be supposed to present one side of the story.

Collaboration on Development Cooperation

For many years, the Nordic countries have had a particularly high profile in international development cooperation. Denmark, Norway and Sweden have been described as 'humane internationalists', which is defined as 'an acceptance of the principle that the citizens of the industrial nations have moral obligations towards people and events beyond their borders; it implies a sensitivity to cosmopolitan values such as the obligations to refrain from the use of force in the pursuit of national interests and respect for human rights' (Stokke 1989: 10–11). This international solidarity manifested itself very clearly in the relatively huge development budgets and Denmark, Sweden and Norway were the first to achieve the UN target of devoting 0.7 per cent of GDP to official development assistance (ODA). It was important that the distribution of ODA from the Scandinavian countries was not tied narrowly to national commercial and strategic interests, 'but was more driven by the goal of helping those in greatest need' (Browning 2007: 35; Bergman 2007; Lawler 2007). Because of many years of bilateral cooperation with a limited number of African countries, the aid bureaucracies of the three countries – Danida, Norad and Sida – have achieved a solid knowledge of the local economic and political environment in the recipient countries (Stokke 2005; Danielson and Wohlgemuth 2005; Olsen 2005). Due to the somewhat technical nature of this particular policy field, the policy formulations and the implementation of policies on a daily basis have been left to the aid bureaucracies and thus to the civil servants.

In the current century, the three Scandinavian countries have had a close and positive working relationship with the UK, which includes aid harmonisation and the improvement of the delivery of development aid in particular. The countries have joined forces under the headline of 'Nordic Plus', which refers to the 'Joint Action Plan for Effective Aid Delivery through Harmonisation and Alignment of Donor Practices'. The basis for the close cooperation is a general agreement on the principles of how to deliver aid and also that the countries share the same understanding and the same professional attitude to development aid. Apparently, France does not find it in its interest to participate in this type collaborative work.

The cooperation between the British and the Nordics has set an example on how to deliver aid in the current century and as such it has had considerable impact, pushing forward the principles of good development aid as they are written down in the Paris declaration principles as well as in the Accra principles. Not only is there agreement on the principles of aid delivery, there are also frequent high level meetings between the heads of the development aid departments from the countries involved. There are joint visits to countries receiving aid from Britain and the Nordics as well as joint programming in these countries. On the other hand, the picture becomes much more ambiguous when other British organisations apart from DfID get involved in the collaboration. When the British Foreign Office and the British Ministry of Defence become involved, there is clearly a tendency to focus more on British national interests and less on the principles of delivering good development assistance. This is particularly obvious in situations where the three British organisations cooperate and have to share a common pool of money to finance initiatives.

As far as French development assistance policy is concerned, it is obvious that Paris pursues an agenda which is influenced by national priorities and concerns. It appears that France to a larger extent sees its aid policy within a commercial and foreign and security policy context, which is very much aimed at taking care of its national interests (Chafer 2002; Renou 2002). For obvious reasons this type of policy makes it difficult to cooperate with 'humane internationalists' like the Nordics. Moreover, France has traditionally focused on the Francophone countries and on the construction of a regional 'space' in West Africa. Outside, this zone Paris has played a reticent role (Gabas 2005: 248ff). Because the Nordics have only been present in West Africa to a limited extent, their experience of cooperating with France within the field of development assistance is limited.

The limited cooperation may also have to be explained by the differences between the Nordic and the French approaches to development aid and by the fact that the countries simply do not share a similar understanding of what development policy is about. Historically, Nordic development aid has been driven less by strategic and economic concerns and more by an ideological commitment to global welfare as a 'logical extension' of the Nordic emphasis on 'social solidarity at home' (Stokke 1989; Bergman 2007). Nevertheless, France is welcoming every donor as a partner under the more or less unspoken expectation that the donor in question is willing to sign up to the political interests of France. The dilemma was exposed in 2009 and 2010 when the political crisis in Niger led Denmark to postpone a new phase of its cooperation in the water sector and to consider adjustments in the overall country programme, whereas France made it clear that it was very interested in maintaining the Danish involvement in the country.

The pattern of cooperation between the Nordics and the two old colonial powers becomes more and more ambiguous with the increasing intensity of cooperation within the framework of the EU, simply because the Commission in Brussels becomes more and more important when it comes to European development assistance in Africa. Even though Denmark and Sweden differ on their national positions towards the common EU development programmes, the two countries generally join forces with the UK and a few others, forming one side of what appears to be a North-South divide within the Union's development aid policy. France and its Southern partners are found on the other side.

In spite of the fact that it is not a member of the EU, Norway has been working closely with the Union both in its development assistance and in other policy fields related to Africa. Oslo finds the EU is a very heavy and difficult organisation to work with and it is particularly slow in making decisions and also in implementing its decisions. Therefore, Norway has preferred to work on a bilateral basis, at least in situations where there has been an obvious need for quick responses. Neither the status of Norway within Europe nor its specific policy initiatives within the field of development assistance have created particular problems with the UK or with France bilaterally.

It appears that France on several occasions has been sceptical towards Norwegian engagement in Africa. In its traditional Anglophone-Francophone perspective, France has located Norway in the Anglophone camp, meaning the relations and contacts between Paris and Oslo have automatically been strained. At least, this was the situation until Bernard Kouchner became French Foreign Minister in 2007. He brought with him a strong focus on humanitarian issues and was much less preoccupied with narrow French interests in Africa. In many respects, Kouchner has meant a change compared to the situation under the previous French governments.

Summing up, the three Nordics are among the biggest development aid donors if measured by ODA/GNI and moreover, Scandinavian development aid is known to be largely altruistic as well as efficient. These elements give them much prestige within the global policy community dealing with development assistance and this is supposed to give the Nordics a unique possibility to influence policies within this particular area. Based on the empirical information presented in this section, it appears that the Nordics have cooperated closely with the UK in Africa in order to influence this particular policy field. When the collaboration is to be explained, it is possible to do so by referring to the perceptions of the Scandinavian and British civil servants of what is good development assistance and what is not. These like-minded countries more or less share the same norms, values and ideas of development aid and therefore cooperation has been natural for all parties involved. In comparison, the level and intensity of cooperation between the Nordics and France are significantly lower, probably because France has such a strong focus on its own national interests and national priorities. This particular focus appears to be an impediment to close cooperation both with Britain and with the Nordics, stressing that the like-minded countries and France are simply not sharing the same norms, values and principles for giving aid.

Collaboration on Foreign Policy and Security Issues

During the Cold War years, Denmark and Norway kept a low profile on general political issues and security topics related to sub-Saharan Africa. Nevertheless, both countries were actively involved in the struggle against apartheid and Denmark even established a special anti-apartheid appropriation. In comparison, Stockholm pursued a much more active policy aimed at fighting the apartheid regime in South Africa and moreover, Sweden cooperated with a number of socialist countries such as Angola. When hardly any Western country was represented in Luanda, Sweden maintained an embassy in the country. Even though the Nordic countries have increasingly moved away from the traditional Nordic exceptionalism, pursuing a morally and normative-driven foreign policy, it does not imply that these elements have disappeared totally.

When Denmark in early 2002 decided to close down its development programmes in Malawi, Eritrea and Zimbabwe, it was done with explicit reference to political-moral arguments such as the lack of good governance (Olsen 2003: 77ff). A proposal to make Ethiopia a future recipient of Danish development aid was turned down in 2005 with the argument that the Ethiopian government did not live up to the requirements for good government and respect for human rights. In comparison, Britain maintained its cooperation with Ethiopia based on realpolitik reflections, which simply were that Ethiopia was and still is considered an important actor in global and regional security. In spite of this disagreement, the Danes and the British have cooperated closely in many African countries such as Zambia, Tanzania and Kenya, where the two countries have been engaged in programmes supporting general elections, development of free media etc.

Compared with Denmark, Norway has been in a much more direct conflict with the Ethiopian authorities. Back in 2007, no less than six Norwegian diplomats were expelled from the country because Oslo had been critical of the human rights situation in Ethiopia. At the same time, it is recognised by the Norwegian authorities that even though the regime in Addis Ababa is totalitarian, it has a clear political strategy to promote development and, most remarkably, it actually tries to implement its policy declarations. It is evaluated that Norway gets a lot of value from its aid money because the Ethiopian authorities have a firm commitment to promote development. As far as Eritrea is concerned, the Norwegian authorities consider the country as extremely important for the whole region. The local authorities in Asmara may be difficult to handle, but nevertheless some Western powers such as Norway have to remain in the country. Thus in some situations, Norway has pursued a high moral profile towards some African countries, but at the same time it is also very pragmatic in its approach.

Looking at the increasing significance of the EU in Africa, Swedish policy towards Zimbabwe is particularly interesting. For a long time, Stockholm kept a high and very critical profile towards the regime in Harare, based on clear principles such as respect for human rights, democracy and good governance. Denmark strongly supported this policy line too. Sweden was so committed to its morally-based policy towards Zimbabwe that it could not participate in the attempts to formulate a common EU policy towards Zimbabwe. Nevertheless after years of disagreement, this high profile policy stance showed the way as the EU finally ended up agreeing with the Swedish moral arguments which have also been advanced by Britain for a long time. Thus since 2007/8 EU member states have been in agreement on a common policy towards Zimbabwe, building on the principles of good governance, democracy and respect for human rights.

In spite of the agreement, it is still possible to identify a North-South division within the EU on Zimbabwe. Thus an informal group of like-minded countries consisting of at least Denmark, Sweden, the UK, Ireland, Holland and Germany meet from time-to-time to discuss issues related to Zimbabwe. The Zimbabwean case shows at least two things. First, it is possible for small Nordic countries to influence the policies of the EU, although it must be acknowledged that Sweden was hardly the most influential country in forming the common EU policies towards Zimbabwe. The UK played a very active role and London's position most probably was decisive in changing the EU's common position towards Zimbabwe. Second, Zimbabwe may illustrate the growing Nordicisation of the common European policies towards Africa, meaning that occasionally the EU appears as a principle-based actor.

As far as security policy is concerned, Sweden shows a new and interesting pattern in its Africa policy. It deployed troops in two of the EU's ESDP missions in

Africa, both in Ituri in DRC in 2003 and in the huge mission in Chad in 2008–9. In both cases, Swedish troops had to work closely with the French forces. In spite of the fact that the Swedish decision-makers were fully aware of the strong national French interests in both cases, the decision-makers in Stockholm were happy to support both missions, simply because there was an obvious need and because France and Sweden had common goals in both instances. The Swedish conclusion to the two operations is that the cooperation with France worked very well indeed. In this particular context, it is worth noting that Norway, a non-EU-member country, actually contributed troops to the ESDP mission in Chad. Moreover, Norway has been very active in relation to finding a solution to the Darfur conflict. Therefore Oslo tried to involve both France and the US in these efforts. As far as the relationship with France is concerned 'it was a mistake. France simply does not like that anybody finds out what it is up to' (confidential interview).

In the current century, the three Nordic countries have been in agreement that 'peace and security are seen as the most important regional capacities in need of support' (Norberg 2009). There is a clear recognition that cooperation among the Nordic countries is necessary simply because 'we are so small' (Mosgard 2009). Also, there seems to be a recognition that it is obvious to cooperate with the armed forces of the UK, particularly in East Africa where there is a special focus on the East African brigade of the African Standby Force, EASBRIG, with respect to developing a regional rapid deployment capacity. In spite of the tradition of close cooperation with the British, there have been tensions and latent conflicts between at least the Danes and the British. According to the Danish side, this is to a large extent caused by the British insistence on their special knowledge of military issues and an attitude that 'we know best'. The cooperation among the three Nordic countries in East Africa has developed a division of labour whereby Denmark has taken the lead working with the African land forces whereas Norway has taken the lead when it comes to the maritime component, in particular the development of a coastguard (Mosgaard 2009).

Concerning the cooperation on security issues between the Nordics and France, Denmark and France have an ongoing dialogue on security issues in West Africa, concretely in Niger and Mali. When it comes to the bilateral relationship between Norway and France, it is characterised by strong French scepticism towards the Norwegians. 'The French do not like to be watched too closely. Moreover, the French are very preoccupied with their specific national interests. France analyses Africa from a perspective of power, whereas Norway looks at the continent from a moral standpoint' (confidential interview). Paris considers Norway as too Anglophone and a country which plays the game of the United States in Africa.

Parallel to the bilateral discussions, consultations on security issues take place within the framework of the EU, where it is noted by Nordic government observers that to a large extent France dominates the Union's policy in West Africa. In general, Swedish decision-makers consider France as a very difficult partner in an African context. During the Swedish presidency of the EU in the second half of 2009, a number of Francophone countries were on the agenda.

Because France considered Mauritius, Guinea Conakry, Niger and Madagascar as its genuine interests, it was very difficult for the Swedish Presidency to find common ground among the member states for policy initiatives towards the four countries. Nevertheless, Sweden considers the EU as the most appropriate forum for formulating policies as well as launching initiatives towards Africa.

It has to be noted that the French have a tendency to opt for traditional or hard core security policy, including reliance on training of local armed forces and military equipment. Therefore, French thinking on security in this region comes easily into conflict with the Nordics' thinking, as the latter argue in favour of understanding security as also being about development, dialogue and about the opportunities to be involved in the political processes. It has to be emphasised that the disagreements between the Nordics and France on security have not changed very much since Paris announced its change of policy towards a more pragmatic, and also multilateral, i.e. EU, approach. To Nordic civil servants, it is an open question if French Africa policy differs in fundamental ways from its traditional, pre-1990s policy, that is, before significant changes were announced (see Chapter 3).

Summing up, the foreign policies of the three Scandinavian countries towards Africa show a dual picture. It appears that the Nordics have not given up pursuing a morally and value-based policy, but at the same time they also tend to conduct a less principled policy depending on the specific time and on the concrete case. This manifested itself in Norwegian policy towards Ethiopia and in its strikingly realpolitik position towards Eritrea and Ethiopia, which is based on a crude power analysis. A similar picture appears in the case of Sweden, stressing that the country, in certain situations, has pursued a principle-based policy, but that it has also taken a realpolitik approach, emphasising the importance of coordinating initiatives towards Africa within the EU.

When cooperation and the coordination of policy initiatives take place within the framework of the EU, two things are worth noting. First, often it involves lengthy and difficult processes which make Norway prefer other ways, including bilateral ones. Second, if the policies are developed within the EU, it appears that Nordic values and Nordic principles have a considerable impact on the common decisions. This Nordicisation of the EU's policies seems to be a crucial explanation for the Swedish as well as the Norwegian support for the ESDP missions. When cooperation is on narrow security issues outside the realm of the EU, the previously mentioned pattern repeats itself, insofar as the Nordics tend to cooperate rather closely with the British armed forces whereas bilateral cooperation with France is limited.

In conclusion, when the Nordics pursue principle- and value-based foreign policies, they very easily end up taking positions different from both Britain and France, as was the case with the Danish and British positions on Ethiopia. The two former colonial powers tend to make realpolitik choices in many situations. Therefore, the risk of conflict is particularly pronounced when it comes to countries where the former colonial powers feel they have special interests, such as Zimbabwe, Niger, Madagascar, Chad etc. Overall, the foreign policies of the Nordics aimed at Africa seem to differ somewhat, confirming the expectation that the new post-Cold War international system leaves small states with more foreign policy choices. On the other hand, they are still influenced considerably by their domestic values and norms which push them towards cooperating within the EU and towards cooperating with the UK, which seem to share a number of values and ideas with the Nordics.

Denmark in the UN Security Council, 2005–6

During the years 2005–6, Denmark served as one of the 10 elected members of the UN Security Council. The Danish foreign minister declared that one of the goals for the two-year Danish membership of the Council was to turn its attention to Africa and in particular towards the many violent conflicts on the continent (Løj 2007: 34ff). During these two years, Denmark was involved in developing a comprehensive approach to the conflicts on the continent and it was working in favour of involving the African Union in conflict management by providing support for African mediation efforts in conflicts such as the ones in Côte d'Ivoire and Sudan (Løj 2007: 37). Sudan became a showcase of the lessons to be learned from the years serving on the Security Council. First, France, the UK and to some extent the US tried to use the Council to promote a normative agenda for international involvement in crisis resolution and management, whereas China and Russia were highly reluctant to follow such a line. Nevertheless, Denmark, the UK and France plus eight other members of the council agreed on Resolution 1593 (2005) on the first referral on Darfur to the International Criminal Court. Another lesson learned was that there were difficulties in setting the agenda of the Council. Denmark fought hard to put the situation in northern Uganda on the agenda, and it was only in cooperation with strong partners like the UK and France that it succeeded (Løj 2007: 46). The Danish UN ambassador's general conclusion to the two years is that 'we worked extremely closely with powerful allies: France, the United Kingdom' (Løj 2007: 47) and others. For this reason, a significant number of actions were taken on Africa by the Council, including the authorisation of the two operations in Sudan, UNMIS and AMIS.

In summary, the EU appears to be an adequate framework for cooperating within the UN, as Denmark together with the UK and France launched a number of important initiatives towards Africa. This observation stresses two things. First, a small state like Denmark can promote a value-based international agenda by working actively within an international organisation such as the UN. Second, there is a certain amount of common interest among the EU member states, based on normative and non-power reflections, when it comes to the evaluation of a number of issues related to Africa. Again, this can be taken as an indication of the increasing Nordicisation of the EU.

The Nordics and the African Union

In the current century, the Nordic countries have been strongly involved in supporting regional institutions in Africa. This is explained by the priority the Scandinavian countries have given to regional approaches to the continent and the emphasis they have given to promoting peace and security. In the Danish Africa strategy, it is established that 'since 2004, Denmark has given support to … strengthen the African Union and the regional organisation's capacity to deal with crises and contribute to peace-keeping operations'. The Swedish government states that 'Africa's political integration and the African peace and security architecture are laying the groundwork for more advanced Swedish initiatives'. Finally Norwegian policy emphasises 'taking part in conflict resolution and reconstruction efforts has become an important part of Norwegian involvement in Africa' (Norberg 2009).

From the start in 2002, Denmark has been one of the closest partners of the African Union. Denmark has strongly supported the concept of the African Peace and Security Architecture (APSA). Therefore, it is no coincidence that Denmark in 2004 was the first country to open an embassy directly accredited to the African Union. It became the beginning of an era when Denmark and Sweden put a lot of emphasis and a lot of resources into supporting the AU. As far as capacity building of the African Union is concerned, there has been close cooperation between the Nordics and the UK, whereas France has been reluctant to participate in the building of the capacity of the Union. Instead Paris has given priority to political dialogue in and around the organisation. Based on its strong focus on national interests, France has tended to follow its own policy priorities and from time to time this has led to conflicts with the AU in situations where the organisation has taken unilateral positions towards countries and regions deemed important to France, such as for example Madagascar.

The Nordic countries have not only been active in promoting Nordic priorities towards Africa within the EU, they have also been prominent in the implementation of the joint Africa-EU strategy. Sweden has been active in the group dealing with peace and security and has been involved in democratic governance and human rights issues, whereas Denmark has been engaged in the work on climate change. Both Norad and Danida have made evaluations of the effects of the support to the AU and the reports are generally positive. However, the Danish evaluation has pointed at the lack of donor coordination, including the lack of clear responsibilities between the embassy level and the level of the headquarters (Norberg 2009).

Summing up, two observations are worth emphasising. First, the Nordics have strongly supported the African Union and its attempts to establish the APSA. This is based on the conception that regional cooperation is a necessary means to promote security and development on the continent. The smooth and uncomplicated cooperation both with the UK and France within the EU on the Africa-EU strategy once again illustrates the growing Nordicisation of the EU's Africa policy. However, this conclusion should not disregard the fact that there have been conflicts with

France when the African Union has taken positions on issues related to countries considered by Paris to be important to French national interests.

Conclusion

It is the argument of this chapter that it has been increasingly difficult to maintain the idea of an exceptional Nordic policy towards Africa during the current century. The chapter has confirmed this argument. It was most obvious within the field of foreign and security policy, but the same picture was also found within the traditionally high profile area of the Nordics, namely development assistance. In spite of the fact that the three countries have increasingly adopted realpolitik considerations, their foreign policies are still highly influenced by domestic values and norms of international solidarity. The particular norm-based or value-based foreign policies in general brought the Scandinavians into a close relationship with the British. The closeness is not without exceptions. On the other hand compared with their limited cooperation with France, there is still a basis for talking about the UK and the Scandinavian countries as like-minded.

It was expected that the traditional inclination of small states towards international cooperation would manifest itself in an African context. It was shown that the EU has developed into a very crucial forum for formulating, coordinating and implementing the Africa policies of the Nordics, even though one of them, Norway, is not even a member. It was considered as a confirmation of the hypothesis that an increasing Nordicisation of the European Union has taken place, at least when it comes to its Africa policy. The observation may point towards a possible future scenario for Europe's approach to the challenges of Africa, i.e. that the EU becomes the main actor which in turn implies that French Africa policy has to become more Nordicised and less focused on national interests.

Finally turning towards the theoretical framework, two elements were emphasised: first the significance of the foreign policy bureaucracies and their quality and second, the importance of values, norms and principles influencing the foreign policies of the three Nordic countries. As to the bureaucratic element and the importance of having a qualified and competent foreign service, the analysis seems to confirm the argument about the significance of this variable. Its significance shows in relation to formulating and presenting policy initiatives and in relation to finding international partners and forming coalitions with these partners. The analysis clearly emphasised the significance of the special Nordic norm on peaceful conflict resolution and also the norm of third world solidarity. These elements influenced the Africa policies of all three states and to a certain extent the principles linked Denmark, Sweden and Norway to the UK, while the very same norms and values created a distance between them and France.

As mentioned, the analysis confirms the argument or the hypothesis that a Nordicisation of the EU's soft policy fields has taken place. At the same time, the analysis is also an indication that a considerable Europeanisation of the Africa policies of the three countries has taken place. This means that more and more policy initiatives are coordinated with EU partners, leaving less and less policy space for launching high profile bilateral initiatives. Adding these conclusions together, a preliminary prediction can be that in the future we will see more norm-based and values-based policy initiatives launched by the European Union and correspondingly fewer traditional principle-based polices promoted by the Nordic countries bilaterally.

Chapter 7

US-UK Cooperation in Africa

Paul D. Williams[1]

Although it is often camouflaged by the missionary rhetoric coming out of Washington and London, Africa is not a strategic priority for either the United States or the United Kingdom. With the exception of some high-profile development initiatives, the extraction of some precious commodities especially oil, gas and minerals, and the odd counter-terrorism operation, Africa remains near the bottom of the global pile in strategic terms. As a result, with a few notable exceptions (such as Sudan and Sierra Leone), neither state has been keen to expend considerable amounts of political capital on tackling 'African problems' nor have they been willing to pursue policies which risk generating American or British casualties. Africa's low strategic importance has also meant that successive US and UK governments have been able to muddle along with fairly woolly objectives on the continent. The good news is that this has afforded them considerable scope for pragmatism and compromise. The bad news is that without a clear strategic vision initiatives are likely to become fragmented and uncoordinated.

The closest either state has come to devising a grand strategy for Africa lies in the articulation of shared liberal goals – in terms of economic growth, open trade, conflict resolution and democratic governance. Not surprisingly, therefore, Washington and London also generally hold similar views about the nature of the challenges facing them in Africa: warfare, underdevelopment and disease, illiberal governance and more recently, transnational terrorism. Both states have also struggled with the continent's huge diversity. Indeed, it is impossible to design a single 'Africa policy' because there are actually many different 'Africas' with which policy-makers have to engage. Nevertheless, both the US and the UK have tried to exert influence over the continent by operating through a variety of channels (e.g. multilateral and bilateral, formal and informal) and utilising a range of instruments (e.g. diplomacy, coercion, aid, and trade). In recent years these efforts have been complicated by the fact that US and UK policies towards Africa have been influenced by four interrelated crises concerning climate change, energy supplies, transnational terrorism and more recently the global recession (Williams 2010: 39).

---

1   This chapter is informed by my discussions with government representatives from both the US and UK. I am grateful for their insights and, as agreed, they will remain anonymous.

As discussed elsewhere in this book, neoclassical realism assumes that state foreign policies are primarily driven by systemic imperatives concerning their relative position within the international system but that such imperatives are mediated by the values held by political leaders, the constraints of domestic politics and bureaucracy, as well as limited resources and instruments. While Africa is not entirely devoid of strategic concerns for both the US and UK, their policies are not reducible to geostrategic calculations about the relative distribution of state power in world politics. For example, although Washington has clearly been concerned about resource extraction (especially oil), countering Chinese influence, and transnational terrorism (especially emanating from Sudan, Somalia and across the Sahel), *realpolitik* is just one of the contending currents of thought which have shaped US-Africa policies; the other two revolving around economics and humanitarianism (see Hentz 2004). Similarly, although the UK does have significant commercial links with South Africa and some of the continent's oil-producing states and retains political ties related to the legacy of colonialism, in the 21st century Britain's Africa policies have been shaped more by the twin concerns of damage limitation and promoting the UK's image as a liberal and benevolent actor (see Williams 2004; Gallagher 2009).

Within this context of relative strategic indifference commentators have identified a core set of underlying problems and challenges facing each country's attempts to devise and implement its Africa policies. Both countries want their businesses to get a slice of Africa's natural resources, to limit the negative effects of armed conflicts, and to contain Africa's health crises. But they have gone about it in different ways and thus faced different problems. Over the last decade Washington's central problems have revolved around the lack of a coherent strategic vision for the continent, the worsening institutional fragmentation within its relevant foreign policy apparatus, contradictions in the core objectives of policy, and the erosion of the State Department's institutional capacity, especially when compared to the dramatic rise in resources given to several autonomous aid initiatives and the Pentagon's Africa projects (Copson 2007; van de Walle 2010). Critics have also argued that, particularly under the George W. Bush administration, US Africa policies were increasingly influenced by the military and evangelical groups – the latter because of their interest in the 'suffering church' on the continent (Huliaras 2008). In the British case, the central challenges have also involved issues of clashing bureaucratic cultures, coordination problems and insufficient institutional capacity to generate real leverage on the ground. But in contrast to the US, Britain has faced a different set of challenges, stemming largely from the 'developmentalisation' of its Africa policies and the ways in which the Department for International Development (DfID), not the Ministry of Defence (MOD), often pushed the Foreign and Commonwealth Office (FCO) to the sidelines (Porteous 2008; Williams 2010).

This chapter examines the extent to which the special US-UK relationship has shaped their responses to these challenges in relation to contemporary African affairs. The overall argument is that the special relationship is real and forms a significant structural backdrop which affects the overall positioning and framing of Africa within both country's foreign policies but it does not generate let alone determine particular policies on specific issues. Rather the special relationship provides a congenial forum in which the formulation of policies can occur and which often enhances the prospects for them being successfully implemented. These policies often share common elements but they are usually distinct, emerging from different domestic political trajectories and bureaucratic architectures. It is also important to emphasise that this is not a relationship between equals: as the world's sole superpower the United States usually brings far more leverage and resources to the table than the UK. This situation is not about to change and the US is quite capable of being dominant when it wants to be. Yet this inequity does not prevent both states realizing that they often stand to gain from cooperation and the multiplier effect it can bring to their foreign policies – although particularly from the US side of the equation the multiplier effect is usually quite small. Of course, there have been arguments, including over the appropriate role for the International Criminal Court in Sudan or whether deploying a UN peacekeeping operation in Somalia was a wise move. But generally the relationship has been characterised by relatively healthy divisions of labour and tactical differences rather than strategic disagreements. Consequently, it would be incorrect to see the relationship in purely instrumental terms for there remains a significant convergence in the official worldview and foreign policy values of these two states. I was frequently told by officials on both sides of the Atlantic that although there were differences of emphasis and sometimes substance, with regard to African affairs US-UK relations were usually qualitatively closer than with any other state.

The rest of this chapter discusses these issues in three parts. After providing a brief summary of the central characteristics of the contemporary US-UK special relationship and how it relates to Africa, the second section maps the institutional architecture and informal mechanisms within which US-UK interaction takes place on African issues. The final section summarises the extent of, and limits to, US-UK cooperation on two important issues, three important African countries, and one important initiative, Tony Blair's Commission for Africa.

The Special Relationship

The special relationship can be understood as shorthand for the fact that official US-UK relations involve three sets of shared expectations (Hodder-Williams 2000). First, there are unique expectations – higher than for any other US ally – about policy agreement. Rooted in the experience of war (both hot and cold), these expectations reflect the idea that as advanced industrial and liberal democratic states, the US and UK share some fundamental values about the nature and purpose of foreign policy. Of course, they sometimes disagree about the best strategies and tactics for achieving particular objectives but a special relationship does not require 'unanimity of policy positions'. Instead, it is revealing that it is policy divergence, not agreement, that 'causes raised eyebrows'. Second, although secrets remain, there are expectations that considerable amounts of sensitive information will be exchanged through the unique sets of structures that have developed between the two states, perhaps most remarkably in the military and intelligence fields.

The third set of expectations involves the presumption of friendship, not solely at the highest levels of government but also at many levels of state and societal structures lower down the official hierarchy. At times, these collegial and often friendly relationships keep US-UK relations special even when the respective leaders have fallen out. The health of the relationship is thus not dependent on good personal chemistry between the top decision-makers. For one thing, it is simply good sense for the UK to develop a mutually beneficial relationship with the world's superpower. Second, it is not at all clear that there is an obvious alternative strategic anchor for British foreign policy. As Lawrence Freedman concluded, 'if only because of the lack of credible alternatives, no prospective post-Blair government will change course significantly and move away from the special relationship' (2006: 73). So far, Freedman is right. This is clearly the case in African affairs where the UK's main alternative is cooperation with France. Despite expending an unprecedented amount of effort on forging better relations since the St Malo declaration of 1998, UK-French cooperation remains distinctly limited and based on intermittent coincidences of interest rather than any genuine commitment to work together through joint structures and common procedures (see Chapters 4, 5 and 10).

Understood in this fashion, the pertinent question is not whether such a relationship exists (it does) but what form it assumes at any given moment. In the 21st century these expectations have helped produce the shared worldviews and values of many US and UK decision-makers, the extraordinary levels of trust exhibited after decades of institutionalised intelligence sharing and military collaboration, especially over nuclear issues, and the dense web of societal and cultural links between large segments of the populations and the official bureaucracies of both states. After the 9/11 terrorist attacks, US and UK grand strategies moved into closer alignment around the need to fight a 'war on terrorism' – or more accurately what should have been a war against Al-Qaeda. The two countries also continued to share unique amounts of sensitive military and intelligence information and to plough a lonely joint furrow in relation to the containment of Saddam Hussein's regime in Iraq. This long-running saga culminated in Blair's administration playing the key military and political supporting role in the US-led coalition which toppled Hussein's regime in 2003 (TSO 2004; Select Committee on Intelligence 2004). Compared to such a display of partnership in the face of substantial international criticism, the arguments between Washington and London over Kyoto, steel tariffs, the detainees at Guantanamo Bay, the 'road map' to Middle East peace and the International Criminal Court seemed rather insignificant to many commentators and UN member states.

Of course, politically, the relationship looks different depending where one sits: for Britain, it is principally about emphasising the shared values and historic trust between the two countries in order to influence US policies and thus retain its inflated status on the world stage. For the United States, its close ties to Britain offer a useful sounding board for ideas and add a politically useful tinge of multilateralism to its foreign policies.

The evident inequality in the relationship has also generated far more discussion and angst on the eastern side of the Atlantic where the phrase is more frequently used and debated. It has also endured a variety of criticisms which suggest either no such 'special relationship' exists or, even if it does, an alternative form of strategic commitment should replace its dominant position at the centre of Britain's national security strategy (see Cox 2005; Wallace and Phillips 2009; Dunn 2009; Dumbrell 2009; Porter 2010). One line of attack is that the UK should start embracing rather than denying its European destiny. A second argument is that any relationship that currently exists is heading for the rocks because of a growing 'values gap' between the US and UK evident in a wide range of issues from religion, guns and welfare, to the environment and military power. A third suggestion is that the UK needs to reorient its foreign priorities in light of the forthcoming global power shift from West to East and the inevitable downgrading that Europe will undergo in US foreign policy priorities. A fourth argument suggests that all attempts to exert a special long-term influence over US foreign policies are doomed to fail, at least while it remains the world's sole superpower. Finally, the UK's commitment to the special relationship has been criticised on the grounds that it has encouraged successive British Prime Ministers to engage in counter-productive policies. Most recently, British troops were deployed to Iraq and Afghanistan in part to bolster London's ability to influence Washington. Unfortunately, the perception within some elite US circles that the Brits failed to live up to their own hype about their counter-insurgency prowess has actually weakened Britain's ability to exert any significant influence over US foreign policies.

It is still too early to tell how the new coalition (Conservative-Liberal Democrat) government's foreign policies will develop. But noises from the Conservatives before the 2010 general election suggested that nothing fundamental was about to change in US-UK relations. The shadow foreign secretary, William Hague (2009), for instance listed one of the five big themes of a 'liberal conservative' foreign policy as retaining a 'solid but not slavish' commitment to the transatlantic alliance. The first official document of the Liberal Conservative coalition government stated it would 'maintain a strong, close and frank relationship with the United States'. Perhaps surprisingly, the document's only explicit mention of a 'special relationship' was related to the Coalition's search for 'a new special relationship with India' (The Coalition 2010: 20). But in his first keynote speech outlining the Coalition's vision for UK foreign policy, Hague made it clear that Britain's 'unbreakable alliance with the United States ... is our most important relationship and will remain so' (2010).

Where have African affairs featured in this special political landscape? In sum, they have been almost entirely absent from the general literature on the US-UK special relationship. This underlines the limited strategic importance attached to Africa in both countries and the fact that the fundamental security institution in US-UK relations, NATO, has played almost no role in African security issues, the exception being the provision of logistical and airlift support to some African peacekeeping operations. Instead, Africa issues have tended to capture the spotlight only intermittently. They have revolved around personality and summit politics such as Blair pushing Clinton to get onboard with the Jubilee 2000 debt relief campaign for developing countries and urging Bush to do more in the G8 to help Africa's predicament as part of his Commission for Africa initiative. On the US side of the equation Africa appeared primarily in relation to Bush's programme to alleviate the HIV/AIDS pandemic; as a potential source of Islamic extremism, especially in the Horn and the Sahel; and Sudan, where the Comprehensive Peace Agreement of 2005 ranks as the only major peace deal worldwide mediated by the Bush administration.

The Architecture of Cooperation

Since African affairs cover such a wide range of issues, it is not surprising that both governments have a large number of bureaucratic institutions involved in the design and implementation of various Africa policies. On the US side of the equation a larger number of official (interagency) and unofficial (advisory and analytic groups) moving bureaucratic parts are involved in African issues as is also the case for foreign and security policies more generally. As Nicolas van de Walle (2010: 14) put it, 'Virtually every federal agency is now involved in some African activities'. When the president takes a strong interest in issues related to Africa the White House can certainly play a leading role. Under Bush, this was most evident in his response to the continent's HIV/AIDS pandemic – the President's Emergency Plan for AIDS Relief (PEPFAR), the largest single-disease campaign in history with a 10-year commitment of $63 billion. However, the fragmented nature of the US decision-making system means that without the presidency exercising significant leadership institutional coordination is usually difficult to achieve. This has traditionally left the State Department assuming the lead role. In recent years, however, a lack of resources and some internal problems have dented the Africa Bureau's status and reputation.[2] In addition, since 2006 the State Department's position has come under increasing challenge from the Pentagon and the newly formed Africa Command (AFRICOM). These are not only coordinating security policies in Africa but also playing a significant role in the disbursal of the US

---

2   In August 2009 the State Department's Inspector General issued a damning verdict on the failings of the management and leadership of the Africa Bureau particularly, but not solely, during the Bush administration (Office of the Inspector General 2009).

Government's increasingly fragmented aid programmes (see Ploch 2007).[3] Other parts of the federal government have also provided significant input including the Treasury, the Departments of Justice and Agriculture, and the Department of Commerce, Health and Human Service. The National Security Council and various agencies within the intelligence community are also actively engaged.

In London, the offices of the Prime Minister and the Attorney General as well as at least nine government departments are involved in designing or implementing Britain's Africa policies (AAPPG 2005). Once again, the players are not all equals. Under Blair's leadership the Prime Minister's office often played a key role in promoting particular Africa policies. More generally, despite various attempts to create joined-up structures and mechanisms such as the Africa Conflict Prevention Pool, DfID has consistently been the lead department on Africa with the FCO and MOD playing relatively backseat roles (Porteous 2008). The general context of the increasing 'EU-isation' of UK foreign policies adds an additional layer of complexity to the formulation and implementation of some policies relevant to Africa, including those that fall within the remit of the EU's Common Foreign and Security Policy (CFSP) and Security and Defence Policy (ESDP). Although there is some variation from issue to issue, by and large the smaller UK bureaucratic system requires less clearances to get information to ministers than the larger (some say more cumbersome) US system.

As a consequence of the large number of institutional players, mapping the relationship between the US and UK governments on African affairs is difficult – suffice it to say that there is a dense, complex and periodically changing web of bureaucracies which generate many formal and informal connections. As a result, there is lots of regular contact between officials and politicians at many levels: from senior politicians to representatives in international institutions and government departments as well as among embassies on the ground in African states. This interaction assumes many forms including regular conferences and video conferences, telephone calls and e-mail traffic as well as personnel exchanges and secondments. It occurs so regularly that it can reasonably be described as deep-seated and routine. In political terms, this set up means that not only do both countries get a good sounding board for their policies the UK also gets better access to high-level US officials than other countries. The key question for the Brits, of course, is whether access regularly translates into influence?

There are numerous forums where US and UK representatives discuss African issues. Within the UN system the Security Council has played a particularly important role. Indeed in the 21st century a majority of the Council's activities have focused on African issues and the US and UK often coordinate explicitly on the passage of particular resolutions and/or presidential statements. Often this coordination is quickly extended to France through the informal P3 mechanism

---

3   In 1998, USAID managed 64.3 per cent of US overseas development aid, the State Department 12.9 per cent, and the Defense Department 3.3 per cent. In 2006 the figures were USAID 45 per cent, State 13.4 per cent, and the Pentagon 18 per cent (Oxfam 2008: 12).

where a considerable number of agenda items originate (see Chapters 4 and 5). Other less significant UN forums include the General Assembly and the Human Rights Council, especially now that the US has resumed its place in the latter. A second set of forums are the various international contact groups or 'friends' groups, for example, on piracy, Somalia and the Great Lakes. A third site of regular interaction is the longstanding military-to-military mechanisms that have developed between the US and Britain with the result that military personnel are regularly embedded in each other's key training institutions and special forces units. Fourth, special envoys have regularly interacted on specific issues, perhaps most notably in recent years on the case of Sudan.

Several points about US-UK cooperation follow from these multiple sites of interaction. First, neither government behaves as a monolithic entity with consensus as to its policies and approaches. On most issues, different views will persist across and/or within the distinct branches of government. In this sense, it is not always clear, especially to outsiders, who is the authoritative voice speaking for the government on any given topic. Second, this situation produces significant coordination challenges within governments over how to develop 'joined-up' or 'whole of government' approaches. Bureaucratic turf wars have persisted on both sides of the Atlantic particularly as the traditional understandings of defence, diplomacy and development have blurred into one another. In the US, for instance, the Pentagon has been disbursing significant amounts of development aid while in the UK the DfID has been playing more prominent roles in traditionally military issues such as security sector reform. Third, the multiplicity of institutional perspectives means that shared analysis can develop within entities across different governments. Thus it is quite common for departmental entities on different sides of the Atlantic to agree with their foreign counterparts but reject the positions held by their colleagues in other parts of their own government. Such splits have tended to be more publicly visible on the US side of the equation than the UK – whether for reasons to do with the nature of the inter-agency process or more inquisitive media. For example, differences of opinion within the US government over how to deal with Sudan – particularly between Susan Rice at the US UN mission and the Special Envoy Scott Gration – or debates about the wisdom of the Africa Bureau's push for a UN peacekeeping mission in Somalia in late 2008. In contrast, open rifts between high-profile figures within the British government have appeared less frequently.

As noted above, another factor that influences the relationship is the inequality of resources which each government brings to the table. This is clearly not a partnership between powers with equal material capabilities. In some situations the UK retains some degree of leverage (or perhaps more accurately responsibility) because of its colonial history but in general, British departments, particularly the FCO, do not have nearly as many resources to bring to bear as the US entities. This has meant that Britain has often had to conduct its foreign policies with relatively little diplomatic leverage, sometimes, as in the case of Zimbabwe, precisely because of its colonial history. This, in turn, has made it difficult to project UK power beyond a few select areas of the continent and left many gaps in its coverage. When a UK citizen was kidnapped in Mali, for example, Britain lacked diplomatic representation and expertise in the country. Similarly, when the recent constitutional crisis broke in Madagascar the UK was not helped by the fact that it had closed its embassy on the island several years earlier. This might also help explain why in some senior circles within the State Department, the UK is taken less seriously than it had been previously. But it is important to bear in mind that for all its resources, commentators still bemoan Washington's lack of leverage over the continent's conflict zones. As Nicolas van de Walle recently concluded, 'Without the attention of the White House, US diplomacy was too weak and poorly funded, its presence on the ground too thin and isolated, to make a difference' (2010: 16).

There is also a sense in which the special relationship has had to work around the unique mix of priorities that each country brings to the continent. These priorities have affected not only the amounts but also the type of resources brought to bear on African policies. On the US side, its priorities during the last decade have revolved around security (especially issues of counter-terrorism), energy supplies (notably the fact that one-quarter of US oil imports now come from Africa) and health challenges (especially HIV/AIDS) (see Morrison and Cooke 2001; Rothchild and Keller 2006; Cooke and Morrison 2009). Under successive Labour governments, the UK, on the other hand, has articulated its Africa policies around the interrelated goals of promoting peace, prosperity and democracy (Abrahamsen and Williams 2001; Williams 2004, 2010). Of course, British governments have suffered from inconsistency when it comes to democracy promotion, have often continued to sell weapons systems to African states that could ill-afford them, and turned a blind eye when its friends have used military force. But overall it remains fair to say that the UK's approach has been less militarised than the US and it is DfID which has played the leading role on the continent, not least because its budget has increased consistently since it was (re)established by Blair's government in 1997. But this developmentalisation of policy has brought its own problems. Critics have levelled various accusations including that in Whitehall DfID often lacked personnel to represent its view; its personnel sometimes displayed a poor grasp of military details (as occurred in relation to Operation Palliser in Sierra Leone); it tended to adopt a narrow development lens which underplayed the importance of politics and suggested that while development indicators were improving questions of bad governance could be sidelined; and it tended to see governance as being about creating institutions rather than as creating a particular type of political culture. In some circles, the feeling is that UK aid has gone from being overly politicised (before 1997) to not being politicised enough.

With its focus on counter-terrorism and energy security, Washington has faced a different set of criticisms. With regard to AFRICOM, this was a quite reasonable – indeed, badly needed – bureaucratic restructuring initiative but it was initially sold badly to the Africans who remained confused and suspicious about its primary mission, its role outside of traditional military-to-military issues, where its permanent headquarters would be located, and what it said about the militarisation of American engagement with the continent. It is also notable that of the two countries, only the US has kept a military base on the continent, Camp Lemonnier in Djibouti which houses the roughly 1,650-strong Combined Joint Task Force-Horn of Africa (CJTF-HOA). Interestingly, discussions are now underway as to the future sustainability of this Task Force (USGAO 2010). Even the much touted PEPFAR has come under fire on two main grounds. First, its failure to be sufficiently integrated into a broader health sector development strategy means its achievements on HIV/AIDS are in danger of being undermined if it does not leave behind effective and sustainable healthcare systems. And second, because the evangelical foundations of the initiative have disincentivised the adoption of potentially very effective initiatives such as those revolving around condom use.

In sum, while multiple forums and channels have made interaction between US and UK personnel routine, this does not necessarily ensure cooperation. As the next section discusses, there is a good deal of cooperation but the complex web of bureaucracies and informal ties relevant to African affairs have also generated significant challenges related to policy formulation and implementation as well as obstacles to coherence and coordination. This should not come as any surprise because although the foreign policies of these two states share several common elements, they also retain some different priorities and sometimes emphasise different instruments. These challenges have often been overcome in practice but not always.

Cooperation in Action

Cooperation is a nebulous concept and can come in several forms. For the purposes of this chapter, it is important to distinguish between two broad types of cooperation: implicit and explicit. Implicit cooperation occurs at a deep philosophical level, for example, when actors promote similar values and pursue similar policies because they share a similar worldview and analysis of the situation at hand. In the case of the US and UK their shared worldview revolves around liberal views of politics and economics. This means that differences between the two states' policies often tend to be of degree, timing, pace of action, and over appropriate tactics rather than fundamental objectives. At a more practical level, implicit cooperation might include situations where separate actors work to achieve shared objectives but without those actors necessarily devising specific policies in direct coordination with one another. For example, government representatives may hold similar conceptions of security, perspectives on development, and/or what good governance entails without explicitly coordinating their views. In this sense, policy convergence could give the outward appearance of cooperation when in fact there was no explicit coordination between the different actors. By explicit cooperation, I mean instances where separate actors consciously work together in multilateral forums or bilaterally to pursue similar goals and agendas. Such activity may involve agreeing upon mutually acceptable divisions of labour or developing common instruments. Representatives from both the US and UK acknowledge that unnecessary duplication should be avoided where possible and that they possess comparative (dis)advantages on certain issues, whether because of different abilities to implement policies owing to historical ties, relative influence, or the level of resources available. After both countries had been heavily involved in negotiating the Lomé Accord (1999) in Sierra Leone, for example, the UK took the military lead after the Accord collapsed. Similarly, when military forces were required to address Liberia's civil war in 2003, it was US troops that deployed. Explicit cooperation does not necessarily assume complete agreement on all strategic and tactical issues but these are likely to be discussed openly although not necessarily advertised publicly.

In order to illustrate these types of cooperation in action as well as some of their limits, this section briefly summarises US-UK cooperation in relation to two important issues, peacekeeping and budget support; three countries, Sudan, Somalia and Uganda; and one initiative, Tony Blair's Commission for Africa.

Peacekeeping: here we have seen a high level of explicit cooperation and evidence that the US government's greater resources have made it a more important actor than the UK. Since the so-called Black Hawk Down firefight in Mogadishu, Somalia in October 1993, neither Washington nor London has committed significant numbers of troops to UN peacekeeping missions on the continent. (In fact, the UK didn't provide significant numbers of troops to peacekeeping operations in Africa before this episode either.) This has not stopped each country undertaking unilateral military operations, however. For Washington, these have revolved primarily around small-scale counter-terrorism initiatives in the Horn and across the Sahel as well as the military deployment of troops to Liberia in 2003. In the British case, the major military engagement occurred in Sierra Leone in 2000 with Operation Palliser and the subsequent security sector reform missions within that country. Instead of deploying large numbers of their own troops, each state has helped to train, fund, equip and deploy peacekeepers from other (primarily African) countries to the continent's conflict zones. Most recently, this has taken place under the umbrella of the Global Peace Operations Initiative (GPOI). As of 30 September 2009, 86,969 military personnel from 78 countries had been trained through GPOI-funded activities, of which 77,406 were African troops trained through the US Government's Africa Contingency Operations Training and Assistance program (State Department 2009). There has also been a notable rise in the US government's use of private contractors such as Dyncorp, PAE, PSI and AECOM to implement government policies in Africa, particularly under the Africa Peacekeeping Program (AFRICAP).

Budget support: this has been a source of explicit disagreement between the aid agencies in London and Washington. As Britain strove to develop 'enhanced partnerships' with certain African states, DfID began dispersing a significant amount of its aid programme through 'poverty reduction budget support' i.e. direct financial support provided through the recipient state's own public finance and budgetary systems. By March 2004, Britain was providing budget support to Ethiopia, Ghana, Malawi, Mozambique, Rwanda, Sierra Leone, Tanzania and Uganda (FCO 2004). Today, budget support accounts for approximately a quarter of all British aid. The UK preferred this approach over traditional forms of aid dispensation for three main reasons: it is based on the notion of partnerships between donor and recipient rather than donor-imposed conditions; it is viewed as an efficient form of lending by reducing transactions costs; and when administered selectively it is viewed as supporting 'good' performers while denying or reducing aid to 'poor' performers (Barkan 2009: 68). This is not, however, a popular approach within the US government. The criticism is that in essentially one-party states like Ethiopia, Rwanda, and Uganda – all major recipients of British aid, including budget support – it effectively meant the British government was engaging in a direct partnership with a specific political party. By helping these parties to build their patronage system this type of aid was actually weakening the chain of accountability between the regime and its citizens because the local regime became more accountable to its donors than its citizens.

Sudan: since 2002, Washington and London have devoted more sustained political attention to managing the various armed conflicts in Sudan than tensions in any other African country. Once again, there has been far more evidence of explicit cooperation than policy divergence (see Black and Williams 2010: Chapters 7 and 9). Both countries worked hard as friends of the Inter-Governmental Authority on Development and then within the Troika (with Norway) in the negotiations which eventually produced the Comprehensive Peace Agreement signed between the National Congress Party and the rebel Sudan People's Liberation Movement/Army in 2005. When armed conflict erupted in Darfur in 2002 both countries also followed similar policies, specifically they began by supporting the African Union-led mediation and peacekeeping initiatives before switching to a more coercive strategy which involved advocating for sanctions against Khartoum and pushing for a hybrid UN-AU force to take over from the small AU mission. Although both Bush and Blair apparently took a genuine personal interest in Darfur's conflict, neither pushed strongly for military intervention. They also both appointed a series of special envoys to oversee and coordinate the implementation of their policies. And yet despite these shared strategic objectives, on Darfur at least, there were some notable differences. For one thing, the UK did not follow the Bush administration's lead when in September 2004 it described the violence taking place in Darfur as genocide. The two states also had initially different views on whether to refer the situation in Darfur to the International Criminal Court. This issue was worked through pragmatically, not least in regular telephone conversations between Condoleezza Rice and Jack Straw.

Somalia: Somalia was another case where although the US and UK shared broadly similar strategic objectives there were at times clear public differences between the methods they advocated to promote those objectives. Both states saw a significant threat of terrorism and regional destabilisation stemming from both the long-running absence of a strong central government in Somalia and the rhetoric of factions within the Islamic Courts Union (ICU) which took power in Mogadishu in mid-2006. Both states also supported the various regional mediation initiatives which took place outside Somalia to establish some sort of transitional government and charter for the country. More recently, they also both identified issues of maritime insecurity stemming from piracy as a shared threat. In January 2007, in the immediate aftermath of Ethiopia's expulsion of the ICU from Mogadishu, the AU authorised a peacekeeping force, AMISOM, to support the Transitional Federal Government (TFG) and the institutions it was supposed to create. This mission received political support within the UN Security Council from both the US and UK and both states contributed logistical and/or financial assistance to the AU peacekeepers from Uganda and Burundi. But there were also differences over the best way forward, particularly during the Bush administration's final few months in power. Specifically, the two governments differed over whether to support a UN peacekeeping operation and multinational stabilisation force taking over from AMISOM (Williams 2009: 524–5).

Uganda: this was another case where the US and UK were in broad strategic agreement about the key challenges and desirable objectives and where embassy personnel on the ground worked closely with one another but sometimes adopted different tactical approaches. In the 21st century the two big issues were how to deal with the Lord's Resistance Army (LRA) and what to do about President Museveni's manipulation of the constitution to extend his period in office. In country, it was clear that there were tactical disagreements not only across the two governments but also between different departments within the same government. It was also notable that personalities made a considerable difference to the levels of explicit US-UK cooperation. In relation to the LRA, a central issue was how much faith to place in the ability of the Ugandan People's Defence Force (UPDF) to defeat the LRA. Both Washington and London appeared comfortable with the idea that, if possible, LRA leader, Joseph Kony, should be captured or killed and that after many years of trying there was little scope for genuine negotiations with the LRA because it lacked any coherent political agenda with which to engage. To that end, although it had no illusions about the limited abilities of the UPDF, the US government saw it as the only realistic option and thus provided considerable support for its military operations. During 2006 and 2007, it even seriously debated whether to use its own military assets against Kony. While the UK government did not appear to object in principle, it adopted a more cautious position on engaging in security sector reform with the UPDF and appeared more concerned about the unprofessional manner in which the UPDF operated and the tactics it employed to go after the LRA, particularly its tendency to harm local civilians during its operations and thus make it more difficult to win local trust and support. With regard to Museveni's manipulation of the constitution to extend his presidency, both the US and UK agreed that it would be better if he did not seek a third term by running in the 2006 elections. This message was conveyed in person by the leaders of both countries. But both states faced the structural problem that Museveni's regime was one of the key recipients of their aid programmes, in the UK case his regime received direct budget support. When it became clear that Museveni was going to extend the presidential term limit both states backed away from a serious public confrontation and emphasised the fact that Museveni was making good progress on economic development and combating HIV/AIDS, the right noises about the war on terrorism, and had invited the International Criminal Court to take up the LRA issue.

The Commission for Africa: published in early 2005 – dubbed by British representatives 'the year of Africa' – the Commission's report was supposed to provide leverage for Blair's Government at a time when it occupied the chairmanship of both the G8 and the EU. In essence, the Commission called for the G8 to provide Africa with a massive increase in aid, debt relief, trade and investment – an additional $75 billion of resources by 2010 – as the primary means of stimulating economic development. In the Commission's words, what was required was 'a big push on many fronts at once' (Commission for Africa 2005: 61). In return, African governments promised to do their part in pursuing better governance. In relation to US-UK relations the Commission clearly generated some tensions but also illustrated the depth of the special relationship between Bush and Blair. On the one hand, US representatives did not warm to Blair's Commission because they felt Bush already had a good story to tell about development aid towards Africa and they didn't like being pushed into being defensive over Blair's desire to get a specific dollar commitment placed on the 'the doubling of aid' phrase. Part of the problem here was that US officials are wary of specific future targets because of the hold Congress has over the purse strings. As Permanent Under Secretary of State at the FCO, Michael Jay, recalled in the run up to the G8 summit at Gleneagles, 'Everyone was basically against us because nobody else wanted Gleneagles to be a pledging conference' (in Seldon 2008: 369). Yet despite the tensions, Bush eventually committed a dollar figure and according to the National Security Council's John Simon, it was largely down to Blair's commitment to the issue: 'It never would have happened with any other leader apart from Blair' (in Seldon 2008: 369). Indeed other US officials, including Karl Rove, said that the Bush administration owed Blair a debt of gratitude, especially over Iraq, and wanted to make sure Gleneagles was a success for him (Seldon 2008: 322). In the end, as is suggested in Chapter 2, it didn't matter all that much as several years on it is clear that the Commission has not had the impact on the other G8 states that Blair hoped.

Conclusions

In the first decade of the 21st century the special relationship has continued to influence patterns of US-UK interaction and cooperation on African affairs. Such interaction is deep-seated and routine and embedded in a complex mix of bureaucratic and informal mechanisms. While the influence of personalities should not be exaggerated they clearly have some impact as testimony from various personnel working for both states indicates. This complex mix of institutions and personalities has raised challenges for developing 'joined-up' or 'whole of government' approaches. It has also meant that neither government behaves as a monolithic entity. Rather shared perspectives, analysis and hence alliances are sometimes forged between departments within different governments. Nor does regular interaction always lead to explicit forms of cooperation. But it has done so more often than not on a wide range of African issues. In political terms, it appears that the special relationship has provided both states with a congenial environment in which to exchange views about African policies and has sometimes generated a multiplier effect which enhances the prospects of their policies being successfully implemented. There is little evidence that the UK has managed to exert much influence over the US, at least if this is defined as persuading the US government to change its publicly stated objectives on African affairs. Whether it has had a moderating effect on some US policies behind the scenes remains difficult to determine. It is also important to note that the special relationship does not erase all disagreements: Washington and London have regularly differed but their differences have tended to revolve primarily around questions of tactics, timing and instruments rather than strategic objectives. It is thus fair to say that the US and UK have developed a qualitatively closer relationship on African affairs with each other than any other state.

Chapter 8
Franco-American Ties: Old Foes, New Friends?

Niagalé Bagayoko

The starting point for understanding the relationship between France and the United States in Africa is to appreciate the very different historical significance that the continent has for the two countries. For the former, Africa was central to its entire security strategy. For the latter, most of sub-Saharan Africa has traditionally been seen as of marginal importance. This chapter will analyse the cooperation/ partnership or the lack of cooperation/partnership between France and the US from the Cold War period to the end of the Bush administration. Insights from neoclassical realism are touched upon towards the end of the chapter to shed light on the various contextual factors involved in foreign policy-making in the two countries and also to help us understand the different level of importance that they attach to Africa. As we shall see, while the US takes the view that its superpower status is unlikely to be enhanced by action in Africa, France sees a partnership with the US south of the Sahara as likely to diminish its relative power – hence its turn to the EU in Africa in an attempt to counter US influence.

Africa indeed has never been seen as a priority by American policy-makers. Frequently, the continent has been relegated to one of the lowest ranks in the hierarchy of regions where the US do identify interests. As stated by Peter Schraeder (1995, 2001), most Africanists recognise that since the foundation of the United States of America, American attitudes towards Africa have been characterised at worst by indifference, at best by 'a benign neglect'. Africa has been considered as a 'secondary zone' or region by US decision-makers. One of the most significant indications of this very limited interest in the continent is the fact that Africa has never been linked to the US by a defence agreement: African strategic matters have been dealt with by three different US Unified Commands (CINCs, Commanders in Chief), namely the US-EUCOM (European Command) in charge of West Africa, the US-Central (Central Command dedicated to Middle East Strategic Affairs) in charge of the Horn and the US-PACOM (Pacific Command), responsible for the rest of the African countries. In fact, from the 1960s to the beginning of the 1990s the European Union (EU) has largely tended to the view that the stability of the African continent was better ensured by the former colonial powers, even if such an option was at times a bit ambiguous. Indeed, the US perception of the role to be entrusted to the former colonial powers in Africa has oscillated between two paradoxical rhetorics. On the one hand,

US decision-makers have formally adhered to an idealist anti-colonial rhetoric, which aims to promote the liberal doctrine that has traditionally informed US foreign policy everywhere in the world. Since the 19th century, US anti-colonial discourse has targeted the commercial and protectionist approach which used to be associated with European colonialism and which was seen from Washington as a major obstacle both to the economic interests of people under colonial rule and to the interests of the US itself.

On the other hand, US decision-makers have developed a very pragmatic approach towards Africa which consists of relying on the operational experience of the former colonial powers: both the extension of the Soviet threat and the institutional weakness of the newly independent African states urged the US to pay attention to some African regions likely to embrace communism. From the end of the 1960s, Africa became one of the areas at stake in the bipolar Cold War. Thus, the dialectic between idealism and pragmatism was formed by the East-West confrontation. US decision-makers clearly chose pragmatism by tacitly entrusting former colonial powers with the responsibility for enforcing the 'containment policy' in sub-Saharan Africa. Such a policy was perfectly illustrated by John Satterwhaite, the first Assistant Secretary for African Affairs, who stated 'We are supporting African political aspirations when these are moderate, non-violent, constructive, and when they are taking into account their obligations towards the international community. We are also supporting the principle of continued and strong links between Africans and Western Europe' (quoted by Yekutiel Gershoni, 1992). The tactical and operational experience accumulated by European powers with the pacification of African territories during the colonial conquest, and with law enforcement campaigns just before independence, persuaded US decision-makers to consider African conflicts and crises through European lenses. US decision-makers were also planning to use the military bases which France had kept on the continent. Such an approach has been reflected at the institutional level: within the State Department, decision-making processes on African matters have to a large extent been led by the European Affairs Office, whereas the African Affairs Office was mainly seen as redundant. As a consequence, France, the UK, Portugal and Belgium have, to some extent, benefited from the necessities of the 'strategic out-sourcing' which *de facto* has facilitated the perpetuation of neo-colonial relationships. The US ambassador to the United Nations declared that 'the Cold War has urged Secretary of State Foster Dulles to subordinate the promotion of African liberties to the dire need to support our NATO allies as well as the policy they are leading on their colonies' (quoted by Michael Clough, 1992). Atlantic solidarity as well as the weak interests identified on the continent thus combined to justify the pro-European posture adopted by the US on African matters. Confronting European powers on African matters that were seen as of minor importance was not an option for US decision-makers who had already to deal with a number of disagreements on other major strategic issues, especially with France.

Among the former European colonial powers, France was undoubtedly the one which most successfully exploited the priority given by the US to Atlantic solidarity. French decision-makers have always highlighted the crucial contribution of the African continent to France's own security. Traditionally, they conceived of Francophone Africa as an area to which French forces could retreat if an invading army occupied metropolitan France, or the European mainland. Fundamental strategic plans were made in the early 1960s around this option, in case of a nuclear confrontation: some NATO plans envisioned Dakar as a possible base to welcome around 800 ships, as explained subsequently by De Gaulle himself. This was the very role for which France used the continent in the Second World War, but it was also his core defence against a possible Soviet invasion. Moreover, defence cooperation agreements allowed France to maintain a permanent French military presence in strategic locations such as Senegal, Côte d'Ivoire, Gabon and Djibouti. Thus, French supply and landing bases were retained in Africa and highly trained mobile forces (Foreign Legion and Marines) were maintained on French territory for rapid deployment to the continent when needed. From 1960 to 1990, France conducted 30 or so military operations (Rouvez 1994), intervening directly in the internal affairs of its *de facto* satellites. It is worth noting that between 1960 and 1990, Franco-US relationships in Africa were characterised by a subtle game of influence. Indeed, though French and US postures were supposedly meant to be complementary, French diplomacy has in fact always been highly suspicious towards its American ally. In reality, France was able to keep its pre-eminence in Francophone Africa thanks to a latent competition with America. Contrary to the British who have rather easily allowed the US to penetrate their former colonies, the French have been eager to prevent any significant incursion (political or economic) of the US within the so-called '*pays du champ*'. In fact, French-African policy is far from having been determined by the bipolar confrontation: as stated by Claude Wauthier (1992), the bipolar competition at the global level was only a kind of framework within which the influence struggles took place, particularly those between the Western allies. France was able to exploit the 'strategic out-sourcing' option supported by the US to fight the threat of communist expansion in Africa, without sacrificing its national interests. France has always been very careful not to allow any incursions of its Anglo-Saxon Western allies within its '*pré carré*' – which encompasses its former colonies in West and Central Africa as well as former Belgian colonies. French diplomacy's overarching objective has always been to prevent the Soviet Union and the US (as well as the other European powers, especially the UK) from stepping into the French '*domaine réservé*'. This is testified by the good relationships that France has always had with countries once considered Marxist, such as Benin, Congo, Madagascar, or socialist, such as Mali and Guinea.

Thus, throughout the Cold War period, a tacit arrangement prevailed in Africa between France and the US. The French accepted the role of gatekeeper to Western interests that the US wanted them to play in order to avoid having to involve troops directly in the management of politics on the continent. In exchange, the

US agreed not to interfere within the political order that France established and defended after the independence of its former colonies in order to perpetuate its major influence on the continent.

Franco-American Disputes During the Late 1990s

The end of the Cold War introduced a breach within this well-established order. The disappearance of the Soviet threat made the US less cautious and less prepared to humour France. Whilst Africa was still considered of minor importance for US strategic interests, the US nevertheless allowed itself to step – often on tiptoe – into African countries where economic and business opportunities were identified, including the Francophone ones: it was in the economic area that the first tensions were noted, as the two countries clashed with one another over the franc zone. French policy-makers have increasingly seen any initiatives taken by the US towards Francophone Africa as an inadmissible attempt at down-sizing its own influence within its '*pré carré*'. US support to the Anglophone leader John Fru Ndi in Cameroon during the presidential election of 1992 as well as the military assistance provided to the Rwandan Patriotic Front leader Paul Kagame in Rwanda from 1990 were seen as alarming signs of an American offensive in Francophone Africa. The common perception in French decision-making circles (both diplomatic and military) of a major American offensive against French interests in Africa can be seen as a new 'Fashoda syndrome'. French grievances against the US reached their peak when the US Secretary of State, Warren Christopher, travelled to Africa in October 1996 and officially declared: 'The time is over when Africa could be divided into spheres of influence, when external powers could consider whole parts of African countries as their reserved domains. (…) The time has come to end the exclusive domains. (…) Nowadays, Africa needs all its friends and not the exclusive patronage of some' (quoted by Nicolas Aggiouri, 1996).

　　This statement on the 'end of the reserved domains' gave rise to a serious controversy between French and US diplomatic staff. The French media followed it closely, often reporting the resurgence of French–Anglo-Saxon competition in Africa. Jacques Godfrain, the then minister for cooperation, described the US Secretary of State's statements as 'electoral remarks' and openly condemned US African policy. The French media gave prominence to this Franco-American dispute. For instance, J.-A. Fralon and J.-P. Tuquoi (1996) contended at the time: 'to Paris, the United States has taken over from Great Britain in the role of the Anglo-Saxon, a hereditary enemy, who is ready to do anything to defraud France of the political, military, and linguistic fruits of its African policy'. The controversy continued during the early years of the Great Lakes crisis. Interpreting *a posteriori* the US decision to support Eritrea's self-determination through the ballot as a will to challenge the *uti possidetis* principle of the intangibility of African borders, both the French diplomatic staff and most French media did not doubt that it was the prospect of extending its economic leadership in Africa that was behind US initiatives. Thus some saw in the US policy in the Great Lakes region, but also in the increasingly frequent choice of French-speaking countries as destinations for US officials' trips, the basis for a new 'scramble of Africa': as had happened at the 1884 Berlin Conference, the new American policy in Africa has been interpreted as an attempt 'to set the most favourable conditions for the development of American trade and civilisation in some areas of Africa'.[1] The US media were astonished by the virulence of the French reaction. Referring to the crisis in Zaire, Howard French wrote in April 1996 in the *New York Times*: 'instead of the treacherous hand of the British that France denounced in the past, many people put presently the blame for the chaos on a thoughtless push, which is steered by the United States and aimed at redrawing the political map of Africa at the expense of the traditionally strong French influence in the area (...). Each defeat of the Zaire Government against the rebels is perceived as a reverse inflicted by the Anglo-Saxons on France and the French language' (French 1997).

Such a heated exchange between the French and US diplomatic staff in fact obscured issues relating to military and security cooperation. In fact, Warren Christopher's 1996 tour was not only aimed at widening the basis of US-African relations, but also at launching the ACRF (African Crisis Response Force) programme. The ACRF was meant to develop an all-African military force which would be a rapid reaction capability to deal with hostilities and humanitarian contingencies. The US was offering to fund half of the cost of the force and hoped that the remainder of the cost would be met by EU members. However, the ACRF concept was met with wide scepticism among African partners and also with the anger of France, which was simultaneously launching its own African crisis management initiative, the so-called RECAMP concept (Renforcement des capacités africaines de maintien de la paix). In response to the French critics, relayed by African ones, the US transformed the idea of an African intervention force into a longer-term capacity-building initiative. By mid-1997, the original ACRF concept had evolved quite significantly into the ACRI (African Crisis Response Initiative), a training programme aiming to develop African peacekeeping capabilities. Nevertheless, during the next five years, the ACRI and RECAMP programmes competed with each other. The US unsuccessfully attempted to work closely with France to blend the ACRI and RECAMP into a common peacekeeping initiative that would draw upon the long history of military co-operation which France enjoys with numerous African states. In spite of alleged efforts to harmonise its programme with the American one, France has in fact been more than reluctant to cooperate with the US. On the contrary, French policy-makers have been working hard to develop alternative partnerships, broadening the RECAMP concept in order to put it at the heart of

---

1   As early as 1992, Claude Wauthier wrote: 'The competition in Africa now brings together the major powers from the Western side: [it] is first of all economic, as each of them tries to preserve or conquer new market shares, either on the whole continent or in a determined country or an area of influence inherited from colonisation'.

the multilateralisation of France's African security policy. Whilst the RECAMP programme was initially mainly seen as a means of avoiding the engagement of French armed forces on the African continent (as a result of the abstentionist posture adopted by France after the 1994 Rwandan genocide), the concept has progressively become a means of legitimising the continuing French military presence in Africa: officially, French armed forces permanently stationed on the continent have been reorganised to fit in with the African Union's African Peace and Security Architecture (APSA); in reality, the strengthening of African peacekeeping capabilities is no longer seen as a substitute for French military intervention in Africa but rather as a complement to it.

Trends in US African Policy Under the Clinton and Bush Administrations

It is possible to identify four main trends in US policy on Africa over the past 15 years, the major orientations laid down under the Clinton Administration having not been significantly changed under George W. Bush's administration. These can be summarised as follows:

- The strengthening of economic relations with the continent, symbolised by the passing of the Growth and Opportunity Act;
- The support provided to a generation of new leaders – such as Yowere Museveni in Uganda, Paul Kagame in Rwanda, Meles Zenawi in Ethiopia, Afeworki in Eritrea – who were initially expected to introduce democratic reforms in their countries but who soon adopted an authoritarian style without losing American support;
- The promotion of a so-called sub-regional approach, which has consisted of resolute support to the major regional powers on the continent: Nigeria and South Africa. The major objective of American diplomacy has been to develop relations with these two partners identified as 'key states', i.e. states presenting both a strategic interest for the United States (energy resources and/or emerging market) and a capacity to contribute to the stability of their regional environment. Bi-national Commissions, involving the US Vice-President and the Vice-Presidents of the countries concerned have been set up to manage the new partnerships at the strategic level. Besides, in a complementary way, the sub-regional approach has implied support to sub-regional organisations, such as the the Economic Community of West African States (ECOWAS) and the Southern African Development Community (SADC);
- The reinforcement of security apparatus capacities in a number of countries, through a large set of training programmes which can be mainly divided into two categories: on the one hand, the traditional military programmes, such as the IMET (International Military and Education Training) and the J-CET (Joint Combined Exchange Training), which aim to provide tactical

and operational instruction; on the other hand, programmes specifically devoted to peacekeeping training, in which significant investment has been made. Thus since 1997, a number of African countries (especially Senegal, Ghana, Kenya, Côte d'Ivoire, Ethiopia, Botswana, Mali) have benefited from peacekeeping and humanitarian assistance mission training within the framework of the ACRI. In the autumn of 2002, a new programme was launched, Africa Contingencies Operations Training Assistance (ACOTA), which combines all the existing training programmes.

Under the G.W. Bush administrations, two other important orientations were added to those aforementioned. First, the Department of Defense (DOD) and USAID have been the main beneficiaries of the 'President's Emergency Plan for AIDS Relief', created to fight against the spread of HIV/AIDS in Africa. Second, since 2001, Washington has considered Africa as one of the theatres to which it was urgent to extend the 'global war on terror'. The Bush administration considered African weak and failed states as a significant threat to US interests, as their lack of control over their own borders and territories was seen as likely to attract terrorist and criminal groups. Therefore, the missions assigned to the US commands responsible for Africa (mainly the USEUCOM and the USCENTCOM) have increasingly included the training of African armed forces in anti-terrorist missions. One of the most important programmes in this area was the Pan Sahel Initiative (PSI), which consisted of training the armed forces of Mali, Chad, Mauritania and Niger to enable these countries to better manage the surveillance of their territories. A similar initiative called Fuel Hubs Initiative (FHI) was launched in East Africa. Both the PSI and the FHI programmes have been merged into the Trans-Saharan Counter-Terrorism Partnership, whilst an important set of other anti-terrorist initiatives has been launched on the continent, such as the Terrorism Assistance Program, the Terrorist Interdiction Program, the Counterterrorism Financing Program and the Counter-terrorism Engagement Program. The counter-terrorist programmes have been complemented by initiatives aimed at providing equipment, infrastructure and training to police and other law enforcement units in Africa, for instance under the International Narcotics Control and Law Enforcement Program.

Thus security issues have been uppermost on the American agenda in Africa, which has resulted, since the mid-1990s, in the increasing prominence of the Pentagon as a key actor in US African policy. Indeed, since the early days of the Clinton administration, one of the major characteristics of US policy in Africa has been the isolation of the Department of State (DOS), whose role has been mainly reduced to the promotion, but also the financing, of security-related programmes (notably the ACRI and ACOTA programmes), without having any significant control over their implementation. Though the United States has not carried out any major military operation on the African continent since the Somali fiasco,[2] US African policy has been in practice mostly conducted by the DOD. Such a situation has to be read as the direct consequence of the orientations laid down by the successive National Security Strategies which have stressed the DOD's key role in the diplomatic and strategic offensive aimed at 'shaping the world' according to American standards. The DOD has been responsible for setting up the so-called 'peacetime engagement' by developing both military cooperation and an informal network of partnerships and alliances with civilian and military African leaders.

The DOD has developed an outsourcing strategy to implement the various programmes for which it is responsible. The role of private security companies – notably DynCorp and MPRI companies, mainly staffed by former US military officers – in a number of these programmes has proved to be extremely significant. The DOD has also supervised many 'civilian-military relations' training programmes,[3] which have been implemented in close collaboration with two types of stakeholders: on the one hand, the democratic and republican institutes, NDI (National Democratic Institute) and IRI (International Republican Institute), affiliated to the US Congress, and, on the other hand, USAID. As regards the latter, an unprecedented partnership was inaugurated in 2000: the Defense Security Co-operation Agency and USAID committed themselves through the signing of a memorandum of understanding in August 2000, 'to develop complementary and cooperative approaches in order to design, implement, and assess programs, which will build the foreign civilian governments' capacities to supervise and control the activities of their military apparatuses and the defense-related sectors'.[4]

However, it is clearly the US Commanders (CINCs, Commanders in Chief), in charge of supervising all the actions implemented in their areas of responsibility, that have played a major role in US African policy since the mid-1990s. While supervising all the 'security assistance' programmes as well as the interventions of the US armed forces (mainly the evacuations of non-combatants) in Africa, USEUCOM and USCENTCOM have also assigned their senior officers the task

---

2   The Bush Administration, however, agreed in mid-August 2003, to deploy a 150-Marine rapid action force in the country, supported by SEAL marine commandos in order to provide transitional support to the first West African peacekeeping troops until the complete deployment of the ECOMIL.

3   Such programmes consist in encouraging African states to set constitutional limits to the role of African armed forces by inviting them to respect the primacy of the civilian authorities, while inculcating a professional republican ethics in them. The principles set out in these academic training sessions are based on the model of civilian-military relations that pertains in the US.

4   Memorandum of Understanding between the Department of Defense Security Cooperation Agency and Agency for International Development Center for Democracy and Governance and Office of Transition Initiatives on the Conduct of Building Democracy Programs.

of developing close relationships with African civilian and military authorities. Particular importance has been attached in the last few years to the strengthening of the so-called 'military to military' relations through Counterparts Visits or Bilateral Staff Talks. According to official documents, 'these visits can be used as a channel to deliver diplomatic messages that the US Government sends the host nation', including the civilian authorities. The CINCs have also frequently been associated with the US 'interagency process', which results from the consultations and collaboration between the various executive bureaucracies. 'The type of US military intervention, since the end of the Cold War, has gradually increased the diplomatic responsibilities of the CINCs, who have thus become proconsuls of the new empire, (…) well financed, semi-autonomous, and not very conventional elements of the US foreign policy'(*Washington Post*, 28–9 September 2000).[5] The involvement of the Unified Commands on the African continent has proved to be more significant than those of any Washington-based agency in charge of African policy, which probably explains the increased role of the military instruments to the detriment of the diplomatic ones. The US armed forces have been assigned non-military missions, which has resulted in Africa in the increasing marginalisation of the traditional diplomatic actors.

The decision by the Bush administration to launch a single unified command for Africa, whose acronym is USAFRICOM or AFRICOM (United States Africa Command), is the latest stage of this evolution. AFRICOM will be in charge of supervising all US activities related to stability in Africa and aims to coordinate all US security activities on the continent that were previously supervised by USEUCOM, USCENTCOM and USPACOM. AFRICOM, which was announced by the Bush administration on 6 February 2007, started operating on 30 September 2008. For the time being, the future command's transitional team is based in Stuttgart, Germany, headquarters of USEUCOM. However, the DOD would like it to be transferred later to an African country, with Liberia and Djibouti being the most serious candidates. AFRICOM will be responsible for the whole African continent, except for Egypt, which remains under the Central Command. No new base will be established on the African continent and no new contingent of US troops will be sent to Africa.

The US administration has described AFRICOM as a new type of command, as both its command and the activities that it will supervise will be both civilian and military in nature. The deputy commander of AFRICOM is a diplomat from the US Department of State. Thus, contrary to the unified command centres, AFRICOM is allegedly not designed to wage war. The US administration and, particularly, the Pentagon insist on the mixed, military and civilian, nature of this new command centre, which is presented as a system that could become a model for all US security bodies. While the difficulties encountered in stabilising Afghanistan

---

5   See also W. Arkin, 'Secrets that Make Foreign Policy', *The Washington Post*, 31 January 2000; E.A. Cohen, 'Why the Gap Matters', *The National Interest*, vol. 61, Autumn 2000.

and Iraq have shown the urgent need to consider the interagency coordination issue, thus contributing to giving it renewed visibility, the Clinton Administration had started considering it within the framework of the doctrine called 'Military Operations Other than War' (MOOTW), which structured US security policy in the so-called 'low intensity' areas in the 1990s. Indeed, US interventions in those crises (Somalia, Haiti, Bosnia) have required, in addition to the military component, a significant civilian contribution from the US Government. The interagency coordination problems encountered in those missions were quickly identified and *ad hoc* solutions were adopted to solve them. Reflections on more codified solutions also started emerging at that time, the most well-known of which remains the Presidential Decision Directive 56 (PDD-56) developed by the National Security Council,[6] which, as early as 1996, recommended the development of an interagency process to support the coordination of the civilian and military bodies' actions, particularly between the Department of State, the Pentagon, and USAID.

Under successive G.W. Bush administrations, the diplomatic and military disagreements between France and the United States ironed themselves out, as the United States did not plan to get too involved in African issues. In this regard, the US position on the crisis in Côte d'Ivoire is a perfect example. Thus, despite Franco-US diplomatic confrontations over Iraq, the US administration supported both the French diplomatic effort and the Licorne Operation in Côte d'Ivoire at the UN level. Besides, the strengthening of relations with the Europeans in Africa was one of the strategic objectives identified by the DOD between 2000 and 2008. After 2007, the Bush and Sarkozy administrations also appear to have been quite keen, at least initially, to work together more closely on Africa: for instance, the 2008 military coup in Mauritania was vigorously denounced by French and American officials. Behind such a US policy of rapprochement, it is possible to detect a willingness to return to the approach adopted during the Cold War, which consisted of letting the former colonial powers deal with a continent which, despite an outward show of renewed interest symbolised by the visits of Presidents Clinton (in 1998 and 2000) and Bush (in 2003), remained the lowest priority of US security and foreign policy.

French Reactions to US Policy on the African Continent

French and US policies in Africa have not been set up on a cooperative model: in fact, France has mainly continued in this most recent period to view cooperation with the US on Africa as a low priority. Since Operation Artemis in the DRC in 2003, France has sought to put its interventions on the African continent under the aegis of the EU. The integration of French interventions within the European

---

6   Presidential Decision Directive 56, 'The Clinton Administration's Policy on Managing Complex Contingencies Operations', 20 May 1997.

Security and Defence Policy (ESDP) framework has allowed France to remain involved in African affairs – Africa still being considered a central asset for France's position on the international scene – whilst weakening the accusations of paternalism and neo-colonialism. It has also enabled France to re-engage in the Great Lakes region and beyond in Central Africa, from which it had progressively withdrawn since the much criticised Operation Turquoise in Rwanda in 1994. In addition, the Europeanisation of its Africa policy has enabled France to share the costs of military and defence cooperation. Finally, beyond these central issues, developing military interventions within the framework of ESDP has also been a way to counter-balance the growing influence of the US on the continent. From the French perspective, involving the EU has been seen as a way to prevent NATO – traditionally seen as an exclusively US-driven organisation – from committing itself in Africa. The Artemis operation proved that the EU was able to plan military operations autonomously, without resorting to NATO means and instruments. The operation was, indeed, entirely and exclusively planned within the EU's military structures – the EU Military Committee (EUMC) and Military Staff (EUMS) – which worked in close coordination with France, then qualified as the 'framework nation' in charge of operational planning (see Chapter 5). An alternative to resorting to NATO's Supreme Headquarters of Allied Powers in Europe (SHAPE) was thus tested successfully. Since then, Africa has been seen by France as a field of European influence that could escape the strict implementation of the 'Berlin Plus' option and consequently would escape US worldwide hegemony. As shown by its ongoing support to the AU mission in Darfur (AMIS), NATO has since, however, stepped up its interests and expertise in Africa. Strong French commitments to the EUFOR DRC Operation and the EUFOR Chad Operation have constituted attempts at mitigating NATO's influence. Another important trend of this Europeanisation of French security policy in Africa has been the integration of the RECAMP programme into a European framework, now known as EURORECAMP.

In this context, the launching of AFRICOM by the Bush administration has been more than badly received by French officials. Initially, when they heard about the AFRICOM project, the French were very active in deterring their Francophone African partners from hosting AFRICOM headquarters. They had already felt betrayed when Djibouti – their traditional ally and the cornerstone of French military forces permanently stationed in Africa – had allowed the US to establish an American base at Camp Lemonnier. Today, a number of French officials still tend to present AFRICOM as a purely instrumental initiative, whose main purposes are twofold. First, it is seen as part of an effort to export the 'war against terror' to the African continent. AFRICOM is mostly presented and perceived as an institutionalisation of the set of US security programmes, whose purpose is to fight terrorist movements in African countries that border the Sahara, as mentioned above.[7] Second, it is presented as an instrument for exploiting African resources, especially oil. One of the major preoccupations of French security policy (particularly under the maritime section of the EURORECAMP concept) has been to strengthen the sovereignty of African states over their coasts and in fact French policy has been implicitly designed to counter-balance American influence over offshore oil production in the Gulf of Guinea.[8]

From a French perspective, it appears that any alliance with the US (sometimes referred to in neoclassical realist theory as 'bandwagoning' with a more powerful state) is not regarded by most decision-makers involved in African affairs as likely to enhance France's relative power in the international system. On the contrary, such an alliance is often seen as likely to diminish French relative power: this can explain the French turn to the EU in Africa, in an attempt to bolster its position there against growing US influence. Presumably for France, a junior partner role vis-à-vis the US is perceived as less attractive than leadership within the EU in a multipolar world. French positions vis-à-vis the US in Africa also confirm another assumption of neoclassical realism according to which the perceptions of government officials do matter in the way in which states position themselves in relation to each other. Indeed, suspicion of the US is widespread not only among French decision-makers – particularly the very powerful network of the Marine Troops (*Troupes de la marine*), most of whose members have been dealing with African security matters since African independence – but also more generally among the French media, which have tended to popularise analyses focused on the new American 'scramble of Africa'. This rhetoric has clearly been a major obstacle to the attempts at fostering cooperation made by some French decision-makers – particularly, in diplomatic circles, those called '*les modernes*' by Daniel Bourmaud (see Chapter 3) – but also by US decision-makers (belonging both to the military and diplomatic circles), who see links with France in Africa as shoring up vital security interests. Thus, despite the overall low level of priority attached to Africa by US foreign policy-making elites, it is nonetheless clear that the US does

---

7   US Africa Command (AFRICOM) Operation Enduring Freedom Trans Sahara (OEF-TS) is the US military component that provides support to the Department of State-led Trans-Sahara Counter Terrorism Partnership (TSCTP) programme. Retrieved 23 November 2008 from www.africom.mil/oef-ts.asp.

8   It is however important to note that French policy-makers have been far from the only ones to greet AFRICOM with suspicion. As stated by Forest and Crispin (2009), 'Conceived largely through the efforts of Donald Rumsfeld and his Department of Defense advisors, and launched with high hopes by American policymakers, AFRICOM quickly lost its momentum and became entangled in accusations that African leaders had not been adequately consulted during the initial decision-making processes; that this was a covert attempt to militarize American aid and development assistance in Africa; and that AFRICOM was created to chase terrorists. Soon after President Bush announced the creation of AFRICOM, it was publicly spurned by much of the African community and met with a fusillade of resistance from the NGO community with whom it had originally intended to partner'.

have some strategic interests there, relating notably to the threat of terrorism and the securitisation of its access to oil.

Conclusion

When Barack Obama was elected President of the United States in November 2008, most Africanists expected that he would show a particular interest in African affairs and reverse the tendencies toward a highly securitised African foreign policy. Yet, the speech delivered by Barack Obama in Accra in July 2009 – mainly devoted to urging Africans to assume their responsibilities and take their share of the burden – has defied such expectations. In fact, the Obama administration has been mostly following the same policy that has characterised US strategy for more than a decade. Support to anti-terrorist programmes has been confirmed and in some cases enhanced: this has been particularly the case in Somalia, where in August 2009 the Transitional Federal Government (TFG) was provided with further support to fight Al-Shahab, the Islamic group fighting to overthrow the TFG and presented by US officials, including Secretary of State Hilary Clinton, as a terrorist group with links to Al-Qaeda. The US administration also decided to provide a major new security assistance package to Mali – known as Counter Terrorism Train and Equip (CTTE), in order to assist the authorities in dealing with potential threats from AQIM (Al-Qaeda in the Islamic Maghreb) (Volman 2010).

Franco-US relations have moved from mutual understanding during the Cold War, to limited soft power competition, through to hard and soft power competition in the most recent period. During the time when the US had erected military non-interventionism as a pillar of its African policy, France only had to thwart American soft power in Africa. With the launching of AFRICOM, French officials are faced with a new challenge: keeping American hard power as far as possible from what is still considered as France's exclusive sphere of influence. For this reason, the US may experience some difficulties in developing strong, constructive and above all long-lasting relationships with Francophone African countries, still closely tied to France by a system of economic, diplomatic and cultural agreements which extend beyond military-strategic relationships. It is possible that the common interest in tackling terrorism, especially in the Sahel region, will become the basis for a strategy that paves the way for a closer Franco-US partnership, but this would have to accommodate the 'special relationships' that France maintains with many of its former colonies.

PART IV
Working Together on the Ground

Chapter 9

The UK and France in the DRC: Making Their Own Peace

Gordon Cumming

The Congo was the disputed territory that sparked the scramble for Africa in the late 19th century. By the turn of the 20th century, the Democratic Republic of the Congo (DRC), as it is now known, had become the battleground for a major regional conflict and the focus of a renewed struggle for its enormous mineral wealth. It was against this backdrop that Britain and France pledged to, at their December 1998 summit in Saint-Malo, to set aside past rivalries and 'harmonise their policies' towards Africa. At their Cahors summit in February 2001, the UK and France promised to 'intensify their joint efforts to promote lasting peace' in the DRC (French Embassy, UK 2001b). Then, in November 2004, at their Lancaster House summit, they singled out the DRC as one of only two African states included in their 'Action Plan on Franco-British Development Cooperation' and committed themselves to 'work together in support of country-owned poverty reduction strategies' (French Embassy, UK 2004).

At no time, however, did the UK or France thrash out the details of this much-needed cooperation. Was it merely to involve a process of 'deconflictualisation', where the UK and France avoid public quarrels and play down divergences in their respective agendas? Or was the idea to engage in 'coincidental' cooperation, where London and Paris collaborate actively but do so only at times of crisis or when their agendas 'naturally' converge? Or was the intention to go further and engage in 'sustained and reciprocal cooperation', where Britain and France work in partnership over a prolonged period, while also seeking to align their goals?

Despite the significance of this initiative for the Great Lakes and for Europe's Common Foreign and Security policy (CFSP), there has been no attempt to study recent UK-French relations in the DRC.[1] This chapter fills this gap. It begins by setting out the history of Anglo-French rivalry in the Congo. Drawing upon extensive off-the-record interviews in Kinshasa and with the British and French Foreign Ministries, European Commission and United Nations, it then looks for evidence over the last decade of any enhanced Anglo-French policy dialogue

---

1   The literature on the DRC focuses largely on EU military cooperation (Gegout 2005), and competition between France and 'Anglo-Saxon' donors, notably the United States (Agir Ici-Survie 1997).

and cooperation in the fields of peace-building and poverty reduction. Finally, it explains the evolution of UK-French relations using a theoretical framework, neoclassical realism, that appears – thanks to its inclusion of domestic political variables – particularly well suited to this kind of foreign policy case study.

There is no need to repeat here all the caveats set out in Chapters 4 and 5. It is nonetheless worth stressing that this study will not assess the impact of Anglo-French cooperation in terms of policy outcomes. This would be difficult to demonstrate, given how influential other external actors are in the DRC, not least China (the largest investor), Belgium (the former colonial power and main trading partner), the United States (the key regional peace broker), South Africa and Angola (regional actors with a central role in SSR), the EU (the largest source of aid) and MONUC (the UN's most expensive mission).[2]

Rivalry in the Midst of Turmoil

From the colonial through to the early post-Cold War era, UK and French policies towards the Congo were underpinned by divergent interests that precluded meaningful cooperation. The nature of, and drivers behind, Anglo-French rivalry can best be understood by examining three flashpoints. The first came at the time of colonisation. Having failed to secure an informal paramountcy over the mouth of the river Congo, the UK signed a treaty with Portugal in 1884, backing the latter's claims in the region in exchange for exclusive navigation rights on the river Congo (Anstey 1962: 10–56). France was alarmed by this treaty which, had it not been quickly rescinded, would have hampered its prospects of developing its recently acquired colony, present-day Congo-Brazzaville. The French were even more dismayed at having to recognise claims at the 1884–5 Berlin Congress by Belgian King Leopold II to the vast territory known as the Congo Free State. They managed, with the support of the UK, whose public was outraged by abuses in the Congo, to compel Leopold to hand over his 'fiefdom' to the Belgian state in 1908. They failed, however, to force their smaller neighbour to accept France's *droit de pré-emption* – its right to take over if Belgium proved unable to manage this territory.

A further bout of Anglo-French rivalry occurred in 1960 at the time of Belgium's ill-prepared decolonisation of the Belgian Congo. This second pivotal moment triggered an army mutiny, the secession of the mineral-rich Katanga province, the mounting of a UN operation, the assassination of the Congo's Marxist-leaning Prime Minister, Patrice Lumumba, and, in 1965, a coup by the Western-backed General Joseph-Désiré Mobutu. Amidst the chaos, the UK and France officially supported the UN aim of preserving Congolese territorial integrity. Yet behind the scenes they were helping Katangese secessionists, albeit towards different ends. The British Foreign Minister, Lord Home, and

---

2   In May 2010, MONUC was renamed MONUSCO, the United Nations Organisation Stabilisation Mission in the DRC.

backbenchers in the ruling Conservative government were sympathetic to the demands of UK-owned companies, such as Tanganyika Concessions, which were calling for Katanga's independence or its integration into the Central African Federation (a semi-independent entity grouping three former UK dependencies: present-day Zimbabwe, Zambia and Malawi) (Janes 2000: 162–3). The French government went further and supplied weapons and mercenaries to the rebels. Its aim was to block the integration of Katanga into the CAF, break up the Belgian Congo and facilitate acquisition of Congolese territory by neighbouring Congo-Brazzaville under its pro-French leader, Abbé Youlou (Trefon 1989: 13–14).

The third key moment came in the mid-1990s by which time Britain had become an insignificant player in Zaire (as the Congo was known from 1971–97), whilst France had become the leading donor and military backer (Economist Intelligence Unit 1993: 37). After suspending development assistance in 1991, the French reverted three years later to a policy of unconditional support to Zaire's President Mobutu, largely in recognition of his backing for France's 1990–93 military intervention in Rwanda (Operation Noroît) and his acceptance, in 1994, of over a million Rwandan refugees on to Zairean soil. In effecting this policy reversal, the French set themselves on a collision course with the UK and US who wanted Mobutu removed and who supported, directly or indirectly, the 1996 military campaign by the Alliance des Forces Démocratiques pour la Libération du Congo-Zaire (AFDL: an alliance of Congolese Tutsis, Rwandans, Ugandans and Angolans, led by Laurent Kabila). On 15 November 1996, the French backed, within the UN Security Council (UNSC), a proposed Canadian-led mission to ensure the repatriation of Rwandan refugees based in Zairean camps. The intervention won cautious backing from the US and the UK, which agreed to provide one battalion (IRIN, *Emergency Update 23 on Eastern Zaire*, 14 November 1996). Yet this support was withdrawn when, following an AFDL attack, 600,000 Rwandan refugees suddenly began returning home. The French government responded in January 1997 by covertly levying 300 mercenaries in a failed attempt to save Mobutu (Agir Ici-Survie 1997: 138). Then, on 13 March, France called for an EU militaro-humanitarian operation. However, this was blocked, apparently by the UK (*The Guardian*, 20 March 1997), prompting French officials to grumble privately that Mobutu's downfall was 'all the work of the Defence Intelligence Agency ... and MI6' (*The Independent*, 11 March 1999).

To sum up, UK-French relations in the DRC and wider region were marred by 'competitive clientelism' (Youngs 2004: 306), the pursuit of hard-nosed realist interests and an absence of forums for constructive dialogue. The UNSC and European Community allowed for discussions but were used by the UK in 1996–7 to slow down or block French-inspired proposals. The Anglo-French summit was another potentially useful forum but, although it focused on the Great Lakes in November 1996, it failed to secure any Anglo-French consensus (*Press Association*, 8 November 1996).

Saint-Malo and After: Towards a Multilateral Framework for Partnership?

At the Saint-Malo summit in 1998, the UK and France promised to 'pursue close cooperation on the ground in Africa' (French Embassy, UK n.d.). At subsequent gatherings, they pledged to work together in the DRC to promote peace and reduce poverty. Despite these promises, Britain and France made only perfunctory efforts to deconflictualise their approaches in the early years following Saint-Malo. Thus, while the UK and French Foreign Ministers, Jack Straw and Hubert Védrine, undertook a joint visit to the Great Lakes in January 2001, the two men proved unable to paper over their differences, with Straw focusing solely on the need for the DRC to disarm Rwandan Hutu militias while Védrine called on Rwanda and Uganda to withdraw their troops in tandem with the disarmament of Hutus (*Financial Times*, 22 January 2002). Similarly, while London and Paris both adopted, in December 2001, a common European line on the restoration of aid to the DRC, they did so only after a bitter dispute in which France, together with Belgium, pushed for development assistance to be resumed immediately, while Britain, with support from Holland, Ireland and the European Commission, sought to delay this decision until the Congolese had shown greater commitment to the peace negotiations. Within the UNSC too, there were disagreements. Thus, while the British and French Permanent Representatives were seeking to elide their instructions 'so that it didn't sound as if the UK was harder on Kinshasa and France harder on Kigali' (personal communication, ex-FCO official, 2009), they were unable to conceal a row in November 1999 over the composition of MONUC, which included, in France's view, too prominent a role for British personnel for a mission in a French-speaking state (Gegout 2009: 234). Nor could they disguise divergences over the April 2001 and October 2002 reports by the UN Panel of Experts. The UK rejected the Panel's early findings which exposed illegal practices by UK mining companies and revealed the extent to which the Ugandan and Rwandan regimes, both close to the British government, were plundering Congolese mineral resources. The French by contrast had been the main driving force behind the Panel, providing it with intelligence and 'an unofficial mandate' to criticise Rwanda and Uganda for 'occupying the DRC not so much for security reasons as for economic reasons' (Nest 2006: 86).

This absence of Anglo-French collaboration has to be seen in context. Thus, the Rwandan genocide had created a faultline between the UK, which saw the Tutsi-led Rwandan Patriotic Front (RPF) as a force for good and the Hutu-based Forces Démocratiques de Libération du Rwanda (FDLR) as unambiguous *génocidiaires*, and the French – or rather elements within the French system – who considered the RPF as illegitimate rebels and the FDLR as legitimate political actors.[3] Subsequently, the outbreak of the Second Congolese War in August 1998 widened the rift between Britain, which became a leading backer of the Rwandan

---

3   This helps explain alleged French intelligence support to the FDLR (personal communication, Whitehall insider, 2010).

government, both bilaterally and in Brussels, and France which, after winning over Laurent Kabila in 1999, became the DRC's key Western supporter.[4] This situation was exacerbated by Britain's Secretary of State for International Development, Clare Short, who blindly provided budgetary assistance that was subsequently used, directly or indirectly, to fund Rwandan and Ugandan war efforts in the Congo (Porteous 2008: 22–3). Finally, the prospects for cooperation were further weakened by the unpredictability of President Laurent Kabila, who expelled the number two in the French embassy in December 1997 before throwing out six British diplomats on allegations of spying in March 1999 (*Figaro*, 5 December 1997; *The Guardian*, 13 March 1999).

It was not until the end of the 'official' conflict and the creation, in June 2003 of a Congolese Government of National Unity and Transition (henceforth the 'transitional government') that Britain and France opened meaningful channels for dialogue. Crucially, the UK, which had only three staff in its mission in 2003 (Hilary Benn, *Hansard*, 7 March 2007, column 465WH), began building up a large permanent Department for International Development (DfID) office, while France reopened the Agence Française de Développement (AFD) in 2003 after a closure lasting 11 years (FCO 2009). Closer Anglo-French cooperation was also facilitated by the creation in 2004 of the International Committee for the Accompaniment of the Transition (henceforth the CIAT), a donor steering committee established to oversee the transition. Chaired by the UN, the CIAT included ambassadors from the UK, France, America, China, Russia, Belgium, Canada, South Africa, plus high-level representatives of the African Union (AU), European Commission and European Union (EU). Within the CIAT, the UK 'worked together with the French in practice and in a close way', and 'dissent was never shown in public' (personal communications, Kinshasa, 2009). This closeness was facilitated by a rapport between UK and French Ambassadors, Andy Sparkes and Georges Serre, and by the diversity of views within the CIAT, which made the British and French appear like-minded.

Following the 2006 elections and the disbandment of the CIAT, Britain and France helped create new donor forums, such as the 'Security Council Plus' and the 'P3 plus 2'. The former is an information-sharing session chaired by MONUC and involving the Ambassadors of Security Council member states with a mission in Kinshasa, key African countries and representatives of the AU, EU and European Commission. The latter is more influential, comprising the UK, France and the US ('the P3'), together with Belgium and South Africa, and meeting fortnightly at ambassadorial level. There are, in addition, P3 plus 2 meetings involving heads of development cooperation and political counsellors. Equally, there are regular talks between European Heads of Mission and Heads of Development Cooperation, as well gatherings of the Great Lakes Contact Group and of the 'International

---

4   This war pitted Congolese rebels, Rwanda, Uganda, Burundi and UNITA, against the governments of the DRC, Angola, Chad, Namibia, Sudan, Zimbabwe.

Facilitation', each of which includes UK and French representatives.[5] In New York too, there have been shadow meetings of the P3 plus 2 as well as close consultations on the UNSC between the UK and France, particularly over recent revisions to MONUC's mandate (personal communication, French Foreign Ministry, 2009).

Alongside these gatherings, the UK and France have established informal bilateral ties. By early 2008, the British and French defence attachés had forged good relations and were collaborating on the renovation of a junior staff college in Kinshasa, the reopening of an initial officer training school in Kitona and the training of the Congolese infantry battalion for the African stand-by force.[6] By November 2008, the UK and French Foreign Ministers, David Miliband and Bernard Kouchner, had undertaken a joint visit to the Great Lakes. This was followed up in the spring when the French Foreign Ministry sent a delegation to London to discuss a paper on the DRC prepared by the Foreign and Commonwealth Office (FCO) Strategy Unit. Then, in September 2009, the French President, Nicolas Sarkozy, appointed Christian Conan as his Great Lakes special representative, and one of Conan's first trips was to London, followed by another to Washington where he met UK and US officials (personal communication, French Foreign Ministry, 2009).

It would, nonetheless, be wrong to overstate the significance of these linkages. The UK and France are certainly involved in a plethora of multilateral forums. Yet this alone need not imply a closer relationship since, if the British and French were engaged in 'sustained and reciprocal cooperation', they might be expected to share out the burden of attending these meetings. It is worth adding that some 'bilateral' Anglo-French exchanges that take place within multilateral groupings are not harmonious (e.g. over the UN Panel reports) or come about primarily because the UK (as in the EU Working Group on Human Rights) or France (as in EUSEC: discussed later) happens to head up a particular body. Significantly too, there has been little attempt to prioritise a particular multilateral forum for closer cooperation. As a rule, the UK has preferred to work through the UN, where it has real clout as a permanent Security Council member, while the French have, except on issues specific to the UN (e.g. MONUC's mandate), often been more inclined to work through the EU and to use their influence there to back European civilian and military missions.

At the same time, there has been no concerted effort to formalise bilateral exchanges. Indeed, tentative plans in 2009 to establish a joint UK-French office

---

5   The Contact Group's other founders were Belgium, Holland, the EU and US. The International Facilitation also includes the EU and US, as donors represented in eastern DRC.

6   The UK has provided English language training and French military training (personal communication, French Defence Ministry, 2009).

in Goma seem to have been put on hold.[7] The emphasis has remained upon informal, even personal ties between officials and politicians who happen to 'get on'. In practice this has led to two planned joint Foreign Ministerial visits to the DRC being cancelled in recent years and the 2008 trip coming about almost coincidentally when Bernard Kouchner extended a last-minute invitation to his British counterpart (French Embassy, UK, 2003, personal communication, former UK Minister, 2009).

Towards Meaningful Cooperation on the Ground?

Having shown that the UK and France have opened channels for communication, we must now ask whether they have, particularly since the creation of the transitional government in 2003, followed through on their commitments and intensified 'joint efforts to promote peace' and 'in support of country-owned poverty strategies'. To answer this question, we must return to the three levels of cooperation highlighted in our introduction. The first is 'deconflictualisation', where the UK and France avoid duplication and contradictory policies, while continuing with their own agendas. The second is 'coincidental cooperation', where Britain and France collaborate actively but do so only sporadically or where their agendas converge. The third is 'sustained and reciprocal' cooperation, where the two countries work in partnership over a prolonged period while also seeking to harmonise their goals. Needless to say, these categories cannot be entirely separated out. It is nonetheless useful to draw these distinctions, while noting that there are also areas where the UK and France have failed to collaborate or have worked towards opposing ends.

Working Together for a Lasting Peace

To begin with British and French efforts to promote peace, here the focus will be on securing the democratic transition, peace-keeping missions, and reforms to the police and army.

Shoring Up the Electoral Process

The UK and France have engaged in active, if 'coincidental', cooperation to secure the democratic process in the DRC. They worked together closely over the transition period (2003–6) when they emerged as leading contributors to the elections, with the UK providing over 50 million euros (M€) and France supplying a further 10 M€, together with police officers and troops (French Embassy, DRC, n.d. [a]). In

---

7   The British and French Foreign Ministries both have an official in Goma, but cooperation between the two is not automatic (personal communications, Kinshasa, 2009).

2004, the UK, through its DfID conflict adviser, and France, through its defence attaché, pushed jointly for an election security strategy. Britain and France took the lead, alongside the Congo's Interior Minister, in bringing in other partners and ensuring the establishment of a steering committee for election security (personal communication, DfID, 2009). Subsequently, London and Paris worked together to approve missions aimed at securing the electoral process: EUPOL-Kinshasa in 2005 and EUFOR-DRC mission in 2006 (discussed later and in Chapter 5). Also in 2006, the UK funded a project aimed at training judges to handle electoral disputes and contracted out much of this activity to the Organisation Internationale de la Francophonie (personal communication, DfID, 2009). British efforts to find a project partner were facilitated by the French aid mission, the Service de Coopération et d'Action Culturelle (SCAC).

After the elections, the UK and France were among the donors pushing for a 'governance compact' designed to increase DRC government accountability (Hoebeke *et al.* 2007: 6). They also established a media donors' group with France as co-chair and with Britain's 'views being represented by France' (personal communication, DfID, 2009). Subsequently, in 2007, they created a civil society group, which is headed up by the UK, France and the UN Development Programme (UNDP). At the same time, they set up a four-year 'silent partnership' (an innovative arrangement in which one donor partner provides the funding and the other executes the project) aimed at promoting democratic governance and an independent media. The DfID provided £10 million to this joint media project, Britain's largest in Africa, while the SCAC offered the office space and France Coopération Internationale (FCI), the French state-funded media body, supplied the expertise.

There have, however, also been instances where the UK and France have failed to cooperate. This was the case towards the end of the transitional period when the British were pushing for political space to be created for an effective opposition, whereas the French were advocating unconditional support for Joseph Kabila as head of the transitional government and DRC president since his father's assassination in January 2001 (*Agence France Presse*, 7 March 2006). In other instances, cooperation has been purely coincidental. To illustrate, Britain and France have, in line with their commitments as members of the EU Working Group on Human Rights, signed up to a robust European policy on human rights and local democracy. Yet they have not done so out of any shared conviction. Indeed, the UK has generally been – in the DRC if not in Rwanda – a stout defender of human rights and, with a contribution of £30 million, a stalwart supporter of the local elections.[8] By contrast, France has, in practice, adopted a more politically expedient and uncritical approach towards the Congolese government and its leaders.

---

8   The UK's image has nonetheless been tarnished by its failure to pursue British companies implicated in UN Panel reports.

The 'silent partnership' represents another example of coincidental cooperation. This project came about 'by accident' and as a result of a momentary coincidence of agendas (personal communication, DfID, 2010). Thus, the UK was aiming to rationalise its staffing and seeking a donor (not necessarily the French) with the expertise to deliver its media programme, while the French coincidentally had the capacity (a permanent media attaché in its mission) but lacked the funding to mount a large-scale project. While this convergence of goals was enough to seal the deal, cooperation was initially stilted as the DfID sought reassurances that the FCI could deliver the project effectively. There has, moreover, been no attempt to replicate this partnership in other sectors, despite the fact that the DfID has a need for operators to implement its programmes, while cash-strapped French agencies are keen to offer their services.

ESDP

Turning to peacekeeping missions, here too there has been, since 2003, active though 'coincidental cooperation'. From June to September 2003, Britain and France participated in Operation Artemis, a European Security and Defence Policy (ESDP) military mission designed to stabilise the situation in eastern DRC. The details of this operation, of the active Anglo-French cooperation that it involved and of UK and French motives have been set out in Chapter 5 and need not be repeated here. It is, however, worth adding that the UK's decision to offer diplomatic support plus 100 engineers and France's readiness to provide the headquarters, the intelligence and the majority of the 1,400 troops for this mission (Gegout 2005: 438) were both the result of a timely convergence of British and French agendas around a shared desire to patch up differences over Iraq as well as common security concerns in the Great Lakes. The UK in particular was alarmed at the possibility of genocide in the DRC, while the French were desperate to ensure British participation, as the operation was in an inaccessible area close to the Rwandan border and could bring French troops into contact with Congolese militias close to the Rwandan regime (Gegout 2009: 240).

The second mission, EUFOR DRC (July–November 2006), which aimed to support the UN in supervising the 2006 elections, is also discussed in some detail in Chapter 5. Here, it should suffice to note that while the British did not send troops, partly due to concerns about military overstretch, they did approve EUFOR within the European Political and Security Committee (PSC), as well as supporting it politically in a joint statement by the UK and French Defence Ministers, John Reid and Michèle Alliot-Marie (*Figaro*, 6 March 2006). The French deployed, together with Germany, the largest number of troops for this mission, which involved 1,200 soldiers in and around Kinshasa as well as almost 1,200 troops on-call in neighbouring Gabon. France also provided the force commander and press-ganged Germany into providing the operational headquarters.

As with Artemis, Anglo-French cooperation in the case of EUFOR DRC was coincidental, reflecting a convergence of agendas at the time. As a major contributor to SSR and the largest bilateral funder of the elections, London considered the stability of the DRC to be imperative. For Paris, EUFOR was also about security. But it was even more importantly a means of building EU military capacity, particularly in the context of the 2005 EU Strategy for Africa. Equally, it had 'to do with French–German cohesion' and with bolstering the ESDP's credibility after the rejection of the European Constitutional Treaty (*International Herald Tribune*, 12 June 2006).

Anglo-French collaboration in peacekeeping has therefore been more about convergent agendas than any overriding desire to work together for Africa or on African crises. The patchy nature of collaboration was exposed in Bukavu (2004), Rutshuru (2005) and Sake (2006) when humanitarian missions could have been but were not mounted, ostensibly to avoid undermining MONUC. It was subsequently revealed in late 2008, when the dissident Tutsi general, Laurent Nkunda, looked like taking Goma. In response, Bernard Kouchner mooted the possibility of an intervention, while the UK Foreign Secretary refused to rule this out (*Agence France Presse*, 31 October 2008). Within days, however, Kouchner's enthusiasm had been curbed by President Sarkozy, and the UK, as one of two countries heading up European battle groups, had ruled out military involvement, citing commitments in Iraq and Afghanistan.[9] In the end, the French, who held the EU Presidency, abandoned the idea and lobbied, together with the UK, for more troops for MONUC and a better deployment of existing forces.

Police Reform

The UK and France have partly deconflictualised their approaches to police reform. They began to limit duplication of donor efforts when, in December 2003, they approved a DRC government request to help establish an Integrated Police Unit (IPU) to protect Congolese state institutions.[10] They took a further step towards coordination when they backed the launch, in April 2005, of EUPOL-Kinshasa, a European civilian police mission to mentor IPU actions in Kinshasa during the transition. The UK and France have provided complementary forms of support to EUPOL, with the British – who are short of French-speaking police officers – contributing mainly equipment and funding and the French supplying over a third of the police contingent. The two countries have, moreover, backed extensions of EUPOL's mandate as well as widening the remit of this body (renamed EUPOL DRC in July 2007) to include security issues in eastern Congo. They have also consistently supported EUPOL in negotiations with the Congolese government over future police reforms.

---

9   The other battle-group country, Germany, 'killed the idea', while most EU states were unsupportive (personal communication, MONUC, 2009).

10   Although the IPU was predominantly funded by the European Commission, the UK earmarked money for training, while France provided 12 IPU trainers and separate riot police training (Chivvis 2007: 31).

However, the limits to cooperation were revealed when, in January 2006, a European fact-finding mission observed that there was little donor coordination on policing, 'with the French having trained a unit following its own chain-of-command and the South Africans, financed by the British, having trained police SWAT teams with another chain-of-command, different equipment and different communication systems' (personal communication, Kinshasa, 2009). There have also been disagreements between the UK and France on police reform. Thus, it emerged during the elections that the British were planning, together with South Africa, a national system for police radio communication, while the French had set aside funding for different equipment and a radio transmission centre. This resulted in a stand-off that was eventually resolved in favour of the UK. Other divergences have persisted beyond the elections. For example, the UK has advocated 'community policing' by unarmed officers, while France has remained more inclined towards riot control. Significantly too, the UK has urged EUPOL to follow the template laid down by the British in Sierra Leone, with the appointment of a single police Inspector-General and the provision of large-scale DfID funding. However, while such a solution was possible in a small ex-British colony, it has been deemed unacceptable by the French, Belgians and Congolese to have a UK police officer assume such a key position in this huge francophone country (personal communication, Kinshasa, 2009).

Army Reform

Britain and France have also partly 'deconflictualised' their approaches towards army restructuring. They took their first important step towards coordination when they approved the deployment, in May 2005, of the EUSEC army reform mission.[11] Since then, the UK and France have both contributed to the common costs of this programme through the CFSP budget, supported moves towards weekly meetings and approved extensions of EUSEC's mandate as well as some merging of the functions of EUSEC and EUPOL.[12] London and Paris have also sought to avoid replicating each other's activities within EUSEC. Thus, the UK has acted mainly in a funding capacity, regularly financing – out of the Africa Conflict Prevention Pool and the Whitehall Peacekeeping Budget – a handful of French-speaking staff within EUSEC[13] and contributing heavily to the cost of its biometric schemes to identify Congolese soldiers and its chain-of-payments

---

11   Earlier attempts at coordination included the World Bank-led Multi-Country Demobilisation and Reinsertion Programme and the UN-led Security Sector Reform Coordination Committee.

12   On the funding of missions, see European Security and Defence Assembly (2006).

13   The DfID funds French military personnel on contracts, two French officers and the (Belgian) Head of EUSEC in Goma (personal communications, Kinshasa, 2009).

project to stop soldiers being defrauded of their salaries.[14] By contrast, France has concentrated on supplying the largest military and civilian contingent, as well as heading up the mission, initially under General Pierre-Michel Joana then under General Jean-Paul Michel.[15]

Ultimately, however, Britain and France have not been working to the same agenda on army reform. The UK has sought to ensure that EUSEC 'acts more broadly' and serves as the main channel through which European donors engage with SSR (personal communication, MoD, 2009). For France, by contrast, EUSEC should only have an 'advisory function' and should merely 'coordinate the bilateral military assistance efforts of its member states' (personal communication, French Defence Ministry, 2009). These divergent visions have persisted, partly because the DRC government has undermined donor efforts at coordination on SSR and partly because Britain and France have had rival perspectives on, and roughly equal influence over, questions of army reform (Melmot 2009: 17). In effect, the UK has seen its 'impact devalued' within EUSEC due to its failure to contribute military personnel but is generally held in esteem by other donors on SSR. Conversely, the French have enjoyed greater influence within EUSEC, thanks to their staff contributions and their role – alongside the Belgians – as the original proponents of this mission (Hoebeke *et al.* 2007: 27). Yet they are not at the forefront of donor thinking on SSR and are widely thought to have remained 'within their comfort zone' in the DRC, taking 'a fairly bilateral approach' and focusing on hard military training and the integration of French officers within the Congolese army (personal communication, senior diplomat, Kinshasa, 2009).

Tackling Poverty Together

Turning to poverty reduction, here too the UK and France have only semi-deconflictualised their approaches. In 2006, Britain and France began drafting, together with 15 other donors, a Country Assistance Framework (CAF) for the DRC (World Bank 2008: 5). The CAF (2007–11) was a strategic tool for coordinating development programmes and reducing duplication. It enabled donors to claim to be adhering to the 2005 Paris Declaration on aid harmonisation and even allowed the French embassy in Kinshasa to assert, on its website, that France, Britain, Germany, Belgium, Holland and the European Commission constituted 'a hard core' of European donors working on key sectors identified within DRC-led poverty programmes, notably the 2006 Poverty Reduction and Strategy Paper and the 2007 Programme d'Actions Prioritaires.

Ultimately, however, Anglo-French cooperation has remained limited. Thus, while the CAF has allowed for some analysis and monitoring, it has done little to

---

14   Although the UK supplied two of the original eight-strong EUSEC mission, it was, by 2009, only providing one civilian employee out of a staff of 43, see ROP 2005.

15   France provided 16 of EUSEC's 43-strong team in December 2009, see ROP 2005.

encourage joint donor programmes. It has, in effect, allowed the UK to continue with policies, such as the payment of school and health-user fees, which are viewed as 'naive' by parts of the French administration (personal communication, Kinshasa, 2009). It has also not discouraged France from pumping aid into cultural projects, even though the developmental merit of such activities is questioned by the DfID.[16] Significantly too, the CAF has not resulted in direct bilateral cooperation between the UK and France. Thus, while the DfID and AFD have recently exchanged information on water projects and discussed the possibility of co-funding health and education programmes (personal communication, AFD, 2009), they have not developed joint programmes or agreed a common approach, even on issues, such as primary education and healthcare, where the wider UK and French aid administrations have worked together constructively. This lack of cooperation is all the more striking given that the UK and French Foreign Ministers began calling for joint projects in late 2008. It can be attributed to a number of factors, most of which are covered in our theoretical section but two of which are worth singling out here: the difference in weight between the DfID's spending capacity (with 50 to 60 million US dollars to devote to primary education) and the AFD's budget (with a maximum of 10 million); and the issue of timing: the UK and French aid agencies were, by 2008, already engaged in separate projects that could not easily be stopped (personal communications, DfID and AFD, 2009).

A Neoclassical Realist Perspective

How then is this trend towards greater, if limited, cooperation to be understood in neoclassical realist terms? It will be recalled from Chapter 1 that this theoretical perspective focuses not on 'common patterns of international behaviour over time' but the 'grand strategies of individual states'.[17] It assumes that the structure of the international system is not determinative and that domestic political variables should be included within foreign policy analysis.

Pressures for Closer Collaboration

So what were the key drivers towards greater Anglo-French cooperation in the DRC? The initial catalyst was the election in 1997 of new 'policy-making elites' in the form of Tony Blair's reformist UK Labour government in 1997 and Lionel Jospin's modernising socialist administration. This cleared the way for the 1998 Saint-Malo agreements and for closer collaboration across Africa. Yet these accords did not give rise to any immediate or meaningful cooperation in the DRC.

---

16   France has allocated 64 M€, almost a third of its 2007–11 budget, for teaching French, cultural diversity and governance (French Embassy, DRC, n.d. [c]).

17   Lobell, S., Ripsman, N. and Taliaferro, J. (eds), *Neoclassical Realism, the State, and Foreign Policy* (Cambridge: Cambridge University Press, 2009), p. 6.

Three events helped ensure a less conflictual approach. The first was the end of the official 'conflict' and the emergence of a transitional government by mid-2003. In such a fraught security context, there was 'simply no scope for nasty little games' between rival external powers (personal communication, European Commission, 2009). The second was the Iraq War which began in March 2003. Although this resulted in competition between the UK and France over the second UN Resolution, it also encouraged London and Paris to seek common ground elsewhere, notably in Africa where they could 'make friends again' (Viscount Slim, *Hansard*, 12 June 2003, column 397). The war also fortuitously provoked the resignation of Clare Short, who had, through her friendship with Rwandan President Paul Kagame and Uganda's Yoweri Museveni, been a major obstacle to Anglo-French cooperation. The third event was the publication in October 2003 of the final and most authoritative UN Panel Report, which shamed the UK into adopting a less indulgent stance towards the Rwandan and Ugandan regimes, even if Rwanda still enjoys a comparatively easy ride,[18] as the muted UK reaction to a damning 2008 UN Group of Experts report revealed (UNSC 2008).

It was against this backdrop that the UK and France came to appreciate how cooperation could better serve their interests. By working together, particularly on military training and SSR, these two former colonial powers with costly commitments in other troubled regions, could make a more meaningful contribution to the near-apocalyptic crisis facing the DRC. Together, they could garner a majority of the votes on the Security Council, not least since France is the lead country on the DRC and views cooperation with the UK as 'the key' to passing UNSC Resolutions (personal communication, French Foreign Ministry, 2009). By aligning their positions within the EU, they could swing votes within the PSC, thereby securing approval for ESDP military missions and overcoming resistance from states such as Germany. By banding together, the UK and France could, moreover, compensate for the fact that they are ultimately only two players in a country where dynamic new suitors now include South Africa, Angola, India, Japan, the Middle East countries and above all China, whose 9.25 billion US dollars ('resources for infrastructure') loan is almost as large as the DRC's national debt (*Africa Research Bulletin*, 16 April–15 May 2008: 17692–3). Furthermore, by working together, the UK (as Rwanda's largest donor) and France (as the DRC's most stalwart backer) could help rein in Rwandan support for Tutsi rebels in the Congrès National pour la Défense du Peuple (CNDP), while also pressuring the Kabila government to do more to disarm the FDLR. Significantly too, Britain and France could, by presenting a more united front on Congolese sovereignty and Rwandan border security, limit the extent to which they are played off against each other by Congolese and Rwandan politicians and negotiators, who are experts at such manipulation (personal communication, EU official, Addis, 2009). By

---

18   The UK government mooted the possibility of suspending aid in 2003 (*Africa News*, 18 August 2003) but failed to follow Sweden and Holland when they halted budgetary assistance to Rwanda in 2008 (*Agence France Presse*, 23 December 2008).

combining their efforts, Paris and London could, moreover, better respond to the threats posed by the DRC, be they from illegal immigration or from regional destabilisation: four of the DRC's nine neighbouring countries are former British colonies and two are ex-French.[19]

These pressures to adopt a better-coordinated approach have not been lost on the UK or French governments who have, as signatories of the 2005 UN Resolution on 'Responsibility to protect populations', been alarmed at the prospect of a genocide of the sort that occurred in neighbouring Rwanda. British policy-makers have been particularly receptive to lobbying by the All Party Parliamentary Group on the Great Lakes region, the UK Congo Forum and Oxfam. Such domestic pressures have been less prevalent on the French side, although officials have, particularly since the 2007 election of President Sarkozy, been anxious to shore up influence throughout the Great Lakes – including in Rwanda where past animosities have come to be seen as obstacles to be overcome (personal communication, French Foreign Ministry, 2008).

Obstacles to Collaboration

Given the above pressures, it might seem surprising that there has been no 'sustained' Anglo-French cooperation in the DRC. The explanation would appear to lie in divergent (or, at best, partially convergent) perspectives on, and interests in, the DRC; institutional constraints; and the different 'extractive capacity' of the British and French states. To begin with the differences in Anglo-French perspectives, the UK has viewed this populous, central African country primarily in terms of its humanitarian and developmental needs. The DRC is 'one of the frontiers of development, where the battle to achieve the MDGs will be won or lost' (Ivan Lewis, *Hansard*, 6 November 2008, column 395). The French, by contrast, adopt a more interest-driven approach, considering the importance of the DRC to lie not in the MDGs – which are viewed as unrealistic and overly technocratic – but in its status as the second largest francophone country (with 15 million French speakers) and as a neighbour of Rwanda, a country that has moved from the francophone to the anglophone sphere of influence and that has had an actively hostile relationship with Paris since 1994 (personal communications, French Foreign Ministry, 2009).

These divergent foreign policy perspectives have restricted collaboration and even engendered mutual suspicion. Thus, DfID officials are increasingly disappointed by France's low level of 'development spending' in the DRC and wary that the French might try to 'take credit for DfID money' (personal communication, former UK Minister, 2009),[20] while French policy-makers are now suspicious of British motives for establishing such a large aid programme

---

19   The DRC is in the top 20 countries of interest for UK Border Agency (FCO 2009: 1).

20   In 2008, France only provided 21M€ (Ministère des affaires étrangères et européennes 2010).

and mission in a francophone country.[21] This lack of trust has been compounded by divergent economic interests which, although quite marginal for the time being, cannot be dismissed altogether. To illustrate, the UK's exports made up only 1 per cent of the total market in 2004 and its diplomatic mission has provided only *ad hoc* support to UK investors (Kisingani and Bobb 2010: 173). Yet, even so, Britain does have important mining interests in the DRC and, through the British-based company Tullow, a stake in offshore oilfields.[22] Similarly, although France currently has little direct investment, it is developing, through the French-based multinational Areva, a strong interest in uranium exploration. It also ranks as the third largest exporter to the DRC, has a sizeable trade surplus (86 M€ in 2008) and actively supports French companies seeking to invest there (French Embassy, DRC (n.d. [a]).

Institutional constraints have further hindered Anglo-French coordination. The main obstacle has been the lack of any French equivalent to the DfID with its 40-strong mission, technocratic expertise and focus on institutional processes (DfID 2008: 7). The much smaller French aid mission, the SCAC, has maintained a strong cultural focus, while the five-strong AFD agency has retained a banking culture and a predilection for profitable investment projects. Another brake on cooperation has come from different institutional procedures. Thus, the DfID, with its shortage of French-speakers, has preferred to channel funds rapidly through budgetary assistance and service providers, such as NGOs, and international organisations, such as the UN Development Programme. The French are, however, cynical about fungible forms of assistance, particularly in countries where corruption is rife. They emphasise more 'visible' project work, focus on supporting individuals rather than institutional processes and route most bilateral aid through their own mission (personal communication, FCO, 2010).

This institutional misalignment has been compounded by different policy styles and internal divisions within the British and French aid administrations. The UK has adopted a low-key, consultative approach, aimed at deflecting DRC government suspicions of Britain's presence, while France has assumed a high-profile, politicised stance, designed to signal support for the Kabila administration. An example of France's readiness to launch grand strategies, even if they end up backfiring, came in January 2009 when the French President announced the 'Sarkozy Plan', a unilateral initiative aimed at unlocking the dispute between Rwanda and the DRC over mineral resources and border security. As regards internal divisions, these have been subtle but important. Thus, while the British mission in Kinshasa won the Civil Service award for joined-up government in 2008, there remain divergences between, for example, the DfID and the Ministry of Defence over the proportion of the SSR budget allocated to defence (DfID 2008: 5). In France's case, divisions have been evident between the Foreign

---

21   The DRC hosts the UK's seventh largest mission in Africa. British aid rose from £6 million in 2001–2 to £100m in 2008–9 (FCO 2009: 1).

22   British-owned companies include AngloGold Ashanti and Katanga Mining.

Ministry and the Elysée, notably over the proposed intervention in the Kivus in 2008.

Finally, coordination has been held back by different 'extractive capacities'. To illustrate, the UK has found it easy to increase aid, both for developmental and humanitarian goals, to this crisis-ridden country.[23] Its task has been facilitated by cross-party support as well as the backing of UK NGOs and the media. The French state has been able to mobilise humanitarian assistance for the DRC (8.2 M€ in 2008), thanks partly to Kouchner's NGO background (Ministère des affaires étrangères et européennes, 2010). But France's capacity to ratchet up long-term development aid has been limited by membership of the 1997 European Stability Pact, recent internal spending cuts across the French administration and the fact that France is the leading contributor to the European Development Fund (French Embassy, UK 2001a). Conversely, the UK has had problems galvanising support for ESDP missions, not least due to its lack of French-speaking and other military personnel, the need for Parliamentary scrutiny of such missions and the fact that MONUC already has a Chapter VII mandate. By contrast, France has found mobilisation easier thanks to the lack of parliamentary oversight over presidential decisions, the pre-positioning of 9,000 French troops in Africa and the way that ESDP missions serve France's aim of making Europe a credible autonomous military force.

Conclusion: Making their Own Peace

This chapter has demonstrated how the UK and France have sought to deconflictualise their stances on the DRC, particularly since the creation of the transitional government in 2003. It has shown how Britain and France have opened new, mainly multilateral, channels for dialogue and engaged in active, though coincidental, cooperation at moments of crisis and on 'hard' security-related matters where the British and French agendas have briefly converged. It has noted, however, that the UK and France have been less successful in deconflictualising their approaches in non-crisis situations and on 'soft' policy issues, such as poverty reduction and the civilian dimensions of SSR.

An effort has been made to explain the significant yet patchy nature of Anglo-French cooperation in one of Africa's most troubled regions. The drivers behind, and constraints on, collaboration have been identified, and the implication would appear to be that, while the UK and France have common interests in tackling the challenges of the DRC together, these interests are not sufficiently important to either the UK or France to give rise to any kind of 'sustained and reciprocal' cooperation or, indeed, to any systematic attempt to harmonise foreign policy priorities towards the Great Lakes region.

---

23 In 2008–9 over a third of the DfID's programme remained humanitarian (DfID 2008: 4–5).

It can be concluded from the above that, while Anglo-French cooperation has been important, particularly in clearing the way for a more meaningful common European foreign policy towards the DRC (personal communication, EU, Addis Ababa, 2010), it has often been 'insufficient' and 'more virtual than real' (personal communication, AFD, 2009). It has also been far from exceptional, as the UK has remained closest to the United States on regional security, to Holland on army restructuring and to South Africa on police reform, while the French have collaborated most with Belgium on water, education and army training projects.

The future of Anglo-French coordination in the DRC is a hard one to call. Clearly the UK and France are facing continuing pressures to engage in more sustained cooperation. Thus, on the security front, collaboration in the DRC and across Africa could help shore up the 'mould-breaking' defence agreements signed by the new British Prime Minister, David Cameron, and French President Sarkozy in November 2010 (personal communication, UK Minister, 2010). The current global financial crisis will also keep governments in both countries under pressure to make savings through greater burden-sharing. Finally, the issue of Rwanda should prove less of an obstacle to collaboration, as London has begun to take seriously Rwanda's democratic shortcomings and as Paris restored diplomatic relations with Kigali in November 2009.

However, a number of indicators suggest that UK-French cooperation in the DRC may well remain largely 'coincidental'. In particular, the election in May 2010 of a Conservative-dominated coalition government in the UK, is likely to militate against increased collaboration. Given the Conservative Party's anti-European credentials and its overt emphasis on British trade, it may struggle to find common ground with a French administration that has pinned its colours to the mast of European integration and that is pushing its commercial interests more aggressively across Africa. Given also the new Conservative-led government's track record of supporting the neo-liberal 'reformist' regime in Rwanda,[24] it is unlikely to wish to align itself to France's now-established policy of unconditional support for Kabila's incompetent and corrupt administration. Nor is there any immediate prospect of the current UK and French administrations moving towards a unified Anglo-French view of the threats posed by the CNDP and FDLR.[25] Yet, unless the British and French governments can agree on a 'common diagnosis' of the problems facing the DRC and act decisively to resolve continuing tensions between the Anglophone and Francophone blocs in the Congo (personal communication, French Foreign Ministry, 2009), then there

---

24 Conservative Development Minister, Lynda Chalker, developed a friendship with Kagame in the mid-1990s. David Cameron visited Rwanda on his first trip to Africa as Conservative Party leader, see Dale 2007.

25 According to one Whitehall insider, the UK and France will 'stick stubbornly to their guns' on the issue of rebel groups, since there are few direct 'political consequences' for failing to cooperate in a region that is marginal to British and French interests (personal communication, 6 June 2010).

seems little hope that this ailing country, the so-called troubled 'heart of Africa', will make any kind of speedy recovery.

Chapter 10

Anglo-French Cooperation vis-à-vis the African Union

Tony Chafer

In launching the Saint-Malo process at the December 1998 Franco-British summit, the UK and French governments declared their intention to set aside a century of rivalry and 'pursue joint cooperation' on the ground in Africa (Saint-Malo Declaration 1998). In so doing, they signalled their readiness to move away from their traditional spheres of influence in their former African empires and towards a continent-wide focus on Africa, including as a central tenet building up the capacity of regional and sub-regional organisations. London and Paris were helped in this latter goal by the winding up of the Organisation of African Unity (OAU) in 1999 and its replacement by the African Union (AU) in July 2002. This chapter therefore examines British and French policy towards the AU. It begins by noting the UK and French neglect of the OAU, and then reviews the key developments and contextual changes that pushed for and facilitated a more coordinated stance on the AU. It then seeks to explain the recent evolution towards a more cooperative approach by examining the key drivers behind this enhanced collaboration and it ends by evaluating the extent and nature of Anglo-French cooperation vis-à-vis the AU. Within a neoclassical framework, it shows how concerns in both the UK and France over their relative power on the international stage have pushed both countries to work more closely together with African regional and sub-regional organisations. However, divergent interests and foreign policy priorities, institutional and resource constraints, and the views of the wider domestic polity on state preference have impinged on policy-making and ultimately limited the extent of cooperation.

Before proceeding, it is important to emphasise that this is not a chapter about the AU *per se*. A number of recent works have examined the history and structure of the organisation and its emerging peace and security architecture (Akokpari *et al.* 2008; Besada 2010; Engel and Porto 2010; Makinda and Okumu 2008). Second, and related to this, AU perceptions of Anglo-French cooperation are not a central feature of this article, although they cannot of course be entirely ignored. In this context it is worth noting that such cooperation has hitherto been broadly welcomed by the AU but, as I argue later, this should not be taken for granted. Finally, the chapter focuses largely on security cooperation, as this represents 90 per cent of the European Union's (EU) engagement with the AU (personal communication, EU official, Addis Ababa, 2009) and, in the French case, almost its exclusive area of engagement. 'Peace and security' is one of the priority areas of the Africa-EU Strategic Partnership, although the AU's strategic plan 2009–12 has three other thematic priorities (*Le Monde Diplomatique* 2009), and the Africa-EU Strategic Partnership has seven other priority action areas.[1] The lack of cooperation in these areas will be touched upon where relevant, as it is a useful indicator of the nature and limits of Anglo-French collaboration with the AU.

From the OAU to the AU: A New Context for Cooperation

Anglo-French relations in Africa have been characterised by rivalry since the beginning of the colonial period. Following the end of the Cold War there was a shift to a more multilateral approach (see Chapter 11) but this did not extend to working with the OAU, which continued to be perceived as a dictators' club (Makinda and Okumu 2008: 30). However, French and British neglect of the OAU was soon replaced by a more supportive, and in some cases more coordinated, approach following the emergence of the AU in 2002. The latter set out to be a quite different type of organisation from the OAU; more outward-looking than its predecessor, its ambition being to create an integrated, prosperous and peaceful Africa, able to play its rightful role on the international stage (AU 2000, art. 3). The launch of the AU was also a significant moment because it signalled the abandonment of one of the OAU's founding principles, the commitment to non-intervention in the internal affairs of member states (*Africa News*, 11 February 2002; Mwanasali 2008: 42–5). This reflected the desire of African leaders to take greater responsibility for peace and security on the continent.[2] More generally, it was born of a desire by African leaders to address the marginalisation of Africa in the context of accelerating globalisation and put the continent 'on track towards sustainable growth and development' (Mathews 2008: 25). The creation of the AU thus marked the emergence of a new and credible African multilateral organisation that appeared to share the ambition of donor countries to address the challenges of governance and security on the continent. (Porteous 2008: 54–6).

At the same time, the UN did not have the resources to respond to the growing number and increased complexity of peacekeeping and security operations on the continent. Moreover, the US was reluctant to undertake military interventions in Africa following its humiliation in Somalia, while the EU for its part was making

---

1   The others are: Democratic Governance and Human Rights; Trade, Regional Integration and Infrastructure; Millennium Development Goals; Energy; Climate Change; Migration, Mobility and Employment; Science, Information Society and Space.

2   Article 4 of the AU's Constitutive Act asserted 'the right of the Union to intervene in a member state pursuant to a decision of the Assembly in respect of grave circumstances', including war crimes and crimes against humanity. The 'responsibility to protect' is the idea of transnational responsibility for human welfare, see http://www.responsibilitytoprotect. org (accessed 17 June 2010).

limited progress on its rapid reaction force prior to Saint-Malo. Both the UK and France thus had a shared interest in supporting Africans to peacekeep themselves by promoting the notion of 'African solutions to African problems'. Against this background, the launch of the RECAMP (Renforcement des capacités africaines de maintien de la paix) programme represented a watershed in French policy, marking a move away from its traditional approach of direct, unilateral, military intervention towards a policy of supporting Africans to peacekeep themselves. The parallel launch of the UK's African Peacekeeping Training Support Programme in 1997 had the same objective.

The final catalyst for improved Anglo-French cooperation vis-à-vis the AU was the shift in the way that the EU engaged with the continent. EU African policy, through the successive Yaoundé and Lomé conventions, was largely driven by the European Commission (EC); its partner was the African-Caribbean-Pacific (ACP) group of countries, and its focus was trade and development. The political dimension of the relationship was left to member states and their bilateral relations with the ACP states. This began to change in the 1990s with the introduction of economic and political conditionalities under Lomé IV, which in 2000 were integrated into the successor Cotonou accords as one of the pillars of the new agreement linking the EU and the ACP countries. In the same year, at a summit held in Cairo, African and European leaders launched a new political dialogue outside the Lomé/Cotonou framework. Building on this and following the launch of the AU, in 2005 the EU developed an Africa strategy for the first time, for which its privileged interlocutor was the AU. At the same time, the EU was developing the European Security and Defence Policy (ESDP), for which Africa rapidly emerged as a key theatre, and responsibility for which fell to the European Council. These developments were crucially important for three reasons. First, they marked a move away from an essentially 'technical' relationship between the EU and Africa (as part of the ACP group of countries), in which the EC took the policy lead, towards a much more overtly political, and indeed military, relationship. Second, reflecting the growing importance of the EU as a foreign policy actor, the European Council now took an increasingly important role in driving African policy. This shift towards intergovernmentalism thrust the UK and France, as the two member states with the largest residual responsibilities and interests south of the Sahara, to the centre of EU policy-making on Africa. Third, the AU, not the ACP group of countries, now emerged as the EU's key strategic partner in Africa, a development that was confirmed by the signature of the Africa-EU Strategic Partnership at the AU-EU summit in Lisbon in 2007. These developments were crucially important in opening the door to increased Anglo-French cooperation within the EU vis-à-vis the AU. They transformed the context for UK and French policy-making on Africa, pushing them to coordinate policy and also to engage with the whole continent, through their partnership with the AU, in a way that they had not done in the past.

The AU and the Saint-Malo Process: Towards Enhanced Cooperation?

With the 1998 Saint-Malo summit promising 'joint cooperation to promote sub-regional integration, in particular between networks of Anglophone and Francophone countries' (Saint-Malo Declaration 1998[3]), the period 1998–2002 thus marked an important moment in UK and French relations with African regional organisations. As we have seen, neither country had sought to engage with the OAU in any systematic way. This changed with the foundation of the AU. Indeed, the pledge to work jointly with the AU, specifically in the field of peace and security, was made explicit in the communiqué issued at the 2004 Lancaster House summit and renewed at subsequent summits in 2006 and 2008 (Franco-British Summit 2006; Saint-Malo Ten Years After 2008). However, while both countries publicly welcomed its creation, the UK has generally engaged more enthusiastically with the AU, reflecting the strategic priority attached by the Foreign and Commonwealth Office (FCO) to engaging with international organisations, whereas France has focused more of its efforts on working with Africa's sub-regional organisations such as ECOWAS and has adopted a more guarded approach to the AU. In the light of this, the question to be addressed here is: how far has Anglo-French cooperation vis-à-vis the AU been taken? In order to do this, we need to understand what has been driving French and British approaches to the AU, the areas in which they have sought to cooperate and examine the obstacles to more systematic cooperation.

The first driver towards cooperation was the election in 1997 of new French and British governments that wanted to overhaul their two countries' approaches to Africa. Prime Minister Lionel Jospin was a moderniser in terms of African policy (see Chapters 4 and 5) and, following the debacle of France's involvement in Rwanda and DRC (then Zaire) in the mid-1990s (Chafer 2005: 17), wanted to move away from France's traditional unilateral approach to Africa, which in the military field had earned it the reputation of the 'gendarme' of Africa, towards a new focus on Africans peacekeeping themselves. His election coincided with the election of a New Labour government in the UK that sought to re-engage with Africa, in particular by promoting an ambitious development agenda through the newly created Department for International Development (DfID). After decades during which Africa appeared largely marginal to British foreign relations, Tony Blair's government was set to make Africa an explicit policy priority (Porteous 2008: 1), though not in the military field (the small and time-limited, albeit effective, intervention in Sierra Leone in 2001 was the exception in this respect), where the UK was keen for Africans to take a much greater role. For both countries this new approach implied moving beyond the traditional Anglo-French 'division

---

3   Full summit declaration obtained from the FCO. The 'Saint-Malo Declaration' is published on several websites but the text is incomplete, even on the FCO website, as it omits the part of the declaration referring to Africa, see www.fco.gov.uk/en/news/latest-news/?view=PressS&id=10435411, accessed 26 March 2010.

of labour' in Africa, whereby France focused its attention on its Francophone '*pré carré*' (sphere of influence), with which it maintained privileged and exclusive relations, and the UK concentrated on maintaining good bilateral relations with key countries, such as Nigeria in the west and Kenya in the east, that had been British colonies (Chafer 2005: 7–23; Cumming 2005: 56–7; Porteous 2008: 7). At the same time, both the Jospin and Blair governments were all too aware that their countries were suffering from resource constraints that prevented them from undertaking all the tasks on the continent that they once had done.

As a result, both governments now perceived it as in their interest to cooperate on African issues. This new approach was not driven solely by a concern for Africa, however. On the French side, relations between President Chirac, Prime Minister Jospin and the German Chancellor Gerhard Schröder were difficult, so that Chirac and his foreign affairs minister Hubert Védrine were looking for EU policy areas where they could work more closely with the UK. At the same time, the UK having opted against joining the euro, Prime Minister Blair nonetheless wanted to 'put the UK at the heart of Europe', and was looking for policy areas in which the UK could play a leading role within the EU.

A further driver of Anglo-French cooperation is that the AU has become an important actor in relation to the UNSC in recent years since it, or more precisely its Peace and Security Council (PSC), is responsible for establishing the AU's position on matters concerning Africa, including Security Council resolutions, that come before the United Nations. This is significant for two reasons. First, some two-thirds of the UNSC's business has in recent years been related to Africa and Anglo-French coordination vis-à-vis the PSC is therefore vital if they are to influence the AU's position on issues coming before the UNSC (personal communication, French official, Addis Ababa, 2009). Second, and even more importantly, two of the other permanent members of the UNSC, Russia and China, are unlikely to support any Security Council resolution on Africa that does not have AU support (personal communication, French official, Addis Ababa, 2009). The PSC's position can therefore have a determining influence over the fate of resolutions relating to Africa at the UN.

Finally, the growing activism of powerful new external actors in Africa, such as China and India, has led to a significant reduction in the importance of the UK and France in Africa's foreign relations since the early 2000s. This has reduced their power to do things in Africa and the resulting decline in leverage provides a further incentive for them to cooperate on African issues. The UK and France thus have complementary interests pushing them towards closer – and mutually beneficial – cooperation vis-à-vis the AU.

Types of Cooperation with the AU

It is possible to discern four different types, or levels, of cooperation with the AU.[4] First, there is 'natural' cooperation, where France and the UK seek to promote essentially the same agenda and priorities, and coordination of positions is relatively straightforward. Since 2002, the two countries have shared broadly similar concerns about Africa, relating to such issues as migration, terrorism, transnational crime, conflict, instability and governance. As a result they have rarely been at daggers drawn over Africa. Second, there is 'coincident cooperation', where the two countries want a similar outcome but seek to reach it in different ways, either because their motivations are not the same, or because they provide support to the AU in distinct ways as the instruments at their disposal are quite different. Third, 'disinterested cooperation' occurs where cooperation is the product of shared liberal norms and values, but working together brings no immediate material benefit to the other party.[5] The fourth type, 'deconflictualisation', is in many instances a pre-requisite for the other three. This involves as a minimum the two countries pursuing their own initiatives independently, but making efforts to ensure that their actions are complementary and do not involve any unnecessary duplication of effort. In political terms it means that they are careful not to 'trip each other up'.

To be sure, these forms of cooperation cannot be entirely separated. For example, although the two countries share broadly the same agenda in relation to Africans taking greater responsibility for security on the continent, they come to the problem from quite different perspectives, so that careful negotiation is needed in order to achieve the desired outcome. The result may be different forms of cooperation situated anywhere on a continuum from actively working together with shared agendas on joint projects at one end to simple deconflictualisation at the other. Moreover, this typology does not fully take account of the different fora and contexts in which cooperation takes place. In particular, a distinction needs to be made between bilateral Anglo-French cooperation that involves just the French and UK governments working together, and 'bi-multi' cooperation that involves them working together within multilateral organisations such as the EU and the UNSC in an effort to bring others round to their view. These different forms of cooperation often take place in parallel, leading in practice to what can perhaps best be described as 'messy multilateralism'. Nevertheless, while there is some overlap between the different types, the analytical distinctions remain useful indicators of the nature of cooperation and are useful for drawing a distinction

---

4   For a discussion of cooperation problems in international relations, see Martin 1992: 768–83.

5   The term 'disinterested cooperation' does not imply that the two countries have no interest in cooperating: from the point of view of diffusing certain norms and values, they clearly have such an interest.

between areas of collaboration and other areas where non-cooperation or limited cooperation have been the norm.

'Natural' Cooperation

Taking 'natural' cooperation first, it should be reiterated that since 2002, France and the UK have rarely had major differences over Africa. As Western liberal democracies, permanent members of the UNSC, key players in the EU and the only major Western powers with significant residual responsibilities and interests south of the Sahara, they share a broad set of common values rooted in notions of human rights, democratisation, good governance and human security. A good example of 'natural' cooperation is in relation to support for the AU's African Peace and Security Architecture (APSA).[6] Both governments want to avoid the costs and risks – in terms of both casualties and potential political damage – of direct military involvement, and therefore prefer to pay others to undertake peacekeeping operations on the continent. Both also agree that peace and security are the prerequisite for development. As the two major EU military powers with the capacity to intervene in Africa, their cooperation on the peace and security agenda was therefore natural, especially as this was an agenda that they shared with both the AU and its emerging APSA. It was therefore to be expected that both countries would play a key role within the EU in obtaining the support of EU member states for ESDP missions in Africa and for capacity-building, peacekeeping and peace support operations under the ESDP, notably in the Democratic Republic of Congo (DRC) and Chad/CAR (see Chapter 5).[7] Both have also played lead roles in generating EU support for the African Standby Force (ASF), the African Union peacekeeping missions in Sudan (AMIS) and Somalia (AMISOM) and, with other partners, the development of the Continental Early Warning System (CEWS). They have also jointly provided backing for map training exercises and support for the MIVAC initiative, an interactive watch and anticipation mechanism that

---

6   The AU established the APSA as 'an operational structure for the effective implementation of … conflict prevention, peace-making, peace support operations and intervention, as well as peace-building and post-conflict reconstruction' (Engel and Porto 2010: 3). The centrepiece of the APSA is the Peace and Security Council (PSC), the role of which is to oversee the establishment of the Continental Early-Warning System (CEWS) and the African Standby Force (ASF). The PSC is supported by a Panel of the Wise, whose role is to advise the PSC on peace and security issues and help in the peaceful settlement of disputes.

7   Although ESDP missions, apart from EU support to AMIS which was provided at the request of the AU, do not directly involve the AU, they cannot be entirely ignored here as the UK and French governments have played a key role in gaining EU member states' support for these missions, which have in turn been a significant factor shaping EU policy towards the AU.

has been developed to help the AU build up its early warning capability.[8] Crucially too, they played a key role, with Portugal, in developing the Africa-EU Strategic Partnership, which was signed at the first joint AU-EU summit in Lisbon in 2007, and in ensuring that this had a strong security focus (Elowson 2009: 27).

'Coincident' Cooperation

'Coincident cooperation' frequently takes place on the ground in Africa, at the level of implementation. Thus the principle of Anglo-French support for the APSA or cooperation to improve UN peacekeeping mandates is 'natural', insofar as both countries share the objective of enabling Africans to take more responsibility for peace and security on the continent. However, if we look at specific instances of cooperation, the two countries often come at an issue from quite different perspectives. With regard to the Sudan/Darfur crisis, for example, the UK has long been interested in stabilising the Sudan and was one of the three countries (with the US and Norway) that helped to deliver the 2005 Comprehensive Peace Agreement (CPA). France has never managed to exert any meaningful influence over the CPA process and only became involved much later, largely because of its concerns about the destabilising impact of the Darfur crisis on two of its key allies in the region, Chad and the Central African Republic (CAR) (personal communication, Foreign Affairs Ministry official, Paris, 2009).

This is an example of what I have called 'messy multilateralism'. There was no formal agreement to work together on this issue. Rather, France effectively deferred to the UK and accepted that, for historical and other reasons, the UK should take the lead on Sudan, while the UK supported France on Chad/CAR. This mutual recognition of the comparative advantage of the UK in Sudan and of France in Chad/CAR in turn facilitated a more coordinated approach to lobbying the AU. This makes sense, as a coordinated approach to lobbying members of the AU's PSC by two of the UNSC's permanent members is more likely to yield results than individual approaches, and because the UK has more influence in Sudan while France has more in Chad/CAR. This is therefore a useful means for both countries to maximise their leverage in pursuit of their shared objective of regional stability (personal communications, EU officials, Addis Ababa, 2009).

Perhaps the most striking example of 'coincident cooperation' is Anglo-French backing for the APSA, where the two countries provide support in quite different ways and using different instruments. After the Lisbon summit France and the UK took the lead in transforming the French RECAMP programme into an EU programme, EURORECAMP. Based in Paris, as France is the EU

---

8   The MIVAC (Mécanisme interactif de veille et d'anticipation conjoint) initiative forms part of the Africa-EU Strategic Partnership. Under it the UK and France sent two AU colleagues to the French Foreign Affairs Ministry's early warning centre and to the BBC monitoring service, Chatham House and the Royal United Services Institute (personal communications, British and French officials, Addis Ababa, 2009).

'framework nation', it has a French general as its director and a British officer as its deputy director. The EURORECAMP programme aims to strengthen African peacekeeping capacity through education and training, and is 'guided by the principle of African ownership', to enable the AU to contribute more effectively to regional security (Africa-EU Strategic Partnership 2007: 5). A good example of this is its first training cycle, Amani Africa ('Amani' means 'peace' in Swahili), which was launched in November 2008 at the AU-EU Ministerial Troika in Addis Ababa. The focus of the cycle (2008–10) was to assist the AU in its decision-making for crisis management at continental level and in its validation of the ASF. France took the lead role in agenda-setting and implementation, while the UK was the largest financial contributor (Elowson 2009: 62–3). Anglo-French strategic-level planning for Amani Africa mainly took place at HQ level in Paris, while the EU Special Representative's Office (EUSR) in Addis Ababa sought to coordinate EU and member states' support for Amani Africa, notably within the African Union Partners Group (AUPG), which was chaired by the UK in 2008 and by the EUSR in 2009.[9]

There have nonetheless been clear limits to this cooperation. Whilst these initiatives have helped ensure a degree of deconflictualisation between member states on the ground, the UK and France do not collaborate actively in Addis Ababa, either by working on joint projects or by working together within the AUPG, despite the fact that other member states acknowledge that they are the key players in the area of peace and security cooperation with the AU and that without them little can be achieved (personal communications, Danish and EU officials, Addis Ababa, 2009). In practice both countries continue to provide a significant proportion of their support for the operationalisation of APSA on a bilateral basis (Bagayoko 2007: 2; Vines 2010: 1106). The UK channels its contributions (additional to those that it provides as a contributor to the European Development Fund) to supporting the APF on a bilateral basis through its Conflict Prevention Pool. It is one of the largest bilateral donors to APSA, and focuses on training African officers and providing funding for training exercises and peacekeeping operations. France, on the other hand, is one of the smallest financial contributors, but plays a much more prominent role than the UK in providing direct support for peacekeeping training exercises, thanks to its pre-positioned forces totalling some 9,000 personnel on the continent. It usually undertakes these initiatives on its own, rather than jointly with other partners.

A further example of coincident cooperation is UK and French support for the AU mission in Somalia (AMISOM), where the two countries have separate and distinct approaches to supporting the AU force on the ground, largely because the instruments at their disposal are quite different. While both countries want

---

9   The AUPG also includes China, India, the US, Canada, Russia, Norway and Turkey. With the creation in Addis Ababa in 2007 of the EU Special Representative's office, representing the European Council and the Commission, the EU became potentially a key forum for Anglo-French policy coordination vis-à-vis the AU.

to avoid direct military involvement, supported the Djibouti peace accords and coordinate their positions on Somalia in Brussels, notably in relation to the ESDP anti-piracy operation EUNAVFOR off the Somali coast, at the bilateral level the British have provided significant financial support to AMISOM, while the French launched a purely French initiative to train Somali troops in Djibouti. The UK put £10m into the UN-administered AMISOM Trust Fund in March 2009, and provided just under £1m in niche support to AMISOM in 2009–10. From May 2008 to March 2009, the UK also gave $16.7m to the AU for AMISOM to cover personnel costs (troop allowances, pre-deployment training and death and injury benefits).[10] The Somali troop training programme, on the other hand, was a purely French initiative, although France did subsequently try, unsuccessfully, to turn this into an EU programme and obtain EU funding for it at a joint meeting of the EU's and AU's PSCs in Addis Ababa in 2009 (personal communications, French and Danish officials, Addis Ababa, 2009; see also *Le Monde*, 14 October 2009). These differences in approach reflect the fact that the UK government, through the Department for International Development (DfID) budget, has money available for bilateral support but no troops on the ground, whereas France has almost no money for bilateral initiatives but has a major garrison and training facilities in Djibouti.[11]

'Disinterested' Cooperation

'Disinterested cooperation' is distinct in nature from the first two forms of cooperation, in that France and the UK do not in this case necessarily have a specific shared agenda or seek a specific outcome from cooperation. Rather, as Western liberal democracies that are permanent members of the UNSC and major players in the EU, they frequently engage with international issues from which they do not expect to derive a direct benefit or reward. This can happen in two ways. There can be a high-level decision at national government level to support the other country's position, even though this will bring the first country no immediate or obvious benefit, or it can happen as a result of personal initiatives by officials at local level. However, while the rhetoric may suggest that these helpful gestures are purely the result of shared Western values, there have been instances where realpolitik-type deals, from which both countries stand to benefit, have also been struck. One example of this was in 2008, when France, which at the time held the EU presidency, agreed to support the UK's stance on Zimbabwe at EU level and then lobbied the AU for support, while the UK supported France on EUFOR

---

10   Payment for these lines has now been taken on by the EU's APF.

11   This difference in approach is also noticeable in relation to the two countries' support for the AU's mission in Sudan, AMIS/UNAMID. The UK has given $62m to the mission, while total French bilateral aid to the AU since 2005 has been only €20m (personal communication, UK official, Addis Ababa, 2009, http://www.ambafrance-et.org/France_Ethiopie/spip.php?article318, accessed 17 June 2010).

Chad/CAR (personal communications, French and British officials, Paris, London and Addis Ababa, 2008–9). This made sense for both countries, as if the UK had lobbied the AU on Zimbabwe or France had lobbied it on Chad, their African interlocutors would likely have turned a deaf ear.

Deconflictualisation

The importance of deconflictualisation as a prerequisite for any form of cooperation cannot be over-emphasised. During the 1990s, before the creation of the AU, there were profound differences between the UK and France on Charles Taylor's Liberia, Côte d'Ivoire and Rwanda/DRC. As late as 2001, the UK saw France as undermining its position on Zimbabwe by inviting President Mugabe to Paris at a time when the UK was attempting to garner EU support for sanctions against his regime (see Chapter 4 for details). It was against this background that Saint-Malo was so significant, as France and the UK recognised that they had little to gain from adopting such conflictual positions and agreed that they would in future avoid such public disagreement on African issues.

These efforts to deconflictualise have extended to UK and French policy towards the AU. As we shall see below, this has been clear in the support that the two countries have provided to the AU's condemnation of unconstitutional changes of government on the continent. Deconflictualisation has also underpinned their approaches to supporting AMIS in Darfur (which was replaced by a UN/AU hybrid force, UNAMID, on 31 December 2007) and AMISOM in Somalia.

Non-cooperation

The creation of the AU provided a new arena for the UK and France to work together and, given their shared interest in cooperating, it may seem surprising that cooperation has not been taken further. Indeed, although considerable progress has been made, cooperation, and even deconflictualisation, is not systematic. At times the UK and France have failed to agree or had difficulty coordinating their stances. These cases are revelatory of their different approaches to the AU and a useful indicator of the constraints that have prevented more systematic cooperation.

Perhaps the most striking recent example of non-cooperation relating to the AU was the contrasting UK and French responses to the Prodi report (Prodi 2008). Romano Prodi was commissioned by the UNSC in 2008 to draw up a report on how the UN could improve its support for peacekeeping in Africa, with a view to providing more predictable, flexible and sustainable funding for AU peacekeeping operations. With the growing demand for peacekeeping operations on the continent, funding was a growing issue as, once an operation was authorised, contributions then had to be sought from member states, whose contributions were entirely voluntary. The report's key recommendation was the creation of a dual system of financial support for the AU's peacekeeping efforts, involving voluntary contributions by member states to support AU capacity-building efforts, and obligatory contributions to establish a UN fund that would be available to support UN-authorised peacekeeping operations undertaken by the AU. The UK supported the report's key recommendation, whereas France, along with the US and Russia, opposed mandatory financing and supported instead a voluntary system of multi-donor transfers. This difference was consistent with the UK's greater enthusiasm for working with the UN and France's preference for working through the EU in support of African peacekeeping efforts (Matlary 2009: 101–2, Vines 2010: 1106–7). In the end, the UK brokered a compromise in the Africa Working Group in Brussels, whereby EU member states agreed to 'keep all options under consideration' (personal communication, EU official, Addis Ababa, 2009), and this was the position eventually adopted by the UNSC on 26 October 2009. However, the question of funding for AU peacekeeping operations remains unresolved, with the UK preferring a reliable UN mechanism and France preferring to focus on developing the EU's support capacity (personal communications, French officials, Brussels and Addis Ababa, 2009).

Moreover, while the UK and France have usually been able to deconflictualise, their positions vis-à-vis the AU, this has not always been straightforward. For example, following the 2008 coup in Madagascar, the British Minister for Africa, Lord Malloch-Brown, publicly condemned the coup, whereas France took a more conciliatory line even than the AU itself (personal communications, AU official, Addis Ababa, 2009; former minister, London, 2009). Although the two governments did eventually align their stances, their different public positions in the immediate aftermath of the coup were symptomatic of deeper differences in reaction to unconstitutional changes of government in Africa. One reason for this is that the French stance on such changes is not always clear. This can lead to a gap between the public discourse of support for human rights and condemnation of unconstitutional changes of government on the one hand, and the actions of individuals close to the government, on the other, that suggest a more qualified position. This happened, for example, in the case of the coup d'état that followed the death of Guinean president Lansana Conté in 2008 (Survie 2009). It can also be the result of differences between government representatives, as happened in the case of the 2009 coup in Mauritania when President Sarkozy appeared to contradict France's official position of condemnation of the coup (*Libération*, 8 April, 17 July 2009). The consequence is that British diplomats sometimes wonder who is articulating the French government's real position on such issues. This uncertainty undermines trust and affects the ability of the two countries to cooperate effectively vis-à-vis the AU.

Constraints on Cooperation

The UK and French foreign policy-making establishments have divergent perceptions of Africa in general, and of the AU in particular, in the context of their countries' broader foreign policy priorities and interests, and in designing policy they are constrained by other factors, notably institutional constraints and the views of the wider domestic polity, on state preferences. These three factors are considered in turn.

Divergent Interests

Despite the common ground between them identified above, Paris and London attach different relative importance to African multilateral organisations at the continental and sub-regional levels. For France, Africa plays a crucial role in enhancing its rank in the international pecking order, with the result that political, diplomatic and military considerations are to the forefront in shaping policy. There is a strong element of defending Francophonie, particularly in west and central Africa, and thus a perception that French influence and power can best be projected by working with African sub-regional organisations, notably the Economic Community of West African States (ECOWAS) and the Economic Community of Central African States (personal communications, British official, Addis Ababa, 2009; French official, Dakar, 2010), and by working closely with key allies in these regions where France has interests or good relations with the government, such as Burkina Faso and Gabon. Moreover, France is sceptical about the AU's capacity to speak on behalf of the whole continent, and believes that international expectations of it are too ambitious, considering that it is an organisation that is still in its infancy (personal communications, French officials, Addis Ababa, 2009).

For UK policy-makers, on the other hand, Africa is primarily a development issue and policy has a continent-wide purview. This is reflected in the rise to prominence of DfID, which has played a major role in shaping UK policy on Africa since 1997. DfID was a product of New Labour's internationalism, with its strong focus on the poorest and most disadvantaged people on the planet. This ethical dimension to African policy was supported at the highest levels of government: Tony Blair's Christian approach (he once described Africa as a 'scar on the conscience of the world') and Gordon Brown's 'moral compass' were key drivers behind the UK approach to the continent (Gallagher 2009: 449–51). New Labour's internationalism was also manifest in the priority it attached to working with international organisations such as the G7/G8/G20, the UN and the AU.

Not only do France and the UK attach different priority to Africa, they also adopt a different approach, with France's focus essentially 'sub-regional' and the UK's continent-wide. France has invested significantly in ECOWAS in recent years. Historically, it has had a strong interest in west and central Africa and this has led the French government to focus on engagement with Africa's sub-regional organisations, particularly in this part of the continent. Although much has been made of French military retrenchment in Africa, what has happened is, rather, a reconfiguration of French pre-positioned forces so as to maintain a presence in the four regions of sub-Saharan Africa that correspond to the four brigades of the ASF: Dakar (West Africa: 1,200 troops), Libreville (Central Africa: 800 troops), Djibouti

(East Africa: 2,700 troops), and La Réunion (Southern Africa: 4,200 troops).[12] The mission of these forces is to cooperate with, and provide peacekeeping support for, the regional brigades of the ASF. In this role they sometimes coordinate with the British, as we have seen, but this is not their sole purpose. They are also there to defend French national interests and support French citizens in each of the major regions of Africa. These twin missions reinforce the 'sub-regional' rather than continent-wide nature of French engagement with Africa, which helps to explain why French engagement with Africa has tended to concentrate on working with the regional brigades of the ASF, such as the ECOWAS standby force. In contrast, the UK has invested less heavily in ECOWAS, has a continent-wide perspective and interests, and is more enthusiastic about the AU.

Institutional Constraints

While both countries have stated their wish to move beyond their traditional spheres of influence on the continent, the fact remains that the UK has a depth of knowledge about Anglophone Africa and France a wealth of expertise about Francophone Africa that means that in practice they generally focus their engagement with the AU on the countries they know best. The result is often a *de facto* 'division of labour', in which France continues to take the political lead on certain countries and the UK on others. The creation of the AU has not overturned this fundamental dynamic, which makes active cooperation on joint projects difficult to achieve as their efforts are simply focused either in different policy areas or on different countries (personal communication, DfID official, London, 2010).

These differences in approach are also reflected in the work of the UK and French ambassadors in Addis Ababa. Both are 'double-hatted', in the sense that they are accredited to Ethiopia as well as the AU, and both also deal with regional issues, as neither the UK nor France has embassies in all the countries of the region. France has significant interests in Djibouti and good links with the Eritrean government, so that a key focus of the work of the French ambassador is regional issues in the Horn of Africa, insofar as they affect French interests in these countries. The French embassy in Addis Ababa has also been heavily involved in crisis management because of the many recent crises in its '*pré carré*'. This priority attached to engaging with regional political and military issues inevitably means that it has less time for engagement with the AU (personal communications, French, British and Danish officials, Addis Ababa, 2009). In contrast, the UK ambassador, for whom long-term capacity-building in cooperation with the AU

---

12   La Réunion is an overseas department of France and troops stationed there are therefore charged with defending French sovereign territory as well as providing support to the ASF. In addition, French forces numbering some 2,450 were deployed on specific operations in Chad, Côte d'Ivoire and CAR at the end of 2009. The Dakar base is currently scheduled to close (*Jeune Afrique*, 27 February 2010).

is a priority, can devote more time to this. The UK embassy in Addis had by 2009 increased to five the number of staff working on the AU, whereas the French embassy only had two such staff.

A more fundamental institutional constraint is that France has no equivalent to the UK's DfID. Not only this, but with the former Development directorate in the Foreign Affairs Ministry subsumed since 2009 within the much larger Globalisation directorate, French engagement with the AU is inevitably mainly political, diplomatic and military. This sidelining of development issues is reflected in the staff present in the embassy in Addis Ababa, whose focus is political and military issues and not long-term capacity-building and development work. In contrast, alongside its defence attaché and diplomatic personnel, the UK has a significant DfID presence within its embassy. As a result, the development agenda is to the forefront in British engagement with the AU. Moreover, with no obvious counterparts in the French embassy with whom they can cooperate on development issues, DfID staff inevitably look to other partners, notably the 'Nordic +' group, with which to work on such issues.

Civil Society and Resource Constraints

Parliamentary and civil society constraints also play a role in shaping UK and French policy towards the AU. The British government faces a powerful and vocal NGO lobby on development and humanitarian issues in Africa, which Labour governments in particular simply cannot afford, politically, to ignore. The French government, in contrast, while it has a prominent lobby for humanitarian intervention, led notably by Médecins sans Frontières and Médecins du Monde, does not face any significant NGO lobby in the development field (Cumming 2009).

Just as importantly, reductions in public expenditure, exacerbated by the 2008–9 global financial crisis, have limited the scope of cooperation. In the case of the UK, this prompted a review of priorities in Africa that led, for example, to cuts in the Conflict Prevention Pool budget and the downgrading of the strategic priority attached to west and central Africa (personal communications, British officials, London, 2009). These ongoing cutbacks, together with the fact that France has troops on the ground in Africa and has cultivated good links with ECOWAS, with the result that it is less dependent on the AU than the UK, accentuate the trend towards the sub-regional (French) versus continent-wide (UK) approach. Moreover, the French government's capacity to maintain troops on the ground in Africa is facilitated by the fact that such deployments are not subject to parliamentary approval in the way that they are in the UK.

Conclusion

In sum, no formal partnership has been established between the UK and France to work together with the AU. While the two countries now enjoy more constructive ties with regard to Africa than in the past, joint Anglo-French working vis-à-vis the AU remains limited in scope. To be sure, they have sought to deconflictualise their approaches to Africa and recognised that they benefit from working together with the AU on certain issues, as this enhances their influence in a context in which their traditional spheres of influence are increasingly under challenge from new external actors. It also plays well in the international arena for them to be seen to be working together to support the AU in managing and resolving crises. At the same time, both countries want to avoid direct military involvement, so it makes sense for them to train and support Africans to take greater responsibility for guaranteeing peace and security on the continent. In these respects the emergence of the AU as a credible interlocutor has opened up new opportunities for Anglo-French cooperation. Yet, at capital level and on the ground in Addis Ababa, there is no systematic effort at joint working. Rather, Anglo-French cooperation vis-à-vis the AU is often ad hoc, driven by personalities on the ground who see the benefits of cooperation or who happen to get on well, or the product of coinciding agendas that are not directly related to African policy *per se*.

The uneven nature of cooperation is also the product of the two countries' different forms and level of engagement with the AU. Although both the UK and France stand to benefit from enhanced cooperation, the neoclassical realist framework of analysis adopted here has helped to explain how divergent foreign policy priorities, institutional and resource constraints have placed limits on the extent of cooperation. Moreover, there is a dialectical relationship between decision-makers' perceptions and the policy choices that flow from them, on the one hand, and the institutional structures that deliver African policy on the other. The former shape the latter and the latter in turn feed back into and reinforce the perceptions and priorities of policy-makers. Both have played a role in shaping the contrasting French and British approaches to the AU. Thus, New Labour's commitment to a new form of internationalism that sought to be morally superior and go beyond the pursuit of naked self-interest in foreign policy shaped the UK government's more value-driven approach to the world's poorest continent between 1997 and 2010. Against this background development and poverty reduction, alongside peace and security, have been the key drivers of policy towards the AU, with DfID playing a lead role in setting the agenda for policy, whereas on the French side, political, diplomatic and military concerns are the key policy motors. This is reflected in the deployment of resources, both material and human, to support the AU: the UK is, through DfID, a significant development aid donor and takes the lead on the MDGs in the Africa-EU Strategic Partnership, whereas France takes the lead on military and security cooperation through the EURORECAMP programme. Cooperation is thus most advanced in the area in which the UK and France have a shared agenda – peace and security – but very limited in other fields.

Furthermore, the whole 'Saint-Malo II' process relating to cooperation in Africa and with the AU was in large part the product of factors that had nothing intrinsically to do with Africa or the AU, such as the coincidence of wider foreign policy objectives in relation to European policy. Personalities also played a key role with, for example, foreign ministers Cook and Védrine, who personally got on well, playing a key role at the outset and Sarkozy and Brown subsequently renewing the two countries' commitment to cooperate on Africa at the 2008 Franco-British summit. This raises the question: how compatible is the bilateral UK-French approach to cooperation with the AU with the 'bi-multi' approach to Africa in multilateral fora such as the EU and UNSC? The analysis presented here suggests that these processes of cooperation are compatible, at least on the security front, despite differences of emphasis between the UK and France. Crucially though, long-term sustainability also depends on continuing AU support for the process. Thus, if security continues to be the virtually exclusive focus for cooperation with the AU and this comes to be seen as driven, ultimately, by European security interests, this will undermine AU member states' support for the process and could lead to the AU withdrawing its support for the Africa-EU Strategic Partnership.

PART V
Other Models of Cooperation

Chapter 11

The New European Security Architecture: An Example of 'Messy Multilateralism'?

Marie V. Gibert[1]

The decision, by Britain and France, to cooperate and establish a joint approach to African issues took place within a particular framework, that of the European Union (EU) and the progressive establishment of a Common Foreign and Security Policy (CFSP). The EU's involvement in Africa's security field is new and gradually developing as security issues are finding their way onto European and international development agendas. This evolution has triggered many hopes that the EU might offer a multilateral alternative to the traditional bilateral relations that have continued to prevail between former colonies and colonial powers after decolonisation. This multilateralisation of the Euro-Africa relationship would also, it was thought, increase the originality and innovative capacities of the EU's presence in Africa through the incorporation of its member states' multiple historical experiences and political approaches to the continent and its development, governance and security issues, which are increasingly seen as closely interlinked. This chapter, based on fieldwork in West Africa's Guinea, Guinea-Bissau and Sierra Leone, will question these two assumptions and show how the EU's Africa security policy, which is still in the making, is especially sensitive to the many interests that shape and feed into it and is often the result of the way they are combined (or not).

The aim of this chapter is threefold: a) to underline and account for some of the inconsistencies of EU security policy in Africa, as well as some of the limits to Anglo-French cooperation in this field; b) to explain why this policy tends to follow international and European trends rather than to be decidedly proactive or innovative; and c) to examine the extent to which the UK and France still have some control over the emerging European security architecture in relation to Africa. Although member states' national interests often play a prominent role on a continent where bilateral relations between former colonies and

---

1   I wish to thank the Central Research Fund, University of London, for providing funding for fieldwork in West Africa, as well as the foundations Compagnia di San Paolo, Torino/Italy, Riksbankens Jubileumsfond, Stockholm/Sweden, and VolkswagenStiftung, Hanover/Germany for making further research in Europe possible. I am also most grateful to my international, European and West African interlocutors for their openness, insights, and time.

colonial powers continue to prevail, other interests are also at play. Four levels of European interests are therefore considered in the first part of this chapter: national, inter-institutional, intra-European and international. These interests do not coalesce naturally. They often compete or even conflict until forced, at times, to agglomerate and feed into a single European policy. Different models of (non-) combination of these interests will be suggested in the second part of the chapter, while the third part attempts to draw some conclusions concerning the nature of the EU's security policy in Africa and its capacity to meet the above expectations.

European Interests and Experiences in (West) Africa

Europe's security agenda in (West) Africa combines four levels of European foreign policy interests:

- National interests when each member state tries to retain as much independence for its own foreign policy and as much influence over the definition of the EU's security objectives as it can;
- Intra-institutional interests when the European Commission attempts to progressively regain or increase its political influence in Africa by extending its field of intervention to conflict prevention and post-conflict reforms, while the Council General Secretariat takes an interest in 'soft' security issues such as conflict prevention that naturally overlap with the Commission's development policies;
- Inter-European interests when agreeing on the EU's agenda in West Africa is an easy way of finding a consensus among member states and with the EU's institutions when they disagree on other issues;
- International interests when the EU aims at increasing its own security and at displaying a consistent, generous and powerful image on the international scene.

The study of the intermingling of these interests sheds an interesting light on the inconsistencies of the EU's security policy in West Africa and on how relations between member states and EU institutions inform and influence it.

Member States' National Interests in West Africa

A quick look at recent European interventions in West Africa proves how much European engagement in West Africa is still characterised by traditional bilateralism. The efforts at peace resolution made by Portugal and the Comunidade dos Países de Língua Portuguesa (CPLP – Community of Portuguese Language Countries) in Guinea-Bissau in 1998–9, the British intervention in Sierra Leone in 2000 and the French intervention in Côte d'Ivoire from 2002 were all driven by the usual partnership between the former colonial power and the former colony.

More than purely material or strategic interests in countries where European economic involvement is limited and which do not attract much international attention or media publicity, it seems that the former colonial power's presence, and its eagerness to remain the sole tutelary power in its former colonies, are motivated by a complex mixture of political experiences, heritages and cultures.

European member states have very different conceptions of their role in and relations with Africa. France has maintained particular relations with its only remaining sphere of influence and its involvement has more often than not attracted accusations of neo-colonialism. While France has recently shown that it was eager to multilateralise its relations with Africa, as with the Europeanisation of its RECAMP military capacity-building programme, it continues to emphasise its own special responsibility, experience and role on the continent.[2] France has, moreover, changed little the qualitative contents of its Africa policy. Aside from its traditional development assistance, cooperation with Africa has mainly consisted in providing military training and equipment, according to the old idea that well-equipped and trained troops can prevent popular revolts or rebel groups from crossing the borders and, to a lesser degree, that some measure of democratic awareness-raising within the army can prevent military coups (Giraud 2000, personal communication, French diplomat, Conakry 2005). It has maintained a tradition of military presence in the West African region – its two remaining military bases in Côte d'Ivoire and Senegal are due to close shortly, however – and still provides substantial assistance to the armies of West Africa's Francophone states.

The UK's involvement in Africa is generally described as very unequal and certainly not comparable to France's. Britain, however, stepped up its concern for and presence in Africa under Tony Blair's New Labour. The support given to Sierra Leone's post-conflict transition and the 2005 Commission for Africa are but two signs of this new form of involvement (Abrahamsen and Williams 2001; Cumming 2005; Gallagher 2009; Porteous 2008; Williams 2004). The latter – which seems to have produced grand announcements rather than tangible results – also underlines that the UK's involvement in Africa is heavily influenced by a concern for public and international approval and humanitarian ethics, more than by hard politics or a sense of historical responsibility such as France's (Porteous 2008: 143; Gallagher 2009). Britain also favours a holistic approach to security, which sees it as intrinsically linked to development and governance issues. Britain is thus involved, through its Africa Conflict Prevention Pool, in a very broad conflict prevention strategy that goes from military assistance to support to state reforms to economic development programmes.

Aside from these two major European member states and former colonial powers, many other European member states share an interest in Africa. Belgium and Portugal have remained involved in their former colonies, in spite of often

---

2 Accounts and analyses of France's relations with Africa abound and range from serious criticism to simple descriptions. See, in particular, Chafer (2001); Charbonneau (2008a, 2008b); Glaser and Smith (1994); Médard (1999, 2005); Verschave (2003).

confrontational decolonisation processes and limited means. They generally seem to share and support France's understanding of Europe's role in Africa and its distrust of the holistic approach adopted by the UK, which is considered too intrusive (Bagayoko 2007: 12, personal communication, Portuguese Institute for Support to Development official, Lisbon 2005). Having more limited political and financial means at their disposal, they may be more eager to see the EU become involved where they cannot; Belgium has thus been supportive of the EU's involvement in the Democratic Republic of Congo (DRC) and Portugal is said to have given the final push for the EU to launch a mission in support of security sector reform (SSR) in Guinea-Bissau, EUSSR Guinea-Bissau. Germany, which has embassies in a vast majority of African states, has been wary of accusations of neo-colonialism and of any kind of military engagement and has therefore maintained its foreign policy in Africa essentially at the level of strong development assistance and through the important network of its political foundations (Mair 1998; Engel 2005).[3]

European Inter-institutional Interests in West Africa

The EU is not made up of its member states only, however. A complex system of institutions now manages it, whose interests and relations also feed into the European policy-making process. The European Commission was the first to recommend that the EU develop a conflict prevention strategy for Africa, its oldest and preferred field for development policy-making (European Commission 1996). A first step towards the implementation of this policy was the creation, in 2000, of a Conflict Prevention and Crisis Management Unit within the Commission's directorate-general for external relations (DG Relex).[4] Meanwhile, the Council was developing the EU's Common Foreign and Security Policy (CFSP) and European Security and Defence Policy (ESDP). The number of ESDP missions led in Africa – 10 missions have been launched since 2003 – alone attests to the fact that the Council has found in the continent an ideal field of experimentation for its external intervention policies (Bagayoko 2004: 101). The General Secretariat of the Council has also significantly expanded its institutional capacities. It has an Africa task force, with a West Africa desk officer, whose work, however, remains essentially limited, for now, to following and maintaining the EU's relationship with the Economic Community of West African States (ECOWAS), to following the only ESDP mission in the region, EUSSR Guinea-Bissau, and, with the Situation Centre, to monitoring the region and the state of its security. The General

---

3   Germany nonetheless headed the EUFOR DRC mission that took place during the elections in 2006 in the Democratic Republic of Congo, but has so far refused to significantly take part in any other EU military involvement in Africa.

4   This unit has since been renamed 'Crisis Response and Peacebuilding Unit' and is part of the Directorate A – Crisis Platform, Policy Coordination in Common Foreign and Security Policy, of DG Relex.

Secretariat of the Council also has a number of institutions in charge of making, implementing and coordinating the ESDP, civilian as well as military, missions.[5]

In West Africa, the EU is however nearly exclusively represented by the Commission's delegations. These delegations, in spite of the deconcentration process initiated in 2000 that gives them more autonomy and influence over the programmes they support, are still far from being the equivalent of European embassies.[6] They lack the financial and material means and the training that would enable them to move from an essentially technical mission in development cooperation to a more diplomatic and political one. As long as their mission and capacities are not significantly transformed, the European delegations' role in political and security matters will very much depend on the determination of the chief of delegation to encourage his/her delegation to acquire capacities in political analysis or on a member state's expressed wish that a member of staff trained in political and security strategies be appointed to a delegation. Such was the case in the European delegations in Conakry (Guinea) and Dakar (Senegal) at the time of my fieldwork (2005–6). It was apparently less so in the European delegations in Freetown (Sierra Leone) or in Bissau (Guinea-Bissau), although a member of the European delegation's staff in Bissau had been asked to contribute to and monitor the government's progress towards an SSR programme. The importance of this human dimension – from the political sensitivity of chiefs of delegations to staff members' individual interest in acquiring a political understanding of the country – seems highly underestimated by the EU, which does not have any clear human resources policy in this regard.[7] In the absence of *ad hoc* decisions such as those taken in Conakry and Dakar, the capacity for political analysis and dialogue essentially rests with the member states' embassies. This partly accounts for the gap between the EU's determination to be involved in political matters and the approach, generally centred on traditional economic development assistance, often adopted.

The Council itself is represented by the EU presidency – i.e. a member state holding the presidency of the EU for six months – and a special representative for the Mano River region, at the time of writing Ambassador Harro Adt. The presidency's presence is most felt when it has a representation in the country, which can lead to some tensions between this representation, the other European national representations and the European delegation when the presidency

---

5   For a comprehensive overview of the EU's institutions and concepts of civilian and military crisis management, see Bagayoko and Gibert (2009).

6   'Sierra Leone is cited as a clear case where some additional problems have arisen due to "deconcentration", the latter making it difficult for diplomats planning overall strategy in Brussels to get information on what work the delegation had been supporting in situ' (Youngs 2006: 345).

7   This information comes from interviews with a policy officer, International Alert, London 2005 and officials at the European delegations, Conakry and Freetown 2005, Bissau and Dakar 2006.

does not follow traditional cooperation rules. As to the Presidency's special representative, his status remains hybrid. He is appointed by the presidency rather than by the High Representative of the Union for Foreign Affairs and Security Policy like his counterparts in the Great Lakes or in Sudan, for example. His mission is therefore extended every six months, and financed by his own state, i.e., Germany for Ambassador Adt (personal communications, West Africa desk officer, Swedish ministry of foreign affairs 2008, desk officer, West and Central Africa unit, German ministry of foreign affairs 2009).[8] Although he takes part in all international summits on the Mano River countries and most EU official visits to the region, exchanges with the in-country delegations, Brussels desk officers or member states seem to remain rather limited and are certainly not systematic. His effective contribution to the EU's West Africa policy is therefore questionable and in the near absence of other long-term Council instruments, the EC enjoys an implicit monopoly in the implementation of this policy. The Council's rather pale presence in West Africa, however, does not prevent it from progressively appropriating the field of security and experiencing some competition and tensions with the Commission. Relations between both institutions are characterised by an increasing number of cooperation problems, essentially to the detriment of the Commission which has considerable experience in the region but is deprived of most of the traditional political and diplomatic instruments essential for a consistent security policy.[9]

Intra-European Interests in West Africa

European multilateral interests in Africa, and in West Africa especially, can also seem quite contradictory. On the one hand, as was underlined in the previous section on national interests, former colonial powers tend to cling to their prerogatives and to consider that they have the monopoly of their former colonies' external – and sometimes even internal – affairs. On the other hand, Africa is not first on Europe's list of strategic focuses; political and economic partnerships with other parts of the world clearly come first. This apparent contradiction makes Africa an interesting experimentation field or laboratory for European consensus and innovative policies (Bagayoko 2005; Bayart 2004: 454). Bargaining strategies and common concerns over a West African state can be an opportunity for cooperation and dialogue between member states when they disagree on a more important issue elsewhere.

This type of intra-European interests in West Africa is certainly among the most difficult to study and grasp. Member state representatives are naturally

---

8   This information comes from email exchanges with a West Africa desk officer, Swedish ministry of foreign affairs 2008 and with a desk officer, West and Central Africa unit, German ministry of foreign affairs 2009.

9   For an analysis of the limits of the 'diplomaticisation' of the EU's role in West Africa, see Gibert (2010).

reluctant to admit to the bargaining game that can take place between them. This often happens implicitly, for example when Britain obtains funding or a political gesture for Sierra Leone, France will expect a similar concession on Côte d'Ivoire (personal communication, FCO desk officer for West Africa, London 2005). This method of policy-making, which rests on member states' bargaining strategies and readiness to compromise, has often been criticised as systematically leading to the 'lowest common denominator'. Stephan Keukeleire however underlines that while an external observer may be tempted to think that the EU has failed as a diplomatic actor on a particular issue, from an intra-European point of view, the EU may have performed well and made a step forward in its 'internal diplomacy', for instance when a member state was persuaded not to act alone and implicitly accept the common European decision (Keukeleire 2003). The EU's relations with Guinea are a case in point, where the EU adopted a harsh position – based on strict conditions of democratisation and liberalisation of the media – with which France disagreed, considering that conditionality was far from being the ideal path to good governance and political stability in Guinea (personal communication, French diplomat, Conakry 2005). But the international image of the EU may suffer from these compromises. They certainly undermine the EU's consistency at the international level and the need to find a compromise often pre-empts any understanding and recognition of African partners' needs and interests.

Europe's International Interests in West Africa

Europe as a whole, finally, also has its own international security concerns, which are at times quite similar to those of other Western powers. This notion of international security, as well as the role Europe intends to play in securing it, are mentioned in the European Security Strategy. Regional conflicts, state failure, terrorism and organised crime are quoted as key threats to Europe's security and are also among real or suspected threats to (West) Africa's security (Council of the European Union 2003). The struggle against these 'public bads' officially justifies and even renders necessary an efficient European security strategy in (West) Africa (Fearon and Laitin 2004; Gibert 2009). This 'enlightened self-interest' serves to justify Western interference in the developing world's affairs. In other words, not only is such interference seen as the moral duty of Western states, but it will also contribute to maintaining international security (Duffield 2007: 2).

Beyond these Realpolitik perspectives, defining a policy for West Africa also represents a means to assert the EU's own identity and values. Europe's traditional influence in (West) Africa and its position as first donor provides the EU with an opportunity to project its influence and further define its own international identity. In this, it also responds to civil society pressure. A number of lobby-type NGOs and think tanks insist on Europe's specific responsibility and comparative advantage, as the most integrated regional organisation in the world, and call for a strong and consistent, political and security EU involvement in Africa.[10] In abiding by these demands, the EU shows that it carefully listens to its civil society and that it shares their moral concerns.

The Making of Europe's Security Agenda(s) in (West) Africa

The above description of the different categories of interests that underlie the EU's agenda in (West) Africa suggests that its making is everything but straightforward and can be the result of different combinations, depending on which interests and actors prevail. The analysis of the interactions that make Europe's agenda in West Africa leads to the definition of three different cases: competition between member states and between member states and the EU institutions; implicit complementarity when the EU institutions and member states adapt their policies one to another without any explicit coordination taking place; and the 'leading nation' configuration when one member state's involvement in a third country is later followed by other member states and the EU institutions once they are convinced of its utility. Studying these cases suggests that the making of the EU's agenda in West Africa tends to be a highly experimental process that essentially evolves by trial and error.

When Competition Dominates

As already underlined, traditional bilateralism often seems to dominate Euro-(West) African relations. This is confirmed by the tensions that arise when one European power tries to intervene in the affairs of another's *protégé*. Important tensions opposed France and Britain over Sierra Leone in 2000 when France and other European states rejected the British request for military assistance under the pretext that it was a 'British problem', while Britain resented France's support to Liberian President Charles Taylor who was directly involved in the Sierra Leonean conflict (Williams 2004: 124).

Competition and tensions in times of peace can also be high, even when it comes to what seem petty matters. In Bissau, France and Portugal seem much keener to win the French vs. Portuguese language race than to add up and coordinate their ideas and efforts. One of my Portuguese interviewees explained how he had been unable to convince the French to get their cultural centres to propose a common cinema programme – the French simply refused the Portuguese proposal to show their films with Portuguese subtitles, even in a Portuguese-speaking country (personal communication, Portuguese diplomat, Bissau 2006).

---

10   Among these are Saferworld (www.saferworld.org.uk), International Alert (www. international-alert.org) and the (International) Crisis Group (www.crisisgroup.org). See their websites as well as Crisis Group (2005), Saferworld and International Alert (2005).

Examples of outright competition between member states and the Commission are more difficult to find and ascertain, but projects led jointly by the EC and a member state are likewise quite rare. Such projects, where the EC, thanks to its significant funds, is clearly the main donor while a member state provides complementary support, are not favoured by member states since they are more likely to increase the EC's visibility than their own and force member states to comply with tight EC rules (personal communication, European delegation official, Bissau 2006). Member states are however fully aware of the extent of the Commission's financial resources and do not hesitate to use their political weight, or to underline their contribution to the European Development Fund (EDF), or their better understanding of their former colonies' needs, to influence the Commission's agenda and encourage it to implement a costly programme in a specific country (personal communication, French diplomat, Conakry 2005). While the deconcentration process has given European delegations a measure of autonomy, member states clearly still retain the upper hand over the bigger programmes and general directions.

It seems unlikely that this state of things will change any time soon. A clear sign is some member states' – and especially former colonial powers' – determination to continue sending Africa regional directors from their capital cities to attend the Council's Africa working group rather than have Africa specialists in Brussels, where they could work together and with the EU institutions on a day-to-day basis. This obviously limits the input of smaller EU member states, which do not always have the means to send out an Africa expert to every Africa working group meeting, and maintains much of the initiative in a small number of capital cities (personal communication, Africa-Caribbean-Pacific specialists, British and French permanent representations to the EU, Brussels 2007). France's lack of enthusiasm for a full Europeanisation of its Africa policies is also visible in its apparently limited interest in placing its own Africa specialists within the EU institutions and, when they are appointed willy-nilly, to support them. One of my French interviewees at the Council General Secretariat deplored that France, contrary to Britain, seemed incapable of – and little interested in – placing its people in intermediary positions, where the small but significant policy details are conceived and heavily influenced.[11]

Finally, as was already briefly mentioned, competition can also characterise the parallel agendas of the Council and Commission in Africa. A recent case has opposed the Council and the Commission before the Court of Justice of the European Communities over which institution was in charge of supporting ECOWAS in the framework of the Moratorium on Small Arms and Light Weapons

---

11 Personal communication, member of the Africa Unit, General Secretariat of the Council of the EU, Brussels 2008. A number of informal conversations and my own observations seemed to indicate, however, that this was much less true of the EU Military Staff, where France seems to have been particularly eager to place its people, and has apparently done so skilfully.

(SALW). While the Court eventually agreed with the Commission, its ruling also leaves a great deal to interpretation as the division of labour depends on whether security elements contribute to fulfilling the social and economic objectives of a development cooperation policy – in which case they should be part of the development agenda implemented by the Commission – or whether they pursue CFSP objectives – and are therefore part of the CFSP and implemented by the Council General Secretariat. The current holistic approach to development thus allows both the Commission and the Council to engage in security policy-making and, in so doing, may multiply the chances of institutional overlaps and competition between the two institutions (Court of Justice of the European Communities 2008).

Implicit Complementarity Rather than Explicit Coordination

The intergovernmental character of the EU has triggered hopes that it would be able to coordinate the external relations of its member states and avoid overlaps and contradictions between these. In (West) Africa, however, the EU tends to be an additional international actor and donor, although certainly not the least. In response to the many criticisms underlining the lack of coordination between development actors, coordination meetings are now numerous, to the extent that some members consider they cannot attend all meetings any more and note that they have not yet managed to impose coordination during the conception – i.e. before the implementation – of development programmes (personal communications, British diplomat, Conakry, UNDP official, Freetown 2005). This is in great part due to the fact that the conception of these programmes, as was previously underlined, essentially takes place in Western capital cities. The EC and its member states do not seem to escape this rule. The European head of delegation attends donor coordination meetings alongside member state representatives but does not exchange with them more information on the EC's development programmes or try to coordinate more than with other members of the international community.

This absence of explicit coordination does not necessarily entail overlaps, however. The EU institutions tend to adapt their strategy to that of other actors and to cover what they consider crucial and others cannot or will not do. A case in point is the EU's current involvement in Guinea-Bissau. It should be underlined that there is a lack of obvious European national leadership in Guinea-Bissau – a major difference with Guinea and Sierra Leone, where France and Britain have been keen and able to maintain their influence. Portuguese diplomats themselves admit that their country has neither the political power nor the financial means to assist Guinea-Bissau in its post-conflict transition efforts (personal communications, Portuguese diplomats, Bissau 2006). Because of this and the EU's increasing willingness to deal with security and state-reform issues, the European delegation in Bissau has been playing a more political role than its counterparts in Guinea and Sierra Leone. It has, in particular, supported the state's reform efforts in sectors such as the rule of law, public administration and security under the 9th EDF (2001–08) and through the instrument for stability managed by DG Relex. This new EC involvement is particularly interesting and in line with its clear determination to provide support where no other donor is ready or has the means to do so. The main risk is that the Commission may increasingly be seen as a 'gap-plugger' more than as an original and proactive actor, but this relative 'contents flexibility' is appreciated both by European member states and their West African partners.

The EU's overall involvement, however, also depends on the Council's – i.e. the member states' – readiness to complete this EC involvement with an ESDP operation that is better able to manage the military dimension, in particular, of post-conflict or conflict prevention reforms. Such complementarity is visible in the ESDP mission launched in 2008 in Guinea-Bissau, EUSSR Guinea-Bissau. The delay – nearly three years – between the initial idea and the effective launch of the mission certainly contributed to the participation, in an apparently consensual manner, of very different EU actors in the mission's preparation. The British Ministry of Defence led two assessment missions in 2005 and 2006, followed by two joint Council and Commission preparatory missions in 2007, while the Portuguese presidency is said to have given the final push, during its presidency of the EU in the second half of 2007, by underlining the urgency of an SSR reform in a state threatened by excessive but weak security forces and the increasing visibility of drug-trafficking networks. Missions such as EUSSR Guinea-Bissau also provide a good example of the potential complementarity between the EU institutions as they make possible an easy division of labour between Council and Commission – the former providing for short-term, more largely staffed missions and the latter for a longer-term preparation and follow-up – in a field, which they now seem resigned to share.

A 'Leading Nation' Concept?

The idea of a 'framework' – or leading – nation, which guided the Artemis Operation in the DRC, seems to gain momentum and can be applied here to further analyse Europe's engagement in security issues in (West) Africa.[12] This consists in one European member state, which has specific interests in a country, giving the lead and proposing new cooperation projects, while the others choose to follow or not.

In West Africa, the 'framework nation' configuration is perhaps most visible at the regional level, where other European member states may also have their say. West African states have for example agreed to establish three military training centres in order to offer a common training to their troops. Germany was the first

---

12   France played the role of the 'framework nation', was in charge of the operational planning and of the field command of the mission and provided the bulk of the ground troops. Other European member states – among them Britain, Belgium, Sweden and Germany – as well as non-European states – Canada, Brazil and South Africa – provided troops, air or logistical support, or equipment (Bagayoko 2004).

to support the foundation of the Kofi Annan International Peace Training Centre (KAIPTC) in Ghana and was followed by Denmark, France, Italy, the Netherlands, Spain, the UK and the EU, which also agreed to support two other training centres in Mali and Nigeria. As already underlined, the EU has also Europeanised France's RECAMP and, through the new European capacity-building programme, is supporting the African Union's project to create five regional standby forces. The Europeanisation of member states' involvement in Africa thus seems to be accompanying a (West) Africanisation of peacekeeping forces and training.

Although these efforts to support collectively capacity-building programmes in West Africa are still tentative, they indicate that European member states closely monitor their co-members' policies in the region and are sometimes ready to follow if they feel convinced by the approach. Trends in international relations and development programmes also inspire a natural convergence in a field where it is important to be visible and sufficiently reactive. France's official reflection, visible in its policy papers and publications, on themes such as post-conflict reconstruction, fragile states and security sector reform, indicate that in spite of some initial reluctance and scepticism, it is ready to yield to global trends and concepts established and implemented in great part by the UK in Africa (Haut Conseil à la Coopération Internationale 2005, Châtaigner and Magro 2007, Ministère des affaires étrangères 2008). To what extent this process of convergence behind a leading nation is due to European integration is however a matter of debate and is certainly impossible to measure, as the coordination and agenda-setting role of the World Bank, the International Monetary Fund (IMF) and United Nations (UN) agencies is admittedly great.[13] There are, moreover, limits to member states' readiness to Europeanise their foreign policies. They may have decided to Europeanise their military training programmes in Africa, but they are much less willing to do so, as we have seen, when it comes to the more political aspects of their relations with African states. The convergence of member states' Africa policies has essentially been, so far, a Europeanisation *à la carte*.

---

13   European member states' representatives like to say that they follow the EU lead, and EU delegates that they respect UN decisions. UN agencies and institutions are however often led and staffed by Europeans, so that some of my West African interlocutors, when asked about Europe's role in their region, underlined that the World Bank and the IMF should also be considered and that Europe seemed to be behind most of the international community's decisions in West Africa (personal communications, Portuguese Institute for Support to Development desk officer, Lisbon, Guinean ministry of cooperation official, Conakry, regional NGO director, Freetown 2005).

The European Union in (West) Africa:
The Co-Existence of Bi- and Multilateralism

The above section underlines how inductive the making of the European Union's agenda in West Africa can be. It evolves by trial and error, follows individual member states' or other international actors' lead, or fills a gap. It is an essentially reactive attitude, which has been more than once criticised for its lack of inventiveness (Gibb 2000). What does this tell us about the evolution of the EU's role in (West) Africa? Is it increasingly acting as a coordinator of European foreign policies in the region? Will the EU multilateral framework replace, one day, the traditional bilateral relations that have linked the former colonial powers and colonies?

The structural organisation of the EU partly explains why the EU often provokes a feeling of confusion among its partners in West Africa even though it is the region's first donor and a major political partner. The EU is, as shown throughout this chapter, a strange animal. Its hybrid, intergovernmental and supranational nature and the many, at times competing, interests that underlie its policies make it a complex actor that others generally find both fascinating and difficult to grasp. Beyond these institutional complexities, the EU's long history of involvement exclusively in development politics in Africa and the fact that the Commission, a notoriously bureaucratic institution, is the dominant – often unique – actor on the continent, also explain the lack of visibility and clarity of the EU's role in West Africa. National ministry staff, local NGOs and even European delegations' staff themselves are weary of the EU's heavy bureaucracy and unending applications for funding (personal communications, Guinean ministry of cooperation official, Conakry, European delegation official, Freetown 2005). Most decisions are, moreover, still taken in Brussels or in European capitals and those countries that are ill-represented in Europe, like Guinea, may face harsher conditions than other, better-supported countries (personal communication, European diplomat, Conakry 2005).

In spite of the reservations expressed by many external observers or even by its own staff, the EU continues to insist on the contribution it can make to Africa's stability and on its added value, derived from its member states' varied experience and from the impressive range of instruments – military and civilian, economic and political – that it can mobilise and fields it can intervene in. This approach, it seems, is as much driven by a sincere adoption of the current holistic approach to development as by the competition between member states and EU institutions described in this chapter. Bargaining over the EU's new strategies and instruments is indeed a way for member states and EU institutions alike to influence these and defend their own interests, values and position (Bagayoko and Gibert 2009). When the Commission published its Communication on conflicts in Africa in 1996, it clearly sought to involve itself in a new field at a time when its development strategies in Africa were facing heavy criticism. Similarly, France's determination to involve the EU in the field of military capacity-building in Africa and to Europeanise RECAMP comes at a time when its Africa policy is increasingly questioned and criticised. While the complexity of the EU thus accounts for the nature of its policies and may partly support its claim that it can intervene in a broad range of fields, it also questions the theoretical bases and consistency of these policies.

The EU's policies in (West) Africa seem to be more about making the EU than about responding to (West) Africa's needs or even strengthening the EU's relations with the region, even if the latter objectives may also play a part and are not necessarily antagonistic with the EU's interest in its own political development. EUSSR Guinea-Bissau is a good case in point; it is a cheap and potentially efficient compromise between member states at a time of controversy over another ESDP mission, EUFOR Chad/CAR, and provides room for the Commission and the Council to work together. While the need for SSR in Guinea-Bissau has been documented at length and has achieved international consensus, the time that elapsed between the original idea of an ESDP mission and its effective implementation, and the size, budget and mandate of EUSSR Guinea-Bissau, which are very limited indeed, seem to have more to do with the EU's agenda at the time the decision was made than with a precise assessment of Guinea-Bissau's needs. Another example of this pre-emption of the EU's own (identity)-making over that of its African partners is to be found in the EU's support to regional integration.

Bruno Charbonneau briefly suggests, in an article about French and EU military interventions in Africa, that 'the French colonial tradition of military intervention is not necessarily incompatible with a multilateral approach' (Charbonneau 2008a: 293). This observation can be taken a little further. Not only are the bilateral and multilateral relations between Europe and Africa not incompatible, but they may also co-exist and strengthen each other for some more years to come. The EU's involvement, as we have seen, serves in many ways to re-legitimise Europe's presence in Africa, when some member states, like France, are the object of increasing criticism, both in academic circles and among African political leaders. By taking over some of France's Africa policies, such as RECAMP, the EU justifies France's relations with Africa and gives it an opportunity to maintain its presence in other, non-Europeanised fields. Meanwhile, the former colonial powers' interest in Africa justifies the EU institutions' involvement and the expansion of their policies on the continent. The EU's multilateral framework does not, therefore, seem about to replace the multiple European bilateral foreign policies. This is clearly visible in the field, where the EC is an additional international actor, rather than one that coordinates the different European positions. The multilateralisation, or Europeanisation, of some specific and often narrow policy fields in effect justifies the existence of both multilateral and bilateral frameworks and is not necessarily a step towards the full Europeanisation of Europe's Africa policies.

This is not to say that the different levels of policy-making remain isolated and foreign to each other. There is, on the contrary, a constant movement of mutual influencing, which often occurs in an informal way, between national and European institutions and their staff. Niagalé Bagayoko underlines this in her analysis of the EU's security policy in Africa, best understood with a multi-level governance model which emphasises the co-existence of different levels of governance with no perspective of one replacing the other. There is a constant adaptation of national policies to the European framework, i.e. while member states try to export their own approaches and policies to the European level, they do so once they have adapted them to European standards (Bagayoko 2009: 197–8). The existence of different, separate levels of governance when it comes to Europe's Africa policy must not be taken to mean the absence of theoretical convergence. This convergence, however, also occurs, as was underlined, at the international level, between the major international organisations in charge of defining and implementing the development agenda – the UN agencies and Bretton Woods institutions, in particular – and donor governments. In this context, it is difficult for the EU to innovate and express the theoretical originality that could be expected as a result of Europe's long experience with Africa's politics. The imperatives of European policy-making – the need to reconcile the above-mentioned intra-institutional, inter-European and international interests – therefore pre-empt Europe's potential understanding of its African partners' political realities and its capacity to offer tailor-made, as opposed to one-size-fits-all, policies.

Conclusion

It was not the object of this chapter to comment in detail on the contents of the EU's security policy in West Africa, the goal being rather to observe the making of this policy. It is obvious, however, that the nature of the policy-making process has a noticeable influence on the contents of the policy itself. The groping and sometimes inconsistent nature of the EU's security agenda, as well as its tendency to follow international and European trends rather than being proactive or innovative, are in fact less surprising when one considers the numerous and complex interests that feed into the policy-making process and the different methods of combination of these interests. The EU institutions' security strategy in (West) Africa is essentially reactive. They fill the gaps left by European member states and other international actors through an implicit multilateral complementarity logic. The nature of the relations between member states, the Commission and the Council General Secretariat do not simplify matters and while the Commission at times attempts to take matters into its hands as in Guinea-Bissau, its role is often limited to what member states, and especially former colonial powers, let it do or want it to do. The fact that the EU finds in Africa an ideal experimentation field also points to the fact that its policies on the continent may be essentially about making the EU and this chapter has indeed tended to show that the EU's security policies in West Africa seem more preoccupied with advancing the 'Europeanisation' of Europe's foreign and security policies than about responding to West Africa's security needs or developing more political or diplomatic relations with the region, which remain essentially confined to the field of development policies and aid.

There is, moreover, little prospect of a replacement of the traditional bilateral system that has prevailed for so long by a multilateral system – under EU leadership – or by a 'bi-multi' system – led by Britain and France. It seems much more likely that the different levels of (non-)cooperation will continue to co-exist, according to actors' interests in the different fields of Euro-Africa security cooperation, leading to a form of 'messy multilateralism' rather than any new 'model' of cooperation. While there are thus clear signs of 'Europeanisation' in SSR and military capacity-building, other fields, such as direct interventions in Africa's conflicts or everyday political relations with African partners, clearly remain in the remit of member states and more particularly of the former colonial powers. The latter skilfully resist any attempt to improve coordination at the European level and obviously consider it in their interest to retain much of the decision-making process in their capitals. This is possible, in spite of the increasing pressure exercised by the Brussels institutions and other member states, because of the effective multilateralisation of a small number of narrow fields. By allowing and promoting cooperation in these fields, Britain and, more importantly, France have regained some legitimacy in Africa and are able to maintain much of their bilateral relations with Africa.

Chapter 12

Sino-African Relations and the Implications for the EU's 'Partnership' with Africa

Ian Taylor

For most sub-Saharan African (SSA) countries, the EU remains the main trading partner and the EU absorbs around 85 per cent of Africa's agricultural exports and 75 per cent of SSA's overall trade (Commission of the European Communities 2008: 3). Even with the rise of interest in the continent by the United States, China and India (the latter two eagerly seized upon in some quarters as finally offering up the chance to move on from Europe), the EU continues to be Africa's key partner and a major source of developmental assistance. The EU is thus a most important factor in Africa's international relations and will remain so for at least the short- to medium-term. In terms of sheer power projection, despite all the brouhaha about China's sudden rise in Africa, the EU (or individual constituent members) remains the key influence in virtually all countries in Africa.

This chapter focuses on the two 'partnerships' which will have the greatest impact on Africa in the future – that of the European Union and that of China. The first is the EU-Africa partnership, which is characterised by only limited policy coherence and by an increasingly uneven relationship, marked by aid conditionalities and distorted by European agricultural policies. The 'partnership' with China, is characterised by relative institutional coherence through the Forum on China-Africa Cooperation (FOCAC) but is also uneven and problematic. The chapter will investigate whether the rise of China in Africa has led to tension and rivalry with the EU, as each strives to maintain or increase its share of Africa's oil and mineral wealth? How have the EU and its major member states, notably the UK and France, with interests in Africa viewed the growing Chinese presence and activism in Africa? How far does the EU perceive China as a competitor in Africa? How far does China consider the EU as a rival?

There are of course significant domestic problems facing any 'partnership' with Africa, be it European or Chinese. The focus of this chapter is neither security matters nor the promotion of democracy *per se*, which has attracted attention given that the EU is perceived as attaching conditions to its aid to Africa whilst China is not. Rather, the issue of the actual extant political economy and dominant political cultures across Africa and how this may affect any putative Sino-EU partnership in Africa is addressed. It has been claimed that the emergence of Chinese actors in

Africa threatens to make much of the EU's policy on governance largely irrelevant. However, it is acknowledged that in the long term Beijing's policy interests are not served by chaotically ruled states. It is here that convergence between the EU and China on governance issues in Africa is a possibility.

Governance as Partnership

In its promotion of 'good governance', one commentary has averred that 'The EU tends to export to third countries the EU model of political and economic development based upon economic liberalisation and the rules of [the] free market, democratic norms and practices, and human rights protection' (Panebianco and Rossi 2004: 6). Commitments to promote democratic principles, the rule of law and human rights are explicitly set out in the EU Treaty (Articles 6 and 11). What is remarkable about this venture is that it is based on the European experience, which is then extrapolated and exported as *universal*. In August 2006, the European Commission launched a new communiqué on *Governance in the European Consensus on Development – Towards a harmonised approach within the European Union*. In paragraph 13 of the document, this reaffirmed that 'development is a central goal by itself, and that sustainable development includes good governance, human rights and political, economic, social and environmental aspects' (Council of the European Union 2005). Among the common values avowed by the declaration was the following: 'EU partnership and dialogue with third countries will promote common values of: respect for human rights, fundamental freedoms, peace, democracy, good governance, gender equality, the rule of law, solidarity and justice'.

Notably, the EU officially presents itself as a qualitatively distinct actor in global affairs (see Söderbaum and van Langenhove 2007). Indeed, [t]he underlying assumption of this self-perception is that the EU, in its global action, follows values and approaches that are somehow different from those of nation states – especially the US, but also individual EU member states – which are mainly (according to neoclassical realists) or exclusively (in the view of most other variants of realism) concerned with their national interests. In the same vein the EU would also be different from international institutions such as the IMF or the World Bank, and from regional organisations, such as Mercosur (South America's premier trading bloc), which are chiefly concerned with economic policies (Fioramonti and Poletti 2008: 167).

According to Hurt (2004), a number of different approaches to the relationship between the EU and SSA exist. The officially sanctioned EU view springs from liberalism and seeks to advance the notion that the relationship is based on mutually beneficial terms grounded in cooperation and interdependence (see Gruhn 1976; Zartman 1976). This in itself is derivative of liberal understandings vis-à-vis integration (Chivvis 2003). From this viewpoint, exploitative relations are absent and, rather, Africa's development is dependent upon greater integration into the global economy, which the EU can help facilitate, on mutually advantageous conditions for both parties. As the EU's *Strategy for Africa* put it:

> The purpose of the EU's action is to work in partnership with the nations of Africa to promote peace and prosperity for all their citizens ... The Strategy will further reinforce the basic principles that govern this relationship, most prominently *equality*, *partnership and ownership* ... Key to the success of the partnership will be its ability to cement the bonds between the two continents beyond the formal political and economic interaction ... objectives should be supplemented, especially for those countries closer to the EU, by support for economic integration and political cooperation with the EU. Taken together, these measures constitute the EU's common, comprehensive and coherent response to Africa's development challenges (European Commission 2005: 3).

A radically different interpretation of the EU's relationship with SSA emerges from Dependency Theory, a critique particularly strong in the 1970s and early 1980s (see Galtung 1976). This approach sees the relationship as being emblematic of typical core-periphery relations and springing from the historical colonial relationship between Europe and Africa – a process that some authors see as having left a legacy of underdevelopment on the African continent (Rodney 1982). In short, the colonisation process resulted in Africa's economies being oriented more towards the needs of European capital than the requirements of the local. This was the quintessential definition of dependency. Rather than picture an ahistorical 'level playing field', as favoured by liberalism, whereby each social formation needed to simply go through the ideal-type stages of growth, Dependency Theory rather asserted that Europe had an advantage from the start in that they never had to – at least in modern times – experience colonial rule, nor had to attempt to integrate themselves into a global economy already replete with richer and more powerful competitors. Comparing then the experiences of Europe and Africa, certainly at the early stages of development, was a futile exercise. Critically, Dependency Theory also pointed out that the relationships of dependency crafted during the Age of Expansionism by the European metropoles were continued long after 'official' rule by the colonisers was over. This was recognised early on by some African elites – Nkrumah (1965) being a famous example.

According to Dependency theorists, only by recognising this can a true appreciation of Europe-Africa relations be realised. Such a position asserts that the main obstacles to real autonomous development were not internal (such as Rostow's caricature of 'traditional' societies, or the *Economist's* innate 'African culture'), but were rather external in origin and contingently bound up with the historical experiences of the spread of international capitalism (Frank 1967, 1975). As Hurt (2004) notes, this approach has placed particular emphasis on agreements such as the Lomé Convention and how this sustained Africa's role as a primary commodity exporter to Europe through the System for the Stabilisation of Export Earnings (STABEX) and the Stabilisation Scheme for Mineral

Products (SYSMIN). On the other hand, core-periphery ties were cemented by the failure to permit duty-free access for manufactured products from Africa, preventing industrialisation. While this approach is helpful in understanding key characteristics of the global capitalist system and how Africa was (unequally) inserted into the world economy, its structuralism serves to deny Africa of any agency and, not least, reduces African elites to the status of willing dupes, something which the evidence of extraversion does not support.

Indeed, while development cooperation itself should be seen as encapsulating particular political and economic relationships, rather than constituting some kind of 'apolitical' or 'technical' assistance (Brown 2000: 368), it should not be seen as a one-way street of neo-colonial impositions. The dialectical role between political and economic elites *on both sides* shapes the relationship. While structures are vital to comprehend, the agency of actors within such structures is equally important. Consequently, the role of resources (political and economic) that emanated from the relationship with Europe was invariably utilised by extant elites for their own purposes (primarily regime survival) and often ran counter to the expressed aims of the Europeans when disbursing such material. As Brown (2000: 371) notes, 'for particular regimes, power lay in the clientelist links and the patronage that occupation of state positions made possible, and access to external resource flows (from both aid and trade) were a major element in this'. Ignoring the extraversion strategies of African elites when discussing EU-SSA ties thus makes little sense.

The Problematic Partners

Obviously, Africa's regeneration was not – and never has been – simply a question of advancing 'good leadership' or 'good government'; the structural impediments to African trade are equally important and here, the European Union is highly culpable, as will be detailed below. Certainly, a voluntarist approach to Africa's development or the neglect of the nature of the continent's relationships within the international system, are central to any evaluation. But, it might be averred that without the construction of transparent and accountable government, ambitious economic plans within the context of its own definitions and pronouncements are profoundly compromised from the start.

According to the Nigerian political scientist Claude Ake, 'we are never going to understand the current crisis in Africa ... as long as we continue to think of it as an economic crisis' (Ake 1991: 316). Indeed, one of the fundamental problems in large parts of post-colonial Africa is that the ruling classes lack hegemony in the Gramscian sense. The early years of nationalism may have been an attempt to build a hegemonic project, but this quickly collapsed into autocracy and failure. Consequently, the ethico-political aspect, which in a hegemonic project serves to assist in building economic configurations but also supplies a justifying and legitimising aspect, is lacking across Africa. As a result, the ruling classes' domination and their modalities of governance are expressed through both the threat and actual use of violence *and* the immediate disbursal of material benefits to supporters in neo-patrimonial regimes (Bratton and van de Walle 1994). Without these twin strategies – both inimical to long-term development and stability – the African ruling elites cannot rule. 'The struggle for power has become so intense and so absorbing that it has overshadowed everything else, including the pursuit of development' (Ake 1991: 318). Non-hegemonic rule often leads to despotism and unpredictability – the latter of course being anathema to the construction of capitalism.

The non-hegemonic nature of much of Africa's ruling elites means that the relative autonomy of the state, which would facilitate the types of reforms demanded by the EU, make autocracy redundant and create the soil in which liberal democracy might be nurtured, is not present. Indeed, the modern state that donors and external actors assume or demand is dependent upon the intrinsically bourgeois liberal distinction between the public and the private, which then grants space for politics to take on an identity that is seen as different from economics. Yet the very kernel of politics in large parts of Africa is the absolute conflation of any separation between the public and the private. Indeed, the formal state is the main battleground through which both political and economic domination can be achieved – a domination that is exercised with no concern over its effect on those upon whom this supremacy is visited.

Central to this milieu is the fact that class power in most parts of Africa is fundamentally dependent upon state power and capturing the state – or at least being linked favourably to those within the state – is an essential precondition for acquisition and self-enrichment. 'The absence of a hegemonic bourgeoisie, grounded in a solid and independent economic base and successfully engaged in a private accumulation of capital, has transformed politics into material struggle' (Fatton 1988: 36). As a result, the bourgeoisie in Africa is generally weak and nascent. This translates into an absence of bourgeois hegemony, resulting in autocracy and economic irrationality. 'Political instability is ... rooted in the extreme politicisation of the state as an organ to be monopolised for absolute power and accelerated economic advancement' (ibid.: 35). Instead of a stable hegemonic project that binds different levels of society together, what we have in much of Africa is an intrinsically *unstable* personalised system of domination. Absolutism reigns and power is maintained through patrimonial power by means of the illegal commandeering of state resources. Corruption, not hegemonic rule, is the cement that binds the system together and links the patron and his predatory ruling class together.

Because the EU's own conception of 'good governance' is technocratic and apolitical the personalisation of political power – either at the low or high social levels – which stakes out well-defined roles within most African polities, is barely understood by the EU's own officers, even in the field. When and where the EU speaks regarding 'governance' this is in a technical sense and misses the *political* dimensions and problems. Indeed, the EU's own prescriptions for designing 'good governance' structures draws upon the international financial institutions 'broadly agreed best international practices of economic management' (International Monetary Fund 1997: 2).

The turn to 'good governance' by the EU can be related to both the dominance of technocratic neo-liberal thinking and a refusal to acknowledge that European policies have not worked in Africa to promote development. Certainly, the refusal by Brussels to acknowledge that policies have not worked is central to the emergence of the 'good governance' discourse within the EU's development rhetoric. Instead of questioning their own prescriptions, European elites have sought to advance 'good governance' as a necessary precondition for reforms to *finally* work, deftly ignoring the elephants in the room – gross levels of subsidisation to Europe's farmers and the effective blocking of much of Africa's export potential by EU policies *and* the reality of neo-patrimonial rule (cheerily supported by key EU states such as France and the United Kingdom). Indeed, when discussing the EU's 'fight against corruption' we should acknowledge that the rigour with which individual European states hold African peers to account is highly context-specific and hostage to the vagaries of national interests and raw economic and political projection.

The turn to 'good governance' itself reflects the conviction amongst major global institutions that neo-liberalism is the only way forward and that what has been wrong is not the content of various assistance programmes, but rather their implementation and wider institutional setting in the borrowing states. This thinking emerged from the institutional culture and specifically the hegemony of narrow-minded economists. As Weaver notes regarding the World Bank, 'governance and anticorruption issues ran head-first into the economistic, technocratic, and apolitical features of the Bank's intellectual culture' (Weaver 2008: 115). After all, there existed 'the dominance of neo-classically trained economists within the Bank ... [many] recruited from academia with little or no experience in government and with little interest in or appreciation of noneconomic factors affecting development' (ibid.: 102).

The result, Fatton notes (1999: 4), has been that policy advice is 'based on a series of deeply flawed assumptions' which:

> posit that development can be 'private-driven,' and that African bourgeoisies can suddenly have a change of heart and become the engine of the take-off, whereas these bourgeoisies have never shown any commitment to sustained productive investment. They posit that privatisation leads necessarily to rational economic decisions and that private agents are inherently more virtuous and efficient than public servants, whereas revenues derived from the sale of state assets can be stolen and squandered, and private agents are bent on defending their own selfish interests rather than the collective good. They posit that democratic governance is compatible with the imposition of fiscal austerity in an environment which is already suffering from acute material deprivation, whereas SAPs' huge social costs are unlikely to be tolerated by docile and passive populations. Finally, they posit that trade liberalisation will promote more efficient African economies

whereas Africa's small industrial base is incapable of withstanding and surviving foreign competition without public protection.

The above accounts for the often distinct naivety that the EU operates from in their dealings with large parts of the continent. As Claude Ake (1991: 319) notes, 'One of the most amazing things about the literature on development in Africa is how readily it assumes that everyone is interested in development and that when [African] leaders proclaim their commitment to development and fashion their impressive development plans and negotiate with international organisations for development assistance, they are ready for development and for getting on with it'.

This is a major problem for the EU in crafting coherent and long-term developmental relationships, as per the EU's stated foreign policy goals, although short-term commercial exchanges of mutual benefit to African elites and European corporations in the realm of energy and resources are evidently possible.

The China Variable

Having said all the above, the entry of the Chinese into Africa may make the EU's governance projects irrelevant. This is because both China and the EU are pushing a similar liberal economic agenda whilst Chinese interests dictate that European-style ideas on economic governance seem to guarantee long-term Chinese interests the best future, rather than the hands-off approach that characterised the earlier incursions into Africa by Chinese business and political interests. Chinese economic and political activities in Africa are growing at exponential rates and this expansion of Chinese involvement in Africa is arguably the most momentous development on the continent since the end of the Cold War (see Taylor 2006, 2009). The People's Republic of China (PRC) is now Africa's second most important trading partner with $91 billion of trade with the continent, behind the United States but ahead of France and the United Kingdom. Along with the rise in Sino-African activity have come accusations that China is a new 'colonising' power, exploiting Africa's natural resources, flooding the continent with low-priced manufactured products whilst turning a blind eye to Africa's autocrats. Senior EU politicians have enunciated this view: for instance, Karin Kortmann, Parliamentary State Secretary in the German Development Ministry, declared in November 2006 that 'Our African partners really have to watch out that they will not be facing a new process of colonisation' in their relations with China (*The Guardian*, 2006: 16 November). But equally, 'thanks to the Chinese' a French official has commented, 'we [have] rediscovered that Africa is not a continent of crises and misery, but one of 800-million consumers' (*Business Day*, 19 October 2007).

It is true that at the moment there appears to be some divergence between EU and Chinese policy aims regarding governance and that this at times suggests a convergence between Beijing and certain types of African leaders. But this can only ever be temporary in nature if China wishes to have a long-running and stable relationship with Africa. China is like all other actors in Africa – it needs stability and security in order for its investments to flourish and for its connections with the continent to be coherent. EU nations have had to learn the hard way that propping up dictators willy-nilly is not sustainable nor desirable (even if this continues), and China will likewise learn this as its relations unfold. As Obiorah notes, 'After an initial phase of snapping up resource extraction concessions, it is almost conceivable that China will be compelled by instability and conflict in Africa to realise that its long term economic interests are best served by promoting peace in Africa and that this is most likely to come about by encouraging representative government in Africa rather than supporting dictators' (Obiorah 2007: 40). This has started to happen:

> China's changing calculation of its economic and political interests has partly driven this shift. With its increased investments in pariah countries over the past decade, China has had to devise a more sophisticated approach to protecting its assets and its citizens abroad. It no longer sees providing uncritical and unconditional support to unpopular, and in some cases fragile, regimes as the most effective strategy (Kleine-Ahlbrandt and Small 2008: 38–9).

Thus, whilst in the current period there sometimes appears to be divergence, there can ultimately only be growing convergence with EU policy aims – maybe not with regard to democracy (though China is itself evolving in interesting directions), but certainly with regard to governance and security and by implication, a greater connection to the downside of supporting regimes that undermine development and China's own notions of human rights, which are largely collective and focussed on economic and social areas.

Furthermore, China's integration into the global economy and the concomitant responsibilities that have come with this greater incorporation necessitate structural and systemic reforms on Beijing, particularly through increasing membership of multilateral bodies. In the long term these could conceivably have an influence on Beijing in the development of a regime that incorporates increased respect for the rule of law and a better safeguarding for universal human rights. For instance, Beijing's key commitments pertaining to its membership of the WTO comprise responsibilities to advance the transparency, consistency and standardisation of China's legal system. And it is more than obvious that over the past 20 years or so, Beijing has signed up to and ratified a growing number of international instruments pertaining to human rights and labour as it embeds itself in various multilateral regimes. The task for EU policy-makers is to encourage such developments, not perpetually criticise Beijing:

> The Western countries should accept that they are not any longer in a position to prevent the rise of China and other actors of global change. The objective should be to design a strategy toward China that does not only constrain competition,

but develop common commitments on how to deal together on pressing global challenges (Jing Gu, Humphrey and Messner 2007: 288).

Finally, the Chinese have actually been quite explicit in their support for African development plans. For instance, at the second Forum on China-Africa Cooperation, Beijing agreed to, 'strengthen cooperation with Africa on priority sectors identified under the New Partnership for Africa's Development (NEPAD)' (*Xinhua News* (Beijing), 17 December 2003). Setting the governance strictures to one side, NEPAD is fundamentally a neo-liberal project aimed at opening up African markets and developing liberalised economies. Just as China has, since 1978, pursued the capitalist path to development, so too now Beijing is *de facto* encouraging Africa to likewise accept and advance the precepts of liberalised capitalism. Clearly there are material interests in the Chinese elites encouraging African states to open up their markets, but this does place a different twist on the much-hyped (within Africa) notion that China presents an alternative 'model' for the continent, one somehow qualitatively different from the West's. In fact, China is, in the sense of being a model for Africa, little more than a metaphor for a non-Western path to development. That the objective conditions in Africa are hugely different from those that China encountered (and continues to encounter) in its quest for capitalist growth appears to escape the notice of many African intellectuals. The fact that China is not the West appears to be good enough for many. What escapes the notice of such commentators is that both the EU and China are, at least in the economic realm, advocating almost identical policies – and policies that have hitherto been rejected by many African intellectuals as 'neo-colonial' and exploitative.

Conclusion

With regard to the EU's 'partnership' with Africa, it is surely naïve to expect elites, whose very modus operandi is based on privatised patronage (in EU eyes, malgovernance) and the prohibition and erosion of democracy, to begin implementing and operating by the rubric of 'good governance'. To do so would not only damage their own holds on power but reduce their ability to maintain lucrative linkages with the external world. That is why this author has little confidence that the commitments to democracy and good government by African leaders will amount to much, despite the EU's rhetorical support.

This implies that any monitoring of governance standards and the improvement in democratic standards on the continent cannot remain elite-driven or, from the perspective of the donor community, dependent upon the whims of the elites within government. Nor can they be detached from a critical restructuring of Africa's global economic linkages and world trade policies. Currently, one of the main positive things about recent African developmental plans is that they are African initiatives and that they have generated a certain level of debate within

Africa with regard to the continent's development impasse. These facets of the project are worth building on. However, whilst Africa's political economy remains so dependent upon the Big Men to advance good governance, something which goes against the very logic of neo-patrimonial rule, then its project to promote the continent's regeneration in the new millennium will likely remain stillborn. Besides, with the rise of China in Africa (as well as other 'new' actors, such as Brazil, India, Iran, Malaysia etc.), the leverage of the EU has been reduced, although both China and the EU desire the same goals in Africa – stability and predictability for their investments alongside liberalised markets.

At the political level, it would be true to say that policy-makers in various European capitals – but particularly in Paris and London – see the rise of China in Africa as posing a potential threat to their relative power. This is most crucial for France, seeing as Africa is arguably the only way that Paris can continue to advance the myth that it is a major global power. Omar Bongo of Gabon once put it that, 'Africa without France is like a car without a driver. But France without Africa is like a car without petrol' (quoted in *BBC News*, 13 June 2009). If the Chinese and their activities in Africa threaten the French car, then Paris will most certainly be feeling the heat, even if Nicolas Sarkozy has sought to downplay (publicly at least) the continuation of the idea of *la Françafrique.*

Of course, this is not the full story and where the EU's claimed 'partnership' sits in a milieu marked out by outrageous subsidies and agricultural barriers to African trade is a moot point, and one generally ignored in discussions of the EU's support for Africa. Oxfam has estimated that cotton subsidies by the United States and the EU in 2002 caused a loss of up to $300 million in revenue to the African continent, which is more than the total debt relief ($230 million) approved by the World Bank and the IMF under the enhanced HIPC Initiative to nine cotton-exporting highly indebted poor countries (HIPCs) in West and Central Africa. Because many African countries are so dependent upon commodities, the continued high level of subsidies and barriers to trade practised by the EU has stimulated a growing call for some type of reform so as to allow exports from Africa to develop. Access to EU markets is a fundamental problem for African exporters, particularly as the bulk of trade barriers (particularly subsidies) are in agriculture, which is where Africa has an arguable comparative advantage.

Indeed, how African agricultural exporters can hope to compete in the West when it is estimated that Western nations pay their farmers $350 billion per year in subsidies (nearly $1 billion a day) is clearly problematic. This inevitably leads to underdevelopment and the associated governance problems that come with the territory. Discussing how this might be addressed vis-à-vis the EU's governance agenda with regard to Africa is outside the remit of this chapter. It does, however, hint at the hypocrisy of Brussels in confronting China in Africa and in lecturing Africa's leaders for their (admittedly profound) flaws in governance, however defined.

PART VI
Concluding Remarks

Chapter 13

Conclusion:
From Rivalry to Partnership?

Gordon Cumming, Tony Chafer and Theresa Callan

This book began by noting how, for much of the post-colonial era, most Northern states considered the needs and challenges of Africa to be of peripheral concern and looked upon this continent primarily as a source of political, economic and strategic advantage. It observed that most Northern donors engaged enthusiastically in unilateral initiatives and to some extent in multilateral schemes, while neglecting bilateral approaches towards the African continent. Against this backdrop, the announcement by the UK and France, at their December 1998 Saint-Malo summit, that they would work together more systematically south of the Sahara appeared to signal a promising 'new' approach to the challenges of Africa. This proposed bilateral or bi-multi cooperation, labelled by some politicians a new Anglo-French partnership or 'entente amicale', has been a central focus of this study. But it has not been the exclusive focus, as other bilateral arrangements between donor states and organisations have been considered partly in their own right and partly as a barometer of progress in Anglo-French relations.

Bilateral Partnerships and Cooperation as a Useful Way Forward?

All of the empirical chapters have focused in one way or another on the issue of 'cooperation' or 'partnership' in relation to Africa. Most chapters have focused on inter-state coordination and cooperation, while others have considered such activity at the intra-state or supra-state level.

Alex Vines concentrates largely on the lack of intra-state cooperation, highlighting the impact of bureaucratic competition between the DfID and FCO, together with a range of other domestic factors, including African diasporas in the UK, on the evolution of British African policy during Tony Blair's premiership. Daniel Bourmaud, too, adopts an intra-state focus, concluding that, while there has been competition between the old guard (*les anciens*) and modernisers (*les modernes*), the key state institutions, political culture and elite consensus in France have all, at least until recently, favoured the continuation of a strong African policy underpinned by the pursuit of French national interests.

Gordon Cumming focuses on the key instance of inter-state cooperation examined in this book, namely Anglo-French collaboration. He finds that the UK and France have collaborated on soft policy issues such as poverty reduction and democracy promotion but observes that this cooperation has been limited, ad hoc and dependent upon informal ties between policy-making elites. Tony Chafer demonstrates that the level of Anglo-French cooperation has been greater in the security domain, particularly in the case of ESDP military missions in Africa and in the training of African peacekeepers. Chafer notes, however, that divergent policies and perceptions remain, especially over NATO, the implications of ESDP missions, and the relative importance of regional forums such as the AU and ECOWAS.

In the following three chapters, the focus turns to cooperation between France, Britain and other bilateral donor states. Gorm Rye Olsen argues that there has been a high degree of Anglo-Nordic cooperation but much more limited Franco-Nordic coordination. He contends that the UK and the Nordic states share an ideational, norm-based approach to the challenges of Africa, whereas France's realpolitik-type stance resonates less with the Scandinavian countries. Ultimately, however, Olsen relativises the importance of bilateral partnerships involving Nordic states by stressing these states' preference for multilateralism, especially within the European context. In the next chapter Niagalé Bagayoko examines cooperative action between France and the United States. She argues that, while the French government under Nicolas Sarkozy and the US administration under George W. Bush were initially keen to work together and shared a common interest in some security matters, Franco-American cooperation, particularly outside the Sahel, has remained extremely limited. Instead mutual suspicion and divergent strategic interests have continued to characterise Franco-American relations in Africa. In contrast, Paul Williams demonstrates that the UK and US share similar ideational perspectives on Africa and contends that Britain and the US have developed a qualitatively closer relationship on African affairs with each other than any other state. Williams suggests nonetheless that, notwithstanding common norms, values and ideas, Africa has remained a very under-developed component of the 'special relationship', not least because successive American administrations' lack of interest and failure to engage in Africa have led the UK to look elsewhere for partners south of the Sahara.

The next three chapters examine cooperation on the ground in Africa. Cumming explores Anglo-French coordination in the Democratic Republic of the Congo and, drawing upon a basic typology, finds that there has been active though coincidental cooperation on security sector reform and in ESDP missions but only a deconflictualisation of approaches on poverty reduction and political reform. Chafer offers an organisational rather than a country case study, with his analysis of the African Union. Drawing upon a more elaborate typology, he argues that the UK and France have worked together vis-à-vis the AU to promote the training of African peacekeepers and secure bilateral and European funding. He notes, however, that cooperation has been limited by competition for influence, by the different forms of support that the UK and France provide and by their divergent perceptions of the significance of the AU relative to other African regional organisations, notably ECOWAS.

The final section examines a different model of cooperation involving a supranational actor, namely the EU. These chapters shed light on the benefits and above all the complexity and shortcomings of multilateral cooperation, some of which at least have acted as a catalyst for states to engage in more explicit forms of bilateral cooperation. Marie Gibert explores various inter-institutional and intra-institutional interests at stake for the EU, particularly in relation to security policy in West Africa. She shows how EU policy-making is variously affected by competition, implicit cooperation and explicit coordination between member states. She finds that the UK and France continue to enjoy considerable influence over EU security policy, particularly when they work together. Finally, Ian Taylor looks at the two 'partnerships' which will have the greatest impact on Africa in the future – those of the European Union and China. The former is characterised by limited policy coherence, an uneven relationship and aid conditionalities while the latter is marked by relative institutional coherence and a lack of conditionalities. Taylor suggests that while there is a competitive relationship in Africa between the EU and China, the Chinese will gradually move closer to the EU model of cooperation with Africa, particularly with regards to the promotion of sound economic governance, a prerequisite for sustainable trade and development.

Overall, bilateral cooperation has become a more salient feature of many donor states' approaches to Africa. In some cases, this coordination has been particularly significant, as it has denoted a move away from or, at least, diminution of past rivalries: UK and French coordination, Franco-American cooperation and the deconflictualisation of EU and Chinese approaches all fit into this category. In other cases (notably the UK and Nordic countries), cooperation has become more pronounced at the ideational level, clearing the way for enhanced bilateral and bi-multi coordination, notably on soft policy issues. Ultimately, however, this cooperation has nearly always been more informal than formal and more hesitant than systematic. Indeed, just because cooperation takes place between two actors in one forum does not mean that it will spread to other forums or even that the same actors will extend their cooperation to other issues. The way that Franco-American collaboration has been limited to security matters is no doubt a case in point.

Collaboration appears most likely in the following circumstances: on high-profile occasions (e.g. Anglo-French summits, the announcement of major initiatives); at the height of major crises (e.g. Operation Artemis, joint Miliband-Kouchner visit); in parts of Africa where neither the UK nor France are the former colonial power (DRC, Guinea-Bissau – ESDP missions); on innovative/new schemes that are likely to raise fresh capital (UNITAID, IFFm); where key officials and politicians individually perceive the advantages of closer cooperation; in the face of common security threats (e.g. Franco-African cooperation in the Sahel) or common economic concerns (e.g. China's future alignment to the EU's governance agenda); as part of a wider relationship based on mutual trust (e.g. UK-

US cooperation); or indeed simply where there is a perception that cooperation will be more effective or will better serve national interests.

Conversely collaboration is unlikely where there are competing commercial or other interests at stake (e.g. between the UK and France in South Africa and Nigeria and between France and the United States more generally in Africa); where one power has a dominant or leading role (France in Francophone west Africa, UK in Sudan and east Africa); where there is no crisis or media attention (e.g. Ghana which had originally been singled out for close UK-French cooperation but where none has taken place); where the administration has not signed up to the new agenda (French Foreign Ministry on joint education initiative, DfID on Saint-Malo as a whole, particularly after the Niger scheme was not reciprocated); where lower-ranking officials are unaware of, opposed to, or simply do not have time to advance the idea of any privileged collaboration; and finally where the gap between the driving forces behind different African policies is too great. On this last point, UK and Nordic claims to be pursuing a normative ethically driven policy towards Africa do not augur particularly well for collaboration involving these donors and France or the US, whose agendas in Africa are driven by more narrowly defined French and US interests.

The patchiness of bilateral cooperation is perhaps not surprising but is disappointing, particularly as all contributors to this volume and almost every official and politician interviewed in the context of this project saw bilateral and bi-multi coordination as a valuable complement to unilateral approaches (which are frequently too expensive) and multilateral initiatives (which can often be bureaucratic and take too long to agree on, as can be inferred from the term 'messy multilateralism', used several times in this volume).

The question therefore arises as to why donor states and organisations have felt the need to engage in more explicit bilateral coordination and why they have stopped short of more systematic, formal or institutionalised partnerships. To help explain the incentives and constraints governing donor collaboration, a neoclassical realist framework has been deployed. Theresa Callan sets out lucidly the key elements of this theoretical perspective, distinguishing it from other realisms and from liberal theories of foreign policy. Callan notes that neoclassical realism has so far been used largely by diplomatic historians to explain the grand strategies of hegemonic powers, but she shows that this framework can have wider applicability, and in particular that it has explanatory potential with regards to donor cooperation in Africa.

The neoclassical realist framework has been used more explicitly by some authors than by others. Williams and Vines, for example, have stressed the role of values and shared liberal ideals as the drivers of state policy as well as highlighting the impact of other intra-state variables, such as intra-bureaucratic competition, in undermining a more strategic approach to policy-making. Gibert and Taylor, too, have used the theoretical framework less explicitly as their respective unit of analysis is not the state but the EU, whose agency and interests are often the result of compromises between its various member states. Bourmaud and Olsen have more fully deployed the neoclassical realist framework. However, Bourmaud has suggested that a more nuanced understanding of French African policy could be gained by drawing on constructivist insights, while Olsen has opted to combine neoclassical realism with theories of small states and adaptation theory. Bagayoko as well as Cumming and Chafer in each of their chapters draw more heavily upon the insights of neoclassical realism and show how this theoretical framework can shed light on the 'messy contextual factors' involved in foreign policy-making.

Theoretical Insights on Bilateral Cooperation

It is worth reminding ourselves of Callan's hypotheses before assessing whether or to what extent the neoclassical realist framework sheds light on the evolution of bilateral cooperation in Africa. They were as follows:

1. that cooperation occurs when it is perceived to be in the 'national interest', that is, it is seen by policy-makers as likely to enhance the state's relative power within international politics;
2. that policy-making within states is not systemically determined and 'that different states will react to the international environment in different ways' due to differences in the composition and ideational outlook of their respective foreign policy executives (FPEs); and
3. that domestic political variables and different 'extractive capacities' will have an influence on foreign policy-making and hence the degree of inter-state cooperation in Africa.

Turning to the first hypothesis, that cooperation is likely where it is perceived to promote the national interest via the enhancement of the state's relative power, this would appear to be confirmed by the various contributions. In this context, Cumming and Chafer demonstrate that the UK and France have, since Saint-Malo, identified collaboration in Africa as a way of enhancing their leverage over EU African policy, shoring up their positions on the UN Security Council and camouflaging their inability single-handedly to cope with the scale of the developmental, humanitarian and conflict-related crises facing Africa in general and the Great Lakes in particular. The tendency of both countries to work through the EU in support of AU peacekeeping efforts is recognition that their continued influence in Africa can be achieved only through multilateral mechanisms over which they hold sway. Olsen argues that the UK and the Nordics have seen cooperation largely in ideational and normative terms, but he recognises that for the Nordic countries in particular the very fact of 'clubbing together' allows them to enhance their relative power and punch above their weight in international donor circles. Olsen notes that France and the Nordic countries cooperate as and where they have common interests (e.g. France and Denmark collaborate on security in West Africa) but fail to do so when they do not (e.g. over development policy).

Similarly, Bagayoko suggests that France and the United States work together insofar as they have shared interests (e.g. the war on terror and on drugs). Finally Gibert argues that neoclassical realists are right to assume that leading individual European member states are driven more by their desire to enhance their own relative power within the international system than by any overriding need to help African countries.

The converse of the first hypothesis is that states will not cooperate where it is not deemed to be in their national interest. This is confirmed by almost all contributors and points to the limitations of bilateral cooperation where perceived strategic interests are threatened, even if the ideational dimension can allow cooperation where there is no direct or immediate correlation with the national interest (e.g., UK-Nordic collaboration on poverty reduction). Thus, Cumming notes how the UK and France are less inclined to work together in former colonies where one power already enjoys a preponderant degree of influence. Chafer draws attention to the NATO factor that has hitherto limited the UK's readiness to support French calls for autonomous ESDP missions. Furthermore, both the UK and France have on occasion sought to enhance their international prestige by becoming the sole champion of the African continent (in the case of the Commission for Africa or the G8 summit at Evian) or of particular regimes (in the case of Rwanda and the DRC respectively). Chafer also notes how the UK has preferred to support AU activities in Africa whereas France has been more inclined to back ECOWAS, as the organisation over which the French hold greater sway. Bagayoko contends that Franco-American cooperation is limited as the two countries have largely divergent interests on the continent, with the US taking the view that its superpower power status is unlikely to be enhanced by action in Africa and France considering that too close an alliance with the US in relation to Africa is likely to diminish its relative power in the international system – hence its turn to the EU in Africa, in an attempt to bolster its position there *against* the US 'threat'. Clearly France views a junior partner role vis-à-vis the US as much less attractive than leadership within the EU in a multipolar world.

Turning to the second hypothesis, namely that foreign policy is not systemically determined but subject to the composition of the FPE, here the evidence in this book has certainly pointed to the influential role played by policy-making elites. In this context, Vines points out that the DfID has systematically won out over the Foreign Office in the battle for control over African policy. He demonstrates how this, together with other variables, led the UK to pursue a humanitarian, value-driven agenda at the expense of its political, commercial and strategic interests. Vines argues that the UK does indeed have 'strategic interests … and a concern with raising its international profile even if these are often taboo subjects'. For his part, Bourmaud notes how French African policy has been marked by continuity over recent decades due to an elite consensus on the necessity of a strong, often unilateralist African policy. He notes however that this consensus is eroding, as France's failure to afford such an approach is cruelly exposed. This change has been facilitated by the fact that the perceptions of a significant proportion of the policy-making elites, (*les modernes*) have changed and opened the way to an approach consistent with France's relative material, strategic and economic power in the world. Even so *les modernes* continue to struggle to mobilise the state or, more particularly, state resources in favour of multilateralism (as opposed to unilateralism) and still have to contend with the competing perceptions of *les anciens*. Cumming and Chafer also draw attention to informal links between UK and French foreign policy-making elites who are ready to cooperate, at least partly because they 'get on' and have developed relations marked by personal trust. Olsen, with reference to UK and Nordic decision-makers, and Williams, referring to UK and US policy-makers, both stress the important role of like-minded elites in securing transnational coalitions in favouring of cooperation in Africa. The UK and US are in effect prepared to work together partly because their interests generally converge and partly because policy-making elites in the two countries share similar worldviews and take on board similar sets of demands from their respective civil societies. Finally Gibert recognises the role of national and Brussels-based policy-making elites in driving forward or constraining EU policy.

The third hypothesis was that domestic political and other variables will have an influence on the degree of inter-state cooperation in Africa. Once again a number of chapters bring out this point, which of course reinforces our earlier claim that foreign policy is not simply determined by systemic pressures. Cumming and Chafer in their various chapters demonstrate how UK and French cooperation has been limited by different institutional set-ups, national policy styles and extractive capacities. Olsen and Williams find that domestic variables favour closer cooperation between the UK and the Nordics and between the UK and the US, as each of these countries is deemed to share similar values, ideals and to some extent interests in relation to Africa. UK elite officials do work more closely with the US than any other state but ultimately run up against the fact that the institutional set-ups and the level of priority the two states attach to Africa are so different. Additionally, intra-bureaucratic competition within both states has undermined the institutionalisation of strategic cooperation. Intra- and inter-institutional competition and above all inter-state rivalries can also limit strategic cooperation within the EU. As Gibert and Taylor show, institutional agency (particularly where this is inter-governmental in nature) is affected by the divergent approaches of more dominant member states – some of which, such as France, adopt a realpolitik approach while others, such as the UK, advocate a more liberal interventionist stance.

On balance, the findings of this volume suggest that neoclassical realism can indeed be deployed to explain more than simply diplomatic history and the actions of hegemonic powers. It sheds valuable light on the complexity of foreign policy decision-making in medium-sized and even small states in a part of the world that is not vital to their economic or security interests. Neoclassical realism does have its limitations, however, notably when it comes to accounting for value-driven and normative approaches to foreign policy. It includes these within the perceptions of policy-making elites but does rather fudge the distinction between values and interests as well as between personal and institutional values. Neoclassical realism is, it would seem, likely to work best when accompanied by detailed off-the-record interviews at different levels of the policy-making machinery.

Whither?

It is of course hard to predict the future of bilateral and bi-multilateral Anglo-French cooperation in Africa or for that matter the future of coordination involving other donor states. The neoclassical realist framework employed in this volume can provide some indicators but the predictive power of this theoretical approach is not great, not least given its encapsulation of such a large number of 'messy contextual variables'.

Clearly the future of bilateral cooperation is likely to depend on how far states continue to or come to consider Africa to be a shared strategic priority and a source of enhanced relative power. The UK clearly views Africa as a source of soft power, whereas for France Africa has been and remains a priority for what it can offer in material economic, security and diplomatic terms. This distinction suggests that UK-Nordic cooperation is on a sounder footing than Anglo-French, whilst Franco-Nordic and Franco-American cooperation will only take place where there are identifiable, even immediate, benefits to be gained from cooperation. The EU-China relationship is likely to become less contentious as the medium-term benefits of deconflictualisation become clearer. Other systemic pressures are also bound to push in the direction of greater cooperation. These include the process of European integration and the creation of the European External Action Service.

That said, divergent interests will continue to impose a brake on cooperation particularly where Northern donors are competing for trade and influence in Africa. Other factors which are also likely to affect the future prospects of cooperation include the emergence of new elites. The elections of new governments will of course influence the African policy of all the donor states considered here. The most recent example relates to the UK, where the newly elected Conservative-led coalition government has given out mixed messages regarding cooperation with the French on Africa. It has reaffirmed the previous administration's commitment to the UN aid target of 0.7 per cent of GNP, largely in an effort to detoxify its brand as the 'nasty party', and has announced enhanced Anglo-French cooperation in the defence field as from November 2010. At the same time, however, this same government is unlikely, given the Conservative party's anti-European credentials and its longstanding Atlanticist tendencies, to be attracted to a strong partnership with France on African issues if it is seen as likely to increase the possibility of a permanent European HQ to run ESDP operations. In France, too, there are signs that *les anciens* are back in the driving seat when it comes to African policy, particularly in and around the Elysée.

The second key factor is a domestic variable, namely the extractive capacity of states. In the current global recession, all Northern states have to justify expenditure on Africa when in crisis at home. While cooperation can play out well in such contexts, it can also slip down the European and wider international agenda, as developed countries look to their own domestic economic and strategic priorities. In Europe this may mean that member states not intrinsically interested in sub-Saharan Africa will push for the EU to look southwards and eastwards as part of the European Neighbourhood Policy. In Europe and other developed countries, it could mean a greater focus on the emerging economies of Asia and the BRICs. The irony is that by prioritising emerging economies at the expense of Africa, the North will lose out in Africa to these same emerging economies. Africa too may lose out, particularly if African governments forge new partnerships with an even less principled and more ruthless set of suitors.

Bibliography

AAPPG. (2005). *UK Government and Africa in 2005: How Joined Up is Whitehall?* London: Africa All Party Parliamentary Group.

Abrahamsen, R. and Williams, P. (2001). Ethics and Foreign Policy: The Antinomies of New Labour's 'Third Way' in Sub-Saharan Africa. *Political Studies*, 49(2), 249–64.

ACPP. (2004). *The UK Sub-Saharan Strategy for Conflict Prevention*. London: Africa Conflict Prevention Pool. Retrieved 30 November 2009 from www. operations.mod.uk/africa/ACPPstrategy.pdf.

Africa Partnership Group. (2007). *Africa-EU Strategic Partnership*. Retrieved 30 November 2009 and 10 May 2010 from www.africa-eu-partnership.org/pdf/ eas2007_joint_strategy_en.pdf.

AFRICOM. *Fact Sheet: United States Africa Command*. Retrieved 26 May 2010 from www.africom.mil/.

AFRICOM. *Program Overview: Operation Enduring Freedom Trans Sahara*. Retrieved 26 May 2010 from www.africom.mil/oef-ts.asp.

Aggiouri, N. (1996, October 18). Douche froide pour M. Christopher. *Marchés Tropicaux*.

Agir Ici. (1997). *France – Zaïre – Congo, 1960–1977: échec aux mercenaires*. Paris: L'Harmattan.

Aicardi de Saint Paul, M. (1984). *La politique africaine des États-Unis: mécanismes et conduite*. Paris: Economica.

Ake, C. (1991). How Politics Underdevelops Africa. In A. Adedeji, O. Teriba and P. Bugembe (eds), *The Challenge of African Economic Recovery and Development*. London: Cass.

Akokpari, J., Ndinga-Muvumba, A. and Murithi, T. (2008). *The African Union and its Institutions*. Johannesburg: Jacana.

Albright, M.K. (1999, February 24). *Testimony Before the Senate Foreign Relations Committee on Fiscal Year 2000 Budget*. Washington D.C.: US Senate Committee on Foreign Relations.

Amin, S. (1973). *Neo-Colonialism in West Africa*, Harmondsworth: Penguin Books.

Angell, N. (1933). *The Great Illusion, 1933*. London: Heinemann.

Anonymous. (2009, November 16). *La France accorde 400.000 euros à la Police nationale congolaise*. Retrieved 18 November 2010 from http://vigilancerdc. afrikblog.com/archives/2009/11/16/15815636.html.

Anstey, R. (1962). *Britain and the Congo in the Nineteenth Century*. Oxford: Clarendon Press.

Archer, C. (2005). Still Nordic After All These Years: Nordic Security in the Post-Cold War Period. *Security Dialogue*, 36(3), 397–401.

Aron, R. (2004). *Paix et guerre entre les nations*. Paris: Calmann-Lévy.

Atlantic Community Initiative. (1998). *Saint-Malo Declaration*. Retrieved 18 March 2010 from www.atlanticcommunity.org/Saint-Malo%20Declaration%20 Text.html.

AU. (2000). *Constitutive Act*. African Union. Retrieved 10 October 2010 from www.africa-union.org/About_AU/Constitutive_Act.htm.

Bagayoko, N. (2003). *Afrique: les stratégies française et américaine*. Paris: L'Harmattan.

Bagayoko, N. (2004a). Les politiques européennes de prévention et de gestion des conflits en Afrique. *Les Champs de Mars*, 16, 93–114.

Bagayoko, N. (2004b). L'opération Artémis, un tournant pour la politique européenne de sécurité et de défense ? *Afrique contemporaine*, 209, 101–16.

Bagayoko, N. (2005). Politique étrangère et de sécurité commune (PESC) et Politique européenne de sécurité et de défense (PESD) en Afrique. *Le débat stratégique*, 79.

Bagayoko, N. (2007). *The EU and the Member-States: The African Capabilities Building Programs*. Paris: Centre d'analyse stratégique.

Bagayoko, N. (2009). Gouvernance multiniveaux et politique de sécurité africaine de l'UE. In R. Schwok and F. Mérand (eds), *L'Union Européenne et la sécurité internationale: théories et pratiques*. Louvain-la-Neuve: Bruylant-Academia.

Bagayoko, N. and Gibert, M.V. (2009). The Linkage Between Security, Governance and Development: The European Union in Africa. *Journal of Development Studies*, 45(5), 789–814.

Ball, G.W. (1968). *The Discipline of Power: Essentials of a Modern World Structure*. London: Bodley Head.

Banégas, R., Marchal, R. and Meimon, J. (2007). La fin du pacte colonial? *Politique africaine*, 105, 7–26.

Barkan, J. (2008). Rethinking Budget Support for Africa. In R.A. Joseph and A. Gillies (eds), *Smart Aid for African Development*. Boulder, Colo.: Lynne Rienner Publishers.

Bassir Pour, A. and Frachon, A. (April 29 1997). Washington dénonce le mythe du 'complot américain' en Afrique centrale. *Le Monde*.

Bayart, J.-F. (2004). Commentary: Towards a New Start for Africa and Europe. *African Affairs*, 103(412), 453–8.

Bayart, J.-F. and Wilson, J.C. (1997). *Politique française et politique américaine en Afrique: convergences et malentendus*. French American Foundation.

Baylis, J. (1997). *Anglo-American Relations Since 1939: The Enduring Alliance*. Manchester: Manchester University Press.

Bedar, S. and Ronai, M. (1999). The US Strategic Debate 1998–1999: Asymetric Challenges and Projection of Power. *Cahier d'études stratégiques*, 25.

Benn, H. (2007). *HC Hansard*. Vol. 457, Col. 465WH.

Bergman, A. (2007). Co-constitution of Domestic and International Welfare Obligations: The Case of Sweden's Social Democratically Inspired Internationalism. *Cooperation and Conflict*, 42(1), 73–99.

Birdsall, N. and Williamson, J. (2002). *Delivering on Debt Relief: From IMF Gold to a New Aid Architecture*. Washington D.C.: Institute for International Economics.

Black, D.R. and Williams, P. (2010). *The International Politics of Mass Atrocities: The Case of Darfur*. London: Routledge.

Blair, T. (February 2006). Carte Blanche Interview with Tony Blair on matters concerning Africa. Retrieved 10 January 2011 from http://tna.europarchive. org/20070807120537/http://www.pm.gov.uk/output/Page9046.asp.

Blair, T. (12 February 2006). The World Must Judge Us on Africa. *Independent on Sunday*.

Blair, T. (January–February 2010). Interview: A Prosperous and Exciting Africa in Our Lifetime. *African Investor*.

Booker, S. (2001a). Bush Global Agenda: Bad News for Africa. *Current History*, 100(646), 195–200.

Booker, S. (2001b). Who Are These People? *Current History*, 100(646), 196–7.

Bourgi, A. (2009). Aux racines de la Françafrique: la dégradation de l'image de la France en Afrique *Annuaire Français des Relations Internationales* (Vol. 10). Bruxelles: Bruylant.

Bourmaud, D. (1996). La politique africaine de Jacques Chirac. *Modern and Contemporary France*, 4(4), 433–42.

Bourmaud, D. (2005). La nouvelle politique africaine de la France: le temps de l'épreuve. *Esprit*, 8(9), 17–27.

Boutros-Ghali, B. (1992). *An Agenda for Peace*. New York: United Nations. Retrieved 1 January 2011 from www.un.org/Docs/SG/agpeace.html.

Bowman, L.W. (1990). Government Officials, Academics and the Process of Formulating US National Security Policy Towards Africa. *Issue: A Journal of Opinion*, 19(1), 5–8.

Bratton, M. and van de Walle, N. (1994). Neo-Patrimonial Regimes and Political Transitions in Africa. *World Politics*, 46(4), 453–89.

Brown, C. and Ainley, K. (2009). *Understanding International Relations* (4th ed.). Basingstoke: Palgrave Macmillan.

Brown, W. (2000). Restructuring North-South Relations: ACP-EU Development Co-operation in a Liberal International Order. *Review of African Political Economy*, 27(85), 367–83.

Brown, W. (2002). *The European Union and Africa: The Restructuring of North-South Relations*. London: I.B. Tauris.

Brown, W. (2006). The Commission for Africa: Results and Prospects for the West's Africa Policy. *Journal of Modern African Studies*, 44(3), 349–74.

Browne, S. (2007). *A Note on Country-Level Donor Coordination in Fragile States*. Washington D.C.: World Bank. Retrieved 2 January 2011 from www. worldbank.org/ieg/licus/conference/presentations/Stephen_Browne.pdf.

Browning, C.S. (2007). Branding Nordicity: Models, Identity and the Decline of Exceptionalism. *Cooperation and Conflict*, 42(1), 27–51.

Buchet, J.-L. (12–18 February 1997). France-Etats-Unis: la guérilla. *Jeune Afrique*.

Cameron, D. and Sarkozy, N. (2010). *UK-France Summit Press Conference* (transcript). Retrieved 15 November 2010 from www.number10.gov.uk/news/ speeches-and-transcripts/2010/11/uk-france-summit-press-conference-56551.

Cargill, T. (2007). Tony Blair and the United Kingdom's Africa Policy. *South African Yearbook of International Affairs 2006/2007*. Johannesburg: South African Institute of International Affairs.

Carr, E.H. (2001). *The Twenty Years' Crisis, 1919–1939: An Introduction to the Study of International Relations* (2nd ed.). Basingstoke: Palgrave.

Chafer, T. (2002). Franco-African Relations: No Longer Exceptional? *African Affairs*, 101(404), 343–63.

Chafer, T. (2008). French African Policy in Historical Perspective. *Journal of Contemporary African Studies*, 19(2), 165–81.

Chafer, T. and Cumming, G. (2010). Beyond Fashoda: Anglo-French Security Cooperation in Africa Since Saint-Malo. *International Affairs*, 86(5), 1129–47.

Charbonneau, B. (2008a). Dreams of Empire: France, Europe, and the New Interventionism in Africa. *Modern and Contemporary France*, 16(3), 279–95.

Charbonneau, B. (2008b). *France and the New Imperialism: Security Policy in Sub-Saharan Africa*. Aldershot; London: Ashgate; Pluto Press.

Châtaigner, J.-M. and Magro, H. (2007). *Etats et sociétés fragiles: entre conflits, reconstitution et développement*. Paris: Karthala.

Chipman, J. (1989). *French Power in Africa*. Oxford: Blackwell.

Chivvis, C.S. (2003). A Liberal History of European Integration. *International Affairs*, 79(5), 1065–9.

Chivvis, C.S. (2007). Preserving Hope in the Democratic Republic of the Congo. *Security*, 49(2), 21–41.

Christensen, T.J. (1996). *Useful Adversaries: Grand Strategy, Domestic Mobilization, and Sino-American Conflict, 1947–1958*. Princeton, N.J.: Princeton University Press.

Clapham, C.S. (2002). *Africa and the International System: The Politics of State Survival*. Cambridge: Cambridge University Press.

Clarke, W.S. and Herbst, J.I. (1997). *Learning from Somalia: The Lessons of Armed Humanitarian Intervention*. Boulder, CO: Westview Press.

Clinton, B. (26–27 June 1994). *Developing a New United States Policy Toward Africa*. Paper presented at The White House Conference on Africa, Washington D.C.

Clough, M. (1992). *Free at Last?: U.S. Policy Toward Africa and the End of the Cold War*. New York: Council on Foreign Relations Press.

Cole, A. (2001). *Franco-German Relations*. Harlow: Longman.

Commission for Africa. (2005). *Our Common Interest: An Argument*. London: Penguin.

Connell, D. and Smyth, F. (1998). Africa's New Bloc. *Foreign Affairs*, 77(2).

Conte, B. *Les dimensions internationales de la crise en Côte d'Ivoire*. Retrieved 1 January 2011 from http:/conte.u-bordeaux4.fr.

Cooke, J.G. and Morrison, J.S. (2001). *Africa Policy in the Clinton Years: Critical Choices for the Bush Administration*. Washington D.C.: CSIS Press.

Cooke, J.G. and Morrison, J.S. (2009). *U.S. Africa Policy Beyond the Bush Years: Critical Choices for the Obama Administration*. Washington D.C.: CSIS Press.

Copson, R.W. (2007). *The United States in Africa: Bush Policy and Beyond*. London: Zed.

Cox, M. (2005). Beyond the West: Terror in Transatlantia. *European Journal of International Relations*, 11(2), 203–33.

Craig, D. and Porter, D. (2003). Poverty Reduction Strategy Papers: A New Convergence. *World Development*, 31(1), 53–69.

Crawford, G. (2001). *Foreign Aid and Political Reform: A Comparative Analysis of Democracy Assistance and Political Conditionality*. Basingstoke: Palgrave.

Cumming, G. (2001). *Aid to Africa: French and British Policies from the Cold War to the New Millennium*. Aldershot: Ashgate.

Cumming, G. (2004). UK African Policy in the Post-Cold War Era: From Realpolitik to Moralpolitik. *Journal of Commonwealth and Comparative Politics*, 42(1), 106–28.

Cumming, G. (2005). From Realpolitik to the Third Way: British African Policy in the New World Order. In U. Engel and G.R. Olsen (eds), *Africa and the North: Between Globalization and Marginalization*. Oxon; New York: Routledge.

Cumming, G. (2009). *French NGOs in the Global Era: France's International Development Role*. Basingstoke: Palgrave Macmillan.

Dale, I. (20 July 2007). Rwanda Trip Shapes David Cameron's View. *Daily Telegraph*. Retrieved 25 May 2011 from www.telegraph.co.uk/comment/columnists/iaindale/3641430/Rwanda-trip-shapes-David-Camerons-view.html.

Danielson, A. and Wohlgemuth, L. (2005). Swedish Development Co-operation in Perspective. In O. Stokke and P. Hoebink (eds), *Perspectives on European Development Co-operation: Policy and Performance of Individual Donor Countries and the EU*. London: Routledge.

Department of State. (2009). *U.S. Global Peace Operations Initiative: Phase II Strategy (Summary)*. Washington D.C.: US Department of State.

DfID. (2008). *Democratic Republic of Congo Country Plan*. London: Department for International Development. Retrieved 12 February 2010 from www.dfid.gov.uk/Documents/publications/DRC-countryplan08-10%5B1%5D.pdf.

DfID. (2009). *Annual Report and Resource Accounts 2008–09*. London: Department for International Development.

Dueck, C. (2006). *Reluctant Crusaders: Power, Culture, and Change in American Grand Strategy*. Princeton, N.J: Princeton University Press.

Duffield, M.R. (2007). *Development, Security and Unending War: Governing the World of Peoples*. Cambridge: Polity.

Duignan, P. and Gann, L.H. (1990). *Les États-Unis et l'Afrique: une histoire*. Paris: Economica.

Dulles, F.R. and Ridinger, G.E. (1955). The Anti-Colonial Policies of Franklin D. Roosevelt. *Political Science Quarterly*, 70(1), 1–18.

Dumbrell, J. (2009). The US-UK Special Relationship: Taking the 21st Century Temperature. *Journal of Politics and International Relations*, 11(1), 64–78.

Dunn, D.H. (2009). Assessing the Debate, Assessing the Damage: Transatlantic Relations After Bush. *British Journal of Politics and International Relations*, 11(1), 4–24.

Dunne, T. (2004). 'When the Shooting Starts': Atlanticism in British Security Strategy. *International Affairs*, 80(5), 893–908.

Dyson, T. (2008). Convergence and Divergence in Post-Cold War British, French, and German Military Reforms. *Security Studies*, 17(4), 725–74.

EIU. (1993). *Zaire, Rwanda, Burundi 1992–93*. London: Economist Intelligence Unit.

Elowson, C. (2009). *The Joint Africa-EU Strategy: A Study of the Peace and Security Partnership*. FOI [Swedish Defence Research Agency].

Elysée. (2006). *Franco-British Summit*. Retrieved 22 March 2010 from www.elysee.fr/elysee/elysee.fr/anglais_archives/speeches_and_documents/2006/franco_british_summit/28th_franco-british_summit-communique.51064.html.

Engel, U. (2005). Germany: Between Value-Based Solidarity and Bureaucratic Interests. In U. Engel and G.R. Olsen (eds), *Africa and the North: Between Globalization and Marginalization*. London: Routledge.

Engel, U. and Porto, J.G. (2010). *Africa's New Peace and Security Architecture: Promoting Norms and Institutionalising Solutions*. Aldershot: Ashgate.

Ero, C. (2001). A Critical Assessment of Britain's Africa Policy. *Conflict, Security and Development*, 1(2), 51–72.

EU. (2005). *Joint Statement by the Council and the Representatives of the Governments of the Member States Meeting Within the Council, the European Parliament and the Commission on European Union Development Policy: 'The European Consensus on Development'* (No. Document 14820/05, Annex 1). Brussels: Council of the European Union.

European Commission. (1996). *Communication from the Commission to the Council: The EU and the Issue of Conflicts in Africa: Peace-Building, Conflict Prevention and Beyond*. Brussels: Commission of the European Communities.

European Commission. (2005). *EU Strategy for Africa: Towards a Euro-African Pact to Accelerate Africa's Development*. Brussels: Commission of the European Communities.

European Commission. (2008). *The EU, Africa and China: Towards Trilateral Dialogue and Cooperation*. Brussels: Commission of the European Communities.

European Commission. (2009). *Assessment Report: Joint Africa-EU Strategy*. Brussels: European Commission. Retrieved 5 January 2010 from ec.europa.eu/development/ icenter/repository/jaes_assessment_report_20091010_en.pdf.

European Security and Defence Assembly (2006). European Union Operations in the Democratic Republic of the Congo. Retrieved 2 June 2010 from www.assembly-weu.org/en/documents/sessions_ordinaires/rpt/2006/1954. php#P201_44933.

Fatton, R. (1988). Bringing the Ruling Class Back In: Class, State, and Hegemony in Africa. *Comparative Politics*, 20(3), 253–64.

Fatton, R. (1999). Civil Society Revisited: Africa in the New Millennium. *West Africa Review*, 1(1), 1–18.

FCO. (2003a). *Franco-British Summit Declaration*. Retrieved 5 December 2009 from www.fco.gov.uk/resources/en/pdf/pdf5/beu_ukfr_nov03_defence.

FCO. (2003b). *Franco-British Summit: Strengthening European Cooperation in Security and Defence*. London: Foreign and Commonwealth Office.

FCO. (2004). *Governance in Africa: What Do We Mean and Why Does It Matter?* London: Foreign and Commonwealth Office Africa Research Group.

FCO. (2008). *Saint-Malo Ten Years After*. Retrieved 20 October 2009 and 22 March 2010 from www.fco.gov.uk/en/news/latest-news/?view=PressSand id=10435411.

FCO. (2009). *Country Business Plan for the Democratic Republic of Congo for 2009–10*. London: Foreign and Commonwealth Office.

FCO. (29 March 2009). *Hansard*. Retrieved 4 January 2010 from http://services. parliament.uk/hansard/Commons/ByDate/20090325/writtenministerial statements/part005.html.

Fearon, J.D. and Laitin, D.D. (2004). Neotrusteeship and the Problem of Weak States. *International Security*, 28(4), 5–43.

Fenton, N. (2004). *Understanding the UN Security Council: Coercion or Consent?* Aldershot: Ashgate.

Fioramonti, L. and Poletti, A. (2008). Facing the Giant: Southern Perspectives on the European Union. *Third World Quarterly*, 29(1), 167–80.

FitzGerald, G. (1979). *Unequal Partners: North-South Dialogue, a Balance-Sheet on the Eve of UNCTAD V*. New York: United Nations.

Foltz, W.J. (1986). United States Military and Strategic Interests in Africa. In E.P. Skinner (ed.), *Beyond Constructive Engagement: United States Foreign Policy Toward Africa*. New York: Paragon House.

Fontaine, R. (2001). Un autre Bush pour l'Afrique. *Géopolitique africaine*, 2, 193–8.

Forest, J.J.F. and Crispin, R. (2009). AFRICOM: Troubled Infancy, Promising Future. *Contemporary Security Policy*, 30(1), 5–27.

FPAE. (June 2008). *Perceptions et représentations par les acteurs et les décideurs de la coopération française au Cameroun – rapport final*. Yaoundé: Fondation Paul Ango Ela.

Fralon, J.-A. and Tuquoi, J.-P. (10 October 1996). Afrique: la fausse querelle franco-américaine. *Le Monde*.

Frank, A.G. (1967). *Capitalism and Underdevelopment in Latin America: Historical Studies of Chile and Brazil*. New York: Monthly Review Press.

Franke, B. (2009). *Security Cooperation in Africa: A Reappraisal*. Boulder, CO: FirstForumPress.

Freedman, L. (2006). The Special Relationship: Then and Now. *Foreign Affairs*, 85(3), 61–74.

French Embassy, DRC. (n.d. [a]). Retrieved 2 December 2009 from www. ambafrance-cd.org/spip.php?article282.

French Embassy, DRC. (n.d. [b]). Retrieved 2 June 2010 from www.ambafrance-cd.org/spip.php?article522.

French Embassy, DRC. (n.d. [c]). Dossier France. Lettre IV. Retrieved 2 June 2010 from www.ambafrance-cd.org/IMG/pdf/dossier_special.pdf.

French Embassy, UK. (n.d.) *Political Cooperation: France in the United Kingdom*. Retrieved 21 January 2010 from www.ambafrance-uk.org/Political-cooperation.html.

French Embassy, UK. (2001a). *France's Africa Policy, 11.01.2001*. Retrieved 30 April 2009 from www.ambafrance-uk.org/France-s-Africa-Policy-11-01-2001.html.

French Embassy, UK. (2001b). *Franco-British Summit Conclusions*: Cahors 9.02.2001. Retrieved 6 April 2010 and 23 June 2010 from www.ambafrance-uk.org/Franco-British-summit-conclusions.html.

French Embassy, UK. (2004). *Franco-British Summit – Action Plan*. Retrieved 2 December 2009 from www.ambafrance-uk.org/Franco-British-summit-Action-plan.html.

French Embassy, UK. (2003). *Franco-British Summit Declaration*. Retrieved 2 December 2009 from www.ambafrance-uk.org/Franco-British-summit-Declaration,4688.html.

French, H.W. (1997, 24–30 April). La main de Washington, la paranoïa de Paris. *Courrier International*.

Gabas, J.-J. (2005). French Development Co-operation Policy. In O. Stokke and P. Hoebink (eds), *Perspectives on European Dvelopment Co-operation: Policy and Performance of Individual Donor Countries and the EU*. London: Routledge.

Gallagher, J. (2009). Healing the Scar? Idealizing Britain in Africa, 1997–2007. *African Affairs*, 108(432), 435–51.

Galtung, J. (1976). The Lomé Convention and Neo-capitalism. *African Review*, 6(1), 43–54.

Gänzle, S. and Grimm, S. (2010). The European Union (EU) and the Emerging African Peace and Security Architecture. In H. Besada (ed.), *Crafting an African Security Architecture: Addressing Regional Peace and Conflict in the 21st Century*. Aldershot: Ashgate.

Gaulme, F. (2001). Intervenir en Afrique? Le dilemme franco-britannique. *Les Notes de l'IFRI*, no. 34. Paris: La Documentation française.

Gaulme, F. (2003). Le sursaut africain du New Labour: principes, promesses et résultats. *Afrique contemporaine*, 207, 71–97.

Gegout, C. (2005). Causes and Consequences of the EU's Military Intervention in the Democratic Republic of Congo: A Realist Explanation. *European Foreign Affairs Review*, 10(3), 427–44.

Gegout, C. (2009). The West, Realism and Intervention in the Democratic Republic of Congo (1996–2006). *International Peacekeeping*, 16(2), 231–44.

Gershoni, Y. (1992). The United States and Africa – The Fundamentals of a One-Dimensional Policy. *Asian and African Studies*, 26(2), 119–32.

Gibb, R. (2000). Post-Lomé: The European Union and the South. *Third World Quarterly*, 21(3), 457–81.

Gibert, M.V. (2009). The Securitisation of the EU's Development Agenda in Africa: Insights from Guinea-Bissau. *Perspectives on European Politics and Society*, 10(4), 621–37.

Gibert, M.V. (2010). The European Union in West Africa: From Developmental to Diplomatic Role? In E. Gross and A.E. Juncos (eds), *EU Conflict Prevention and Crisis Management: Institutions, Policies and Roles*. London: Routledge.

Giraud, H. (2000). Efforts at Conflict Prevention and Resolution: The French Experience. In D. Philander (ed.), *Monograph n° 50*. Tshwane (Pretoria): Institute for Security Studies (ISS). Retrieved 23 February 2006 from www.iss.co.za/Pubs/Monographs/No50/Chap12.html.

Glaser, A. and Smith, S. (1992). *Ces messieurs Afrique: le Paris-village du continent noir*. Paris: Calmann-Lévy.

Glaser, A. and Smith, S. (2005). *Comment la France a perdu l'Afrique*. Paris: Calmann-Lévy.

Godefrain, J. (1996, November 16). Afro-optimisme. *Le Monde*.

Gounin, Y. (2009). *La France en Afrique: le combat des Anciens et des Modernes*. Paris: De Boeck.

Gray, C. (2006). Peacekeeping and Enforcement Action in Africa: The Role of Europe and the Obligations of Multilateralism. *Review of International Studies*, 31 (Supplement S1), 207–23.

Gregory, S. (2000). The French Military in Africa: Past and Present. *African Affairs*, 99(396), 435–48.

Gruhn, I. (1976). The Lomé Convention: Inching Towards Interdependence. *International Organisation*, 30(2), 241–62.

Gu, J., Humphrey, J. and Messner, D. (2007). Global Governance and Developing Countries: The Implications of the Rise of China. *World Development*, 36(2), 274–92.

Gya, G. and Herz, J. (2009). ESDP and EU Mission Updates. *European Security Review*, (43).

Hague, W. (12 July 2009). *The Future of British Foreign Policy with a Conservative Government*. Speech given at the International Institution for Strategic Studies, London. Retrieved 15 May 2011 from www.iiss.org/recent-key-addresses/william-hague-address-jul-09/?locale=en.

Hague, W. (1 July 2010). *Britain's Foreign Policy in a Networked World.*
    Speech given at the Foreign and Commonwealth Office, London. Retrieved
    1 August 2010 from www.fco.gov.uk/en/news/latest-news/?view=Speechand
    id=22462590.

HCCI. (2005). *L'action des acteurs français dans le «post-conflit».* Haut Conseil
    à la Coopération Internationale.

Heap, S. (2000). NGO-business Partnerships: Research-in-Progress. *Public
    Management,* 2(4), 555–63.

Helly, D. (2009). Operation Artemis. In G. Grevi, D. Helly and D. Keohane (eds),
    European Security and Defence Policy: The First 10 Years (1999–2009). Paris:
    European Union Institute for Security Studies.

Hentz, J. (2004). The Contending Currents in US Involvement in Sub-Saharan
    Africa. In I. Taylor and P. Williams (eds), *Africa in International Politics:
    External Involvement on the Continent.* London: Routledge.

Hodder-Williams, R. (2000). Reforging the 'Special Relationship'. In R. Little
    and M. Wickham-Jones (eds), *New Labour's Foreign Policy: A New Moral
    Crusade?* Manchester: Manchester University Press.

Hoebeke, H., Carette, S. and Vlassenroot, K. (2007). *EU Support to the Democratic
    Republic of Congo.* Paris: Centre d'Analyse Stratégique.

Home Office. (2009). *UK Border Agency 2009.* London: Home Office.

House of Commons International Development Committee. (2004). *Commission
    for Africa and Policy Coherence for Development: First Do No Harm.* London:
    House of Commons.

Howorth, J. (2007). *Security and Defence Policy in the European Union.*
    Basingstoke: Palgrave Macmillan.

Hugueux, V. (2010). *L'Afrique en face.* Paris: Armand Colin.

Huliaras, A. (1998). The 'Anglosaxon Conspiracy': French Perceptions of the
    Great Lakes Crisis. *Journal of Modern African Studies,* 36(4), 593–609.

Huliaras, A. (2008). The Evangelical Roots of US Africa Policy. *Survival,* 50(6),
    161–82.

Human Security Gateway. *Human Security Gateway – Home.* Retrieved 15 May
    2011 from www.humansecuritygateway.com/.

Hurt, S. (2004). The European Union's External Relations with Africa After the
    Cold War: Aspects of Continuity and Change. In I. Taylor and P. Williams
    (eds), *Africa in International Politics: External Involvement on the Continent.*
    London: Routledge.

Hurt, S. (2007). Mission Impossible: A Critique of the Commission for Africa.
    Journal of Contemporary African Studies, 25(3), 355–68.

ICG. (2006). *Security Sector Reform in the Congo: Africa Report no.104.* Nairobi;
    Brussels: International Crisis Group.

Ikenberry, G.J. (2001). *After Victory: Institutions, Strategic Restraint, and the
    Rebuilding of Order After Major Wars.* Princeton: Princeton University Press.

IMF. (1997). *The Role of the IMF in Governance Issues: Guidance Note.*
    International Monetary Fund.

IRIN. (1996). *Emergency Update 23 on Eastern Zaire*. Integrated Regional Information Networks.

Jacobsen, P.V. (2009). Small States, Big Influence: The Overlooked Nordic Influence on the Civilian ESDP. *Journal of Common Market Studies*, 47(1), 81–102.

Jalloh, A. and Falola, T. (2008). *The United States and West Africa: Interactions and Relations*. Rochester, NY: University of Rochester Press.

Jamali, D. and Keshishian, T. (2009). Uneasy Alliances: Lessons Learned from Partnerships Between Businesses and NGOs in the Context of CSR. *Journal of Business Ethics*, 84(2), 277–95.

James, A. (2000). Britain, the Cold War and the Congo Crisis, 1960–63. *Journal of Imperial and Commonwealth History*, 28(3), 152–68.

Joannidis, M. (1998). De Ouagadougou à Paris: la sécurité en première ligne. *Dossier RFI/MFI*.

Kabia, J.M. (2008). *Humanitarian Intervention and Conflict Resolution in West Africa: From ECOMOG to ECOMIL*. Farnham: Ashgate.

Kampfner, J. (2004). *Blair's Wars*. London: Free Press.

Kaplan, E. (2005). *British Attitudes to Africa: Briefing Note*. London: Chatham House.

Kaplan, M.A. (1957). *System and Process in International Politics*. New York: Wiley.

Kennan, G.F. (1951). *American Diplomacy, 1900–1950*. New York: New American Library.

Keohane, R.O. and Nye, J.S. (1977). *Power and Interdependence: World Politics in Transition*. Boston: Little.

Keukeleire, S. (2003). The European Union as a Diplomatic Actor: Internal, Traditional, and Structural Diplomacy. *Diplomacy and Statecraft*, 14(3), 31–56.

Kisangani, E.F. and Bobb, F.S. (2010). *Historical Dictionary of Democratic Republic of Congo (Zaire)* (3rd ed.). Lanham: Scarecrow Press.

Kitchen, N. (2010). Systemic Pressures and Domestic Ideas: A Neoclassical Realist Model of Grand Strategy Formation. *Review of International Studies*, 36(1), 117–44.

Kleine-Ahlbrandt, S. and Small, A. (2008). China's New Dictatorship Diplomacy: Is Beijing Parting with Pariahs? *Foreign Affairs*, 87(1), 38–56.

Krasner, S.D. (1983). *International Regimes*. Ithaca: Cornell University Press.

Kuhn, T.S. (1970). *The Structure of Scientific Revolutions* (2nd ed.). Chicago: University of Chicago Press.

Kuisma, M. (2007). Social Democratic Internationalism and the Welfare State After the 'Golden Age'. *Cooperation and Conflict*, 42(1), 9–26.

Lafargue, F. (2008). L'Afrique au coeur d'une rivalité mondiale. *Questions internationales*, 33, 21–7.

Laloupo, F. (1997). L'Afrique et les rivalités franco-américaines. *Le Nouvel Afrique-Asie*, 87.

Larsen, H. (2009). Danish Foreign Policy and the Balance Between the EU and the US: The Choice Between Brussels and Washington after 2001. *Cooperation and Conflict*, 44(2), 209–30.

Lawler, P. (2007). Janus-Faced Solidarity: Danish Internationalism Reconsidered. *Cooperation and Conflict*, 42(1), 101–26.

Leboeuf, A. (2003). L'engagement britannique en Sierra Leone: du volontarisme externe à l'appropriation. *Afrique contemporaine*, 207, 99–113.

Lewis, I. (2008). *HC Hansard*. Vol. 482. Col. 395.

Lobell, S.E. (2009). Threat Assessment, the State, and Foreign Policy: A Neoclassical Realist Model. In S.E. Lobell, N.M. Ripsman and J.W. Taliaferro (eds), *Neoclassical Realism, the State, and Foreign Policy*. Cambridge: Cambridge University Press.

Lobell, S.E., Ripsman, N.M. and Taliaferro, J.W. (2009a). Introduction: Neoclassical Realism, the State, and Foreign Policy. In S.E. Lobell, N.M. Ripsman and J.W. Taliaferro (eds), *Neoclassical Realism, the State, and Foreign Policy*. Cambridge: Cambridge University Press.

Lobell, S.E., Ripsman, N.M. and Taliaferro, J.W. (2009b). *Neoclassical Realism, the State, and Foreign Policy*. Cambridge: Cambridge University Press.

Loisel, S. (2004). Entente cordiale ou moteur européen? *Les Champs de Mars*, 15, 37–62.

Loisel, S. (2005). Les leçons d'Artémis: vers une approche européenne de la gestion militaire des crises? *Les Champs de Mars*, 16.

Løj, E.M. (2007). Denmark's Membership of the UN Security Council: What Came Out of It? In N. Hvidt and H. Mouritzen (eds), *Danish Foreign Policy Yearbook 2007*. Copenhagen: Danish Institute for International Studies.

Lunn, J., Miller, V. and Smith, B. (2008). *British Foreign Policy Since 1997: Research Paper 08/56*. London: House of Commons.

Lynch, C. (2000, January 22). Senator Warner Urges UN to Put Balkans Missions Ahead of Africa. *Washington Post*.

Mair, S. (1998). German-African Relations. *South African Journal of International Relations*, 6(1), 21–34.

Makinda, S.M. and Okumu, F.W. (2008). *The African Union: Challenges of Globalization, Security, and Governance*. London: Routledge.

Malloch-Brown, M. (14 January 2010). How to Reform the British Foreign Office. *Financial Times*.

Mangi, L. (1994). The Role of President and Bureaucracy in US Foreign Policy-Making. *Pakistan Horizon*, 47(4), 33–61.

Marchesin, P. (1995). Mitterrand l'Africain. *Politique africaine*, 58, 5–24.

Maringues, M. (11 June 1997). France et Etats-Unis en Afrique: de la complémentarité à la concurrence. *Le Monde*.

Martin, G. (1985). The Historical, Economic and Political Bases of France's African Policy. *Journal of Modern African Studies*, 23(2), 189–208.

Martin, G. (1995). Continuity and Change in Franco-African Relations. *Journal of Modern African Studies*, 33(1), 1–20.

Martin, L.L. (1992). Interests, Power, and Multilateralism. *International Organisation*, 46(4), 765–92.

Mathews, K. (2008). Renaissance of Pan-Africanism: The AU and the New Pan-Africanists. In J. Akokpari, A. Ndinga-Muvumba and T. Murithi (eds), *The African Union and its Institutions*. Johannesburg: Jacana.

Matlary, J.H. (2009). *European Union Security Dynamics: In the New National Interest*. Basingstoke: Palgrave Macmillan.

McKinlay, R.D. and Little, R. (1986). *Global Problems and World Order*. London: Pinter.

Mearsheimer, J.J. (1994–5). The False Promise of International Institutions. *International Security*, 19(3), 5–49.

Mearsheimer, J.J. (2001). *The Tragedy of Great Power Politics*. New York: W.W. Norton.

Médard, J.-F. (1999). Les avatars du messianisme français en Afrique. In CEAN (ed.), *L'Afrique politique – entre transititions et conflits*. Paris: Karthala.

Médard, J.-F. (2005). France and Sub-Saharan Africa: A Privileged Relationship. In U. Engel and G.R. Olsen (eds), *Africa and the North: Between Globalization and Marginalization*. London: Routledge.

Metz, S. (2000). *Refining American Strategy in Africa*. Carlisle, PA: Strategic Studies Institute, Carlisle Barracks, US Army War College.

Ministère des affaires étrangères et européennes. (2008). *Réforme des systèmes de sécurité: approche française*. Retrieved 22 November 2008 from www.diplomatie.gouv.fr/fr/IMG/pdf/12-MAEE-RSS-final.pdf.

Ministère des affaires étrangères et européennes. (n.d.). *Les écoles nationales à vocation régionale*. Retrieved 26 November 2009 from www.diplomatie.gouv.fr/fr/actions-france_830/defense-securite_9035/cooperation-securite-defense_9037/les-ecoles-nationales-vocation-regionale_12533/une-force-integration_26394.html.

Ministère des affaires étrangères et européennes. (2010). *République démocratique du Congo*. Retrieved 2 June 2010 from www.diplomatie.gouv.fr/fr/pays-zones-geo_833/republique-democratique-du-congo_376/index.html.

Monier, C. (1997). Evolution du concept américain du maintien de la paix en Afrique. *Défense Nationale*, 53(7), 160–63.

Moore, D. (1996). Reading Americans on Democracy in Africa: From the CIA to 'Good Governance'. *European Journal of Development Research*, 8(1), 123–48.

Morgenthau, H.J. (1948). *Politics Among Nations: The Struggle for Power and Peace*. New York: Alfred A. Knopf.

Mosgaard, K. (2009, December 16). *Africa Strategy of the Danish Armed Forces*. Paper presented at the The Danish Defense Staff College, Copenhagen.

Mwanasali, M. (2008). From Non-Interference to Non-Indifference: The Emerging Doctrine of Conflict Prevention in Africa. In J. Akokpari, A. Ndinga-Muvumba and T. Murithi (eds), *The African Union and its Institutions*. Johannesburg: Jacana.

Nest, M.W., Grignon, F. and Kisangani, E.F. (2006). *The Democratic Republic of Congo: Economic Dimensions of War and Peace*. Boulder, Colo.; London: Lynne Rienner.

Ngoupandé, J.-P. (2002). *L'Afrique sans la France: histoire d'un divorce consommé*. Paris: Fayard.

Niebuhr, R. (1932). *Moral Man and Immoral Society: A Study in Ethics and Politics*. New York: Charles Scribner's Sons.

Nkrumah, K. (1965). *Neo-Colonialism: The Last Stage of Imperialism*. London: Nelson.

Noël, A. and Thérien, J.-P. (1995). From Domestic to International Justice: The Welfare State and Foreign Aid. *International Organization*, 49(3), 523–53.

Norberg, C. (25 May 2009). *The Nordic Countries and their Support for African Union, Regional Communities and the African Peace and Security Architecture. Is there a Nordic Model of Support?* Speech given in Oslo.

Obiorah, N. (2007). Who's Afraid of China in Africa? In F.M. Manji and S. Marks (eds), *African Perspectives on China in Africa*. Cape Town: Fahamu.

OECD. (2008). *Development Assistance Committee (DAC) Peer Review of France*. Paris: Organisation for Economic Cooperation and Development.

OECD. (2009). *Geographical Distribution of Financial Flows to Developing Countries*. Paris: Organisation for Economic Cooperation and Development.

OECD. (2010). *Development Cooperation 2010*. Paris: Organisation for Economic Cooperation and Development. Retrieved 1 January 2011 from www.oecd.org/dataoecd/41/31/44449684.pdf.

Office of the Inspector General. (2009). *Report of Inspection: The Bureau of African Affairs* (No. Report No.ISP-I-09-63). Washington D.C.: US State Department.

OISA. (1995). *United States Security Strategy for Sub-Saharan Africa*. Washington D.C.: Office of International Security Affairs, Department of Defense.

OISA. (2001). *Department of Defense Security Strategy for Sub-Saharan Africa*. Washington D.C.: Office of International Security Affairs, Department of Defense.

Olsen, G.R. (2003). Annus Horibilis for Danish Development Aid: Has Denmark's Influence been Reduced? In P. Carlsen and H. Mouritzen (eds), *Danish Foreign Policy Yearbook 2003*. Copenhagen: Danish Institute for International Studies.

Olsen, G.R. (2005). Danish Aid Policy in the Post-Cold War Period: Increasing Resources and Minor Adjustments. In O. Stokke and P. Hoebink (eds), *Perspectives on European Development Co-operation: Policy and Performance of Individual Donor Countries and the EU*. London: Routledge.

Olsen, G.R. (2009). *Conflict Management in Africa: American and European Union Policies Compared*. Paper presented at the ISA 50th Annual Convention, New York.

Olsen, G.R. (2009). The EU and Military Conflict Management in Africa: For the Good of Africa or Europe? *International Peacekeeping*, 16(2), 245–60.

Ottoway, M. (2001). Repenser la politique américaine. *Géopolitique africaine*, 2.

Oxfam. (2008). *Smart Development: Why US Foreign Aid Demands Major Reform*. Oxfam America.

Panebianco, S. and Rossi, R. (2004). EU Attempts to Export Norms of Good Governance to the Mediterranean and Western Balkan Countries. *Jean Monnet Working Papers in Comparative and International Politics*, 53.

Petersen, N. (2000). National Strategies in the Integration Dilemma: The Promises of Adaptation Theory. In H. Branner and M. Kelstrup (eds), *Denmark's Policy Towards Europe After 1945: History, Theory and Options*. Odense: Odense University Press.

Ploch, L. (2008). *Africa Command: US Strategic Interests and the Role of the Military in Africa*: Congressional Research Service.

Pondi, J.-E. (1997). Français et Américains en Afrique noire: nouvelle dynamique ou nouvelle dynamite? *Afrique 2000*, (26), 49–54.

Porteous, T. (2005). British Government Policy in Sub-Saharan Africa Under New Labour. *International Affairs*, 81(2), 281–97.

Porteous, T. (2008). *Britain in Africa*. New York: Zed Books.

Porter, P. (2010). Last Charge of the Knights? Iraq, Afghanistan and the Special Relationship. *International Affairs*, 86(2), 355–75.

Prodi, R. (2008). *Rapport du groupe d'experts Union Africaine-ONU sur les modalités d'appui des opérations de maintien de la paix de l'Union Africaine*. New York: United Nations.

Rathbun, B. (2008). A Rose by Any Other Name: Neoclassical Realism as the Logical and Necessary Extension of Structural Realism. *Security Studies*, 17(2), 294–321.

Renou, A. (2002). A New French Policy for Africa? *Journal of Contemporary African Studies*, 20(1), 5–27.

Ripsman, N.M. (2009). Neoclassical Realism and Domestic Interest Groups. In S.E. Lobell, N.M. Ripsman and J.W. Taliaferro (eds), *Neoclassical Realism, the State, and Foreign Policy*. Cambridge: Cambridge University Press.

Roberts, J.M. (2004). *Alliances, Coalitions and Partnerships: Building Collaborative Organizations*. Gabriola Island, BC, Canada: New Society Publishers.

Rodney, W. (1982). *How Europe Underdeveloped Africa*. Washington D.C.: Howard University Press.

ROP. (2005). *EUSEC – RDCongo: mission de conseil et d'assistance de l'Union européenne en matière de réforme du secteur de la sécurité en RDCongo*. Montréal: Réseau francophone de recherche sur les opérations de paix (ROP). Retrieved 10 April 2010 from www.operationspaix.net/EUSEC-RDCongo.

Rose, G. (1998). Neoclassical Realism and Theories of Foreign Policy. *World Politics*, 51(1), 144–72.

Rosenau, J.N. (1971). *The Scientific Study of Foreign Policy*. New York: Free Press.

Rothchild, D. and Ravenhill, J. (1987). Subordinating African Issues to Global Logic: Reagan Confronts Political Complexity. In K.A. Oye, D.S. Rothchild and R.J. Lieber (eds), *Eagle Resurgent?: The Reagan Era in American Foreign Policy*. Boston: Little.

Rothchild, D. and Ravenhill, J. (1992). Retreat from Globalism: US Policy Toward Africa in the 1990's. In K.A. Oye, R.J. Lieber and D.S. Rothchild (eds), *Eagle in a New World: American Grand Strategy in the Post-Cold War Era*. New York, NY: HarperCollins Publishers.

Rothchild, D.S. and Keller, E.J. (2006). *Africa-US Relations: Strategic Encounters*. Boulder, Colo.: Lynne Rienner.

Rouvez, A., Coco, M. and Paddack, J.-P. (1994). *Disconsolate Empires: French, British, and Belgian Military Involvement in Post-Colonial Sub-Saharan Africa*. Lanham, Md: University Press of America.

Sada, H. (1996). Etats-Unis: le retour en Afrique? *Défense Nationale*, 52(12), 183–5.

Sada, H. (1998). La politique africaine des Etats-Unis. *Défense Nationale*, 54(2), 186–7.

Saferworld and International Alert. (2005). *Developing an EU Strategy to Address Fragile States: Priorities for the UK Presidency of the EU in 2005*.

Schraeder, P. (1994). *United States Foreign Policy Toward Africa: Incrementalism, Crisis and Change*. Cambridge: Cambridge University Press.

Schraeder, P. (1995). The Clinton Administration's African Policies: Some Comments on Continuity and Change Mid Term. In CEAN (ed.), *L'Afrique politique - Le meilleur, le pire et l'incertain*. Paris: Karthala.

Schraeder, P. (2000). Cold War to Cold Peace: Explaining U.S.-French Competition in Francophone Africa. *Political Science Quarterly*, 115(3), 395–419.

Schraeder, P. (2001). 'Finie la rhétorique, bonjour la géopolitique': premières tendances de la politique africaine de l'administration Bush. *Politique africaine*, 82, 133–50.

Schweller, R.L. (1998). *Deadly Imbalances: Tripolarity and Hitler's Strategy of World Conquest*. New York: Columbia University Press.

Schweller, R.L. (2004). Unanswered Threats: A Neoclassical Realist Theory of Underbalancing. *International Security*, 29(2), 159–201.

Schweller, R.L. (2006). *Unanswered Threats: Political Constraints on the Balance of Power*. Princeton, N.J.: Princeton University.

SDA. (2007). *The EU's Africa Strategy: What Are the Lessons of the Congo Mission?* Brussels: Security and Defence Agenda.

Seldon, A., Snowdon, P. and Collings, D. (2008). *Blair Unbound*. London: Pocket.

Select Committee (2004). *Report on the US Intelligence Community's Prewar Intelligence Assessments on Iraq* (No. S. Report 108–301): US Senate.

Short, C. (2005). *An Honourable Deception?: New Labour, Iraq, and the Misuse of Power*. London: Free.

Slim, V. (2003). *HL Hansard*. Vol. 649. Col. 397.

Smith, S. (1994). Afrique Noire: le duel Washington-Paris. *Politique internationale*, 63, 355–67.

Söderbaum, F. and Van Langenhove, L. (2006). *The EU as a Global Player: The Politics of Interregionalism*. London: Routledge.

Sriskandarajah, D., Cooley, L. and Kornblatt, T. (2007). *Britain's Immigrants: An Economic Profile*. London: Institute for Public Policy. Research.

Sterling-Folker, J. (1997). Realist Environment, Liberal Process, and Domestic-Level Variables. *International Studies Quarterly*, 41(1), 1–25.

Stokke, O. (ed.) (1989). *Western Middle Powers and Global Poverty: The Determinants of the Aid Policies of Canada, Denmark, the Netherlands, Norway, and Sweden*. Uppsala: The Scandinavian Institute of African Studies.

Stokke, O. (2005). Norwegian Aid Policy: Continuity and Change in the 1990s and Beyond. In O. Stokke and P. Hoebink (eds), *Perspectives on European Development Co-operation: Policy and Performance of Individual Countries and the EU*. London: Routledge.

Straw, J. (2006). Africa. A New Agenda. Retrieved 10 January 2011 from: http://sudanwatch.blogspot.com/2006/02/africa-new-agenda-how-africa-can.html.

Styan, D. (1996). Does Britain Have an African Policy? In CEAN (ed.), *L'Afrique politique – Démocratisation: arrêts sur images*. Paris: Karthala.

Styan, D. (2007). The Security of Africans Beyond Borders: Migration, Remittances and London's Transnational Entrepreneurs. *International Affairs*, 83(6), 1171–92.

Survie. (2009). Guinée – 2006, 2007, 2009: Les massacres se succèdent, l'impunité demeure. Retrieved 1 April 2010 from http://survie.org/francafrique/guinee-conakry/article/guinee-2006-2007-2009-les.

Tannenbaum, F. (1959). The American Tradition in Foreign Relations. In R.A. Goldwin, R. Lerner and G. Stourzh (eds), *Readings in American Foreign Policy*. New York: Oxford University Press.

Taylor, I. (2005). 'Advice is Judged by Results, Not by Intentions': Why Gordon Brown is Wrong About Africa. *International Affairs*, 81(2), 299–310.

Taylor, I. (2006). *China and Africa: Engagement and Compromise*. London: Routledge.

Taylor, I. (2009). *China's New Role in Africa*. Boulder, CO: Lynne Rienner.

The Coalition. (2010). *The Coalition: Our Programme for Government*. London: Cabinet Office.

Thorhallsson, B. and Wivel, A. (2006). Small States in the European Union: What Do We Know and What Would We Like to Know? *Cambridge Review of International Affairs*, 19(4), 651–68.

Trefon, T. (1989). *French Policy Toward Zaire During the Giscard d'Estaing Presidency*. Brussels: Centre d'étude et de documentation africaines.

UK-France Summit. (2010). *Declaration on Defence and Security Cooperation*. Retrieved 29 December 2010 from www.number10.gov.uk/news/statements-and-articles/2010/11/uk%E2%80%93france-summit-2010-declaration-on-defence-and-security-co-operation-56519.

UN. (1995). *Improving Preparedness for Conflict Prevention and Peacekeeping in Africa* (No. A/50/711-S/1995/911): United Nations.

UNCTAD. (2009). *UNCTAD Handbook of Statistics 2009*.

UNITAID. Retrieved 15 May 2011 from www.unitaid.eu/en/supporters-mainmenu-64/donors-mainmenu-122/html.

UNSC. (2008). Final Report of the Group of Experts on the Democratic Republic of the Congo [S/2008/773]. Retrieved 9 January 2011 from www.humansecuritygateway.info/documents/UN_S2008773_DRCGroupOfExperts_FinalReport.pdf.

USAID. (2004). *Institutional Co-operation Between African NGOs and External Partners: 'Current Constraints and Ways Ahead'*. Paper presented at the International Symposium on Building the Capacity and Resources of African Non-Governmental Organisation, African Union Conference Centre, Addis Ababa. Retrieved 2 January 2011 from www.usaid.gov/our_work/cross-cutting_programs/ private_voluntary_ cooperation/conf_intrac.pdf.

USGAO. (2010). *Defense Management: DOD Needs to Determine the Future of its Horn of Africa Task Force* (No. USGAO-10-504). Washington D.C.: US Government Accountability Office.

Utley, R.E. (2005). Franco-Africa Military Relations: Meeting the Challenges of Globalisation? *Modern and Contemporary France*, 13(1), 25–40.

Utley, R.E. (2006). A Means to Wider Ends? In R.E. Utley (ed.), *Major Powers and Peacekeeping: Perspectives, Priorities and the Challenges of Military Intervention*. Aldershot: Ashgate.

Van de Walle, N. (2010). US Policy Towards Africa: The Bush Legacy and the Obama Administration. *African Affairs*, 109(434), 1–21.

Van Evera, S. (1999). *Causes of War: Structures of Power and the Roots of International Conflict*. Ithaca, N.Y.: Cornell University Press.

Verschave, F.-X. (1998). *La Françafrique: le plus long scandale de la République*. Paris: Stock.

Vines, A. (2005). Commission for Africa: Into Africa. *The World Today*, 61(3).

Vines, A. (2010). Rhetoric from Brussels and Reality on the Ground: The EU and Security in Africa. *International Affairs*, 86(5), 1091–108.

Vines, A. and Cargill, T. (2006). 'Le monde doit nous juger sur l'Afrique': l'héritage africain de Tony Blair. *Politique africaine*, 101, 132–47.

Vines, A. and Middleton, R. (2008). *Options for the EU to Support the African Peace and Security Architecture*. Brussels: European Parliament.

Volman, D. (1993). Africa and the New World Order. *Journal of Modern African Studies*, 31(1), 1–30.

Volman, D. (15 March 1995). The New Republican Congress and African Policy. *Africa Policy*, Report Number 1.

Volman, D. (2010). Obama's National Security Policy Towards Africa: The First Year. *Pambazuka New*, 466. Retrieved 26 May 2010 from www.pambazuka.org/en/category/features/61614.

Waever, O. (1996). The Rise and Fall of the Inter-Paradigm Debate. In S. Smith, K. Booth and M. Zalewski (eds), *International Theory: Positivism and Beyond*. Cambridge: Cambridge University Press.

Wallace, W. and Phillips, C. (2009). Reassessing the Special Relationship. *International Affairs*, 85(2), 263–84.

Walt, S. (1985). Alliance Formation and the Balance of World Power. *International Security*, 9(4), 3–43.

Walt, S. (2002). The Enduring Relevance of the Realist Tradition. In I. Katznelson and H.V. Milner (eds), *Political Science: State of the Discipline*. New York: W.W. Norton.

Waltz, K.N. (1959). *Man, the State and War: A Theoretical Analysis*. New York: Columbia University Press.

Waltz, K.N. (1979). *Theory of International Politics*. New York: Random House.

Wauthier, C. (1992). L'Afrique après la guerre froide: l'enjeu diplomatique. *La revue internationale et stratégique*, 8, 51–62.

Wauthier, C. (1993). La politique africaine de la France: 1988–1993. *La revue internationale et stratégique*, 9, 198–205.

Weaver, C. (2008). *Hypocrisy Trap: The World Bank and the Poverty of Reform*. Princeton, N.J.: Princeton University Press.

Webber, D. (1999). *The Franco-German Relationship in the European Union*. London: Routledge.

WEU. (2006). *The European Union and Security Sector Reform in the DRC: EUPOL Kinshasa and EUSEC RD Congo*. Assembly of the Western European Union.

Wickstead, M. and Hickson, C. (2010). *Still Our Common Interest: Commission for Africa Report 2010*. London: Commission for Africa.

Williams, P. (2004). Britain and Africa After the Cold War: Beyond Damage Limitation? In I. Taylor and P. Williams (eds), *Africa in International Politics*. London: Routledge.

Williams, P. (2004). La Grande-Bretagne de Tony Blair et l'Afrique. *Politique africaine*, 94, 105–27.

Williams, P. (2005). Blair's Commission for Africa: Problems and Prospects for UK Policy. *The Political Quarterly*, 76(4), 529–39.

Williams, P. (2009). Into the Mogadishu Maelstrom: The African Union Mission in Somalia. *International Peacekeeping*, 16(4), 514–30.

Williams, P. (2010). Britain and Africa in the 21st Century. In J. Mangala (ed.), *Africa and the New World Era: From Humanitarianism to a Strategic View*. New York: Palgrave Macmillan.

Wohlforth, W.C. (1993). *The Elusive Balance: Power and Perceptions During the Cold War*. Ithaca; London: Cornell University Press.

World Bank (2008). The Democratic Republic of Congo: Country Assistance Framework (CAF). Washington D.C.: The World Bank.

Youngs, R. (2004). A New Approach in the Great Lakes? Europe's Evolving Conflict-Resolution Strategies. *Journal of Contemporary African Studies*, 22(3), 305–23.

Youngs, R. (2006). The EU and Conflict in West Africa. *European Foreign Affairs Review*, (11), 333–52.

Youngs, R. (2008). *Is European Democracy Promotion on the Wane?* The Centre for European Policy Studies.

Zakaria, F. (1992). Realism and Domestic Politics: A Review Essay. *International Security*, 17(1), 177–98.

Zakaria, F. (1999). *From Wealth to Power: The Unusual Origins of America's World Role*. Princeton, N.J.: Princeton University Press.

Zartman, I.W. (1976). Europe and Africa: Decolonisation or Dependency? *Foreign Affairs*, 54(2), 325–43.

Zimmern, A.E.S. (1939). *The League of Nations and the Rule of Law: 1918–1935* (2nd ed.). London: Macmillan.

Press References

Africa News.
Africa Research Bulletin.
African Investor.
Agence France-Presse.
Courrier International.
Daily Telegraph.
European Report.
Federal News Service.
Financial Times.
The Guardian.
The Independent [London].
Independent on Sunday [London].
International Herald Tribune.
Jeune Afrique.
Le Figaro.
Le Monde.
Le Monde Diplomatique.
Lettre du Continent.
Libération.
Marchés Tropicaux.
M2 PressWIRE.
New York Times.
Observer [London].
Press Association.
Washington Post.
Xinhua News Agency.

Index